Great Composers of the World

By

Gervase Hughes

Published by Forgotten Books 2012

Originally Published 1834

PIBN 1000045013

GREAT COMPOSERS

OF THE WORLD

GERVASE HUGHES

THOMAS Y. CROWELL COMPANY

Established 1834   New York

Contents

Chapter		Page
1	PALESTRINA	9
2	BYRD	13
3	MONTEVERDI	17
4	PURCELL	22
5	SCARLATTI	27
6	HANDEL	31
7	BACH	39
8	GLUCK	46
9	HAYDN	50
10	MOZART	57
11	HAYDN again	63
12	BEETHOVEN	67
13	WEBER	76
14	SCHUBERT	80
15	MENDELSSOHN	88
16	BERLIOZ	92
17	CHOPIN	99
18	SCHUMANN	103
19	LISZT	108
20	WAGNER	113
21	VERDI	123

Chapter		Page
22	BIZET	132
23	FRANCK	139
24	BRUCKNER	145
25	BRAHMS	150
26	BORODIN	157
27	MUSSORGSKY	164
28	TCHAIKOVSKY	170
29	DVOŘÁK	175
30	RIMSKY-KORSAKOV	182
31	FAURÉ	187
32	ELGAR	192
33	PUCCINI	199
34	MAHLER	205
35	DEBUSSY	210
36	STRAUSS	218

THREE NOTES BY THE AUTHOR

(1) This book comprises small-scale pen-pictures of thirty-five great composers. I have done my best to describe in as few words as possible the sort of men they were, and to review their music comprehensively yet concisely in non-technical language intelligible to all.

(2) Since the true stature of a creative artist rarely becomes apparent until after the lapse of a generation or two I have excluded, *ipso facto*, any composer born during the last hundred years, thereby sparing myself the embarrassing responsibility of weighing the rival claims of Sibelius, Vaughan Williams, Schonberg, Ravel, Bartok, Stravinsky and a host of others.

(3) For the anomaly that a book dealing with thirty-five composers runs to thirty-six chapters full respon sibility rests upon the broad shoulders of Joseph Haydn.

GERVASE HUGHES

13th June 1964

CHAPTER ONE

PALESTRINA

On a sun-baked hillside twenty-five miles east of Rome (and in clear weather visible from the *autostrada del sole*) there stands a quaint little town called Palestrina – present-day population 9,000 – with a cathedral dedicated to the memory of the obscure St. Agapit. In the first half of the sixteenth century a respected member of the community was the small landowner Sante Pierluigi; he and his wife Palma, a fellow-citizen, were indirectly responsible for ensuring that the name of their town would become a household word among musicians the world over, for the eldest of their four sons (christened Giovanni) chose to tag his birthplace to his patronymic and be known as GIOVANNI PIERLUIGI DA PALESTRINA.

In fighting which took place all over the region in 1527 when Emperor Charles V (head of the temporal Power known as the Holy Roman Empire) sacked Rome and imprisoned the reigning pope (Clement VII) the municipal records were destroyed; there is consequently some uncertainty as to the exact date of Palestrina's birth but it may have been 17th December 1525. Thereafter his career is remarkably well documented. As a boy he became a chorister at the church of Santa Maria Maggiore in Rome where he carried on with his studies after his voice had broken. In 1544 he was appointed cathedral organist in his home town and began to tackle composition. Three years later he married; it seems to have been a love match and furthermore his bride, a local girl named Lucrezia Gori, brought as dowry a considerable inheritance from her father which included among other valuables a mule, a house – and a fertile vineyard.[1] The union produced three sons, of whom

---

[1] Those who know their *Gianni Schicchi* (see page 203) will be reminded of 'la mula, questa casa – e i mulini di Signa'. ('The mule, this house – and the sawmills at Signa'.)

Angelo and Rodolpho showed musical promise as youngsters but died in their early twenties; Iginio became a doctor of law and later entered the priesthood.

In 1551 Palestrina returned to Rome to direct the Julian choir of St. Peter's already respected as an organist and recognised as a wine-merchant he soon established his reputation as a composer. Although in due course receiving tempting offers to migrate – in one instance to as far afield as Vienna – he stayed in Rome, for all practical purposes, for the rest of his life. Between 1555 and 1580, under the successive patronage of Popes Julius III, Marcellus II, Paul IV, Pius IV, Pius V and Gregory XIII, he was choirmaster of several important churches and cathedrals in turn; they included San Giovanni Laterano (the 'parish cathedral'), Santa Maria Maggiore (where he had been a pupil) and St. Peter's itself. But during the fifteen-seventies pestilence stalked the land in the aftermath of another war, sparing neither prelate nor peasant. Palestrina fell grievously ill and, although he himself recovered, during the space of eight years he lost not only his two elder sons but also his wife Lucrezia; in deep distress he applied to Pope Gregory XIII for admittance to holy orders, was accepted, and was allocated to a vacant canonry. Yet almost immediately (and here one perhaps finds a clue to his personal character) he relinquished the tonsure and married a widow named Virginia Dormuli; she was as well-endowed as Lucrezia had been thirty-four years before, but now it was profit from the sale not of wine but of furs that augmented his income. During the fourteen years that remained to him, however, he went on composing as hard as ever and – thanks partly, perhaps, to the tactful and flowery dedicatory epistles which prefaced his compositions – his abrupt abandonment of priestly ambitions escaped the censure of Popes Sixtus V, Gregory XIV, Innocent IX and Clement VIII. But early in 1594 he succumbed to a seizure and he died on 2nd February; so nearly to reach three-score-years-and-ten was in those days a fairly remarkable achievement although surpassed (as we shall see in the next two chapters) by both Byrd and Monteverdi.

In the sixteenth century music was slowly beginning to escape from bondage to the Church, which in earlier days had pounced on the troubadours and still frowned on their successors the lute-players, but it is not surprising that Palestrina, born and brought up in a Papal state and spend ing most of his life in the shadow of the Vatican, should have concentrated his attention on masses, litanies and motets. He did also compose secular madigrals but not many of them rank among his masterpieces; it was in the masses 'Ecce Sacerdos magnus', 'Aeterna Christi munera' and (above all) 'Assumpta est Maria' that he demonstrated his true genius. Despite – or perhaps because of – the direct and straightforward approach, they possess an other-world quality which has rarely been recaptured. Nevertheless it should be made clear that an apologetic this-is-a-solemn-affair-and-I-must-restrain-myself attitude would here be as inappropri ate as it would be in Verdi's Requiem; this music should always be sung with full-throated sincerity.

During the three centuries preceding Palestrina's birth the purely monodic plainsong intoned by the priests had been gradually developed through a primitive form of harmony known as organum to polyphony, an early manifestation of counterpoint, i.e. two or more melodies sung or played *against* one another; the melodies belonged to one or other of the mediaeval scales – the modes – on which plainsong had been based. A very fair idea of the contrasted modal characteristics can be obtained by playing octave scales on the white notes of a piano: A to A for the Aeolian mode, C to C for the Ionian, D to D for the Dorian, E to E for the Phrygian, F to F for the Lydian, G to G for the Mixolydian. (Since this is neither a history of music nor a text-book there is no need to enlarge on the sub-divisions into Dorian and Hypodorian, Mixolydian and Hypomixolydian and so on.) Palestrina was one of several sixteenth-century com posers who were subconsciously responsible for evolving from these mediaeval modes the modern diatonic major and minor scales, the former being the comparatively rarely used Ionian mode and the latter being based on the Aeolian. Admittedly several of his motets and one at least of his masses – 'Te Deum Laudamus' – harked back to the Phrygian mode, but a critic endowed with a 'tonal' outlook (like Edmund H. Fellowes, see page 15) would have no difficulty in describing the mass 'Papae Marcelli' as a mass in C major. (Incidentally the only modulations – i.e. emphatic digressions to a different key – were to G major, G minor and – once – to D major.) Nor was this the only avenue in which Palestrina showed initiative. In the madrigals *Che debbo far* and *Com' in più negre* and the motets *Paraclito amoroso* and *E, se il pensier* he used a vertical (i.e. harmonic rather than contrapuntal) structure which would appear out of character unless one were prepared to recognize his readiness to experiment. Where he differed from some of his equally enterprising contemporaries was in having the good sense to discontinue such experiments when they proved unrewarding.

In the long run, therefore, Giovanni Pierluigi da Palestrina deserves to be remembered not so much for having been an innovator as for having been a consolidator. He brought church music to perfection in the idiom of his day; his mastery of that idiom has compelled the admiration of posterity and moreover has exerted its own influence on composers who were a hundred, two hundred, three hundred or four hundred years his junior.

CHAPTER TWO

BYRD

Very little is known in detail about the life of WILLIAM BYRD. He *may* have been born at Epworth in Lincolnshire (ten miles north of Gainsborough); it is *surmised* that from 1577 until 1592 he lived at Harlington in Middlesex; he *probably* spent most of the rest of his life at Stondon Massey in Essex. Facts, as distinct from conjectures, tell us that the year of his birth was 1543; that in 1563 he was appointed organist of Lincoln cathedral; that in 1568 he married Joanna Birley who subsequently bore him at least five children; that during his thirties and forties his activities centered largely on London where he was partly responsible for the directorship of the Chapel Royal; that he was later involved in continual law-suits concerning his property at Stondon Massey (a village lying midway between Brentwood and Ongar); that although sometime organist of an Anglican cathedral and generally in good favour at the Protestant court of Queen Elizabeth I he was occasionally in trouble as a staunch Roman Catholic; that he died in 1623 at the age of seventy-nine or eighty. Turning from conjecture and fact to criticism it would be fair to say, with all respect to Christopher Tye, Thomas Tallis, Thomas Morley, John Dowland, Thomas Campion, Thomas Tomkins, John Wilbye, Thomas Weelkes and Orlando Gibbons (one is tempted to add old uncle Tom Cobley and all), that among the many stars of this golden age of English music the star of William Byrd shone the brightest.

For the Catholic Church Byrd composed three masses and more than two hundred motets, most of the latter being published in four collections entitled *Cantiones Sacrae* and *Gradualia*. For the Anglican Church (established by the Act of Uniformity, 1549) he composed two complete services, a handful of shorter liturgical settings and about sixty anthems. In the secular field he was equally prolific, for he wrote some fifty songs (with string or lute accompaniment) and nearly double that number of madrigals. (I use the familiar and well-understood term madrigal rather than follow Byrd himself with his 'songs of sundrie natures' and so on.) Nor was this all: he left a surprisingly large quantity of chamber music for strings and about a hundred harpsichord pieces. (Strictly speaking they were written for the virginal, an instrument built on the harpsichord principle and played in exactly the same manner but as a rule smaller in size and slightly more restricted in compass.)

Of Byrd's masses one was written for three voices, one for four and one for five; when there was an extra voice-part or two to play with he was able to provide greater aural contrast than in a three-part work. In the four-part mass, for instance, separate sections of the 'Angus Dei' were set for two, three and four voices respectively, while in the five-part mass he explored almost every possible threefold, fourfold and fivefold permutation of soprano, alto, tenor, baritone and bass. Of the two complete Anglican services one was 'short' (i.e. a straightforward word-for-word setting of the liturgy) and the other 'great' i.e. an extended setting giving more scope for musical treatment). The short service was four-part; the great service was the most elaborately contrapuntal of all his works (although not, I think, one of the most inspired), being written for a double choir of ten voices and here and there incorporating ten separate vocal lines. His (Latin) motets and (English) anthems were all in anything from three to nine parts, but it is noticeable that what might be called the subsidiary parts were sometimes allotted not to voices but to viols.

Byrd's sacred music was often similar in style to that of Palestrina but at times showed a healthy open-air robustness more closely associated with his native land than with Italy. The 'Gloria' and 'Credo' from the five-part mass; the motets *Vigilate, nescitis enim* and *In resurrexione tua*; the anthems *Make ye joy to God* and *From Virgin's womb this day did spring*: these clearly exemplified that trend – which was also apparent in some of the secular madrigals (e.g. *The Night-*

ingale so pleasant and *Come, jolly swains*). His chamber music, taken as a whole, has been unduly neglected. It con sists of some thirty pieces for three, four, five, six or seven viols (of varying shapes and sizes), all of which are playable on a suitable combination of modern violins, violas and cellos. Some would appear to be little more than madrigal transcriptions but two at least of the 'quintet-fantasies', all the five quintets grouped together as 'In nomine' and the *Pavan and Galliard* (a sextet) are one-hundred-per-cent instrumental in conception – and furthermore ahead of their time. In keyboard music Byrd was no less of a pioneer; indeed in that field he stood alone among his contempor aries of any nationality. The output may be roughly divided into (*a*) dances and marches and (*b*) airs with variations, the airs used being sometimes traditional (*The Carman's whistle*, for instance) and sometimes original (*Go from my window*). These forms he treated with astonishing freedom, often more suggestive of the late seventeenth century than of the Tudor era.

Byrd, being some twenty years younger than Palestrina, did even more than his predecessor to establish the charac teristics of major and minor tonality while the mediaeval modes were falling gradually into disuse. This was partly because he out-did Palestrina in exploiting *musica ficta* (i.e. what would nowadays be called 'accidentals') and so was able to cover a wider range of chromatic expression. This important technical aspect of sixteenth-century music has been thoroughly examined by R. O. Morris in his *Contra puntal Technique* (1925, revised 1939), by the Danish musicologist Knud Jeppesen in *The Style of Palestrina and the Dissonance* (1927, revised 1946) and by Edmund H. Fellowes in his *William Byrd* (1936, revised 1947) – especially in chapter 15 of that indispensable work. Certainly the 'sourest sharps and uncouth flats' of Byrd's madrigal *Come, woeful Orpheus* give the music a modern *look* but there is nothing sour or uncouth in their *sound* – and this is far from being an isolated instance. One is therefore inclined to cavil slightly at Fellowes's tendency to couch his valuable remarks in 'tonal' terms. Here are two quotations from his book, the first concerning a passage from the five-part mass, the second the opening of the motet *Vide, domine.*

> Following a cadence in D major, the modulations run rapidly through G, B flat, F, and A, ultimately arriving at a full close in C major.

> The main key is D minor, but the opening phrases are in D major, soon leading to a close in F major. After passing through B flat, a plagal cadence in E flat is reached.

Comment of this sort would be entirely appropriate if applied to the work of any composer from Handel to Richard Strauss inclusive, who when modulating rapidly from D major through C, B flat, F, and A to C major would do so in the full realisation of the effect of relative key-contrasts in a particular context. Byrd, I submit, had no key-structure, as such, in mind: although in his capable hands the language of music admittedly became more com plex, more chromatic, the real motivation was still the poly phonic interweaving of strands of melody. That in Byrd's case this interweaving led to subconscious mastery of what has since become known as modulation does not mean that in that or other respect he can be judged alongside Handel, Strauss or any intermediary; he belonged, let us face it, to an earlier age. It would therefore be pointless to argue about his stature as compared with that of Handel or Bach, let alone Haydn or Mozart. He merits not a different standard of criticism but a different application of the same standard. Direct comparison with Palestrina (whom we have already met) and with Monteverdi (to whom we shall very soon be introduced) would be almost equally unprofitable, for whereas the two Italians each excelled in specialized fields William Byrd was essentially an all-rounder. In the gallery of illustrious composers he would occupy a niche all on his own did it not perhaps deserve to be shared by one or two compatriot contemporaries like Thomas Morley and Orlando Gibbons.

CHAPTER THREE

MONTEVERDI

CLAUDIO MONTEVERDI was born in 1567. He was the eldest
of four children of a doctor named Baldassare Monte
verdi who practised at Cremona, a fair-sized cathedral-town
on the left bank of the river Po lying roughly in the middle
of the triangle whose apexes are Milan, Parma and Mantua,
three cities which in those days vied with Verona, Bologna,
Ferrara, Padua and Venice as centres of the cultural renais
sance which had had its roots in northern Italy. As a
youngster Claudio's musical promise fell little short of
precocity and before he was out of his teens – probably
while still studying with the local choirmaster Marc'
Antonio Ingegneri – he published four volumes of sacred
and secular madigrals. Few held signs of immaturity; often
(as in *Baci soavi e cari*) they showed greater awareness of
the harmonic implications of the new tonal system than had
the Palestrina examples cited on page 12. Two more volumes
of secular madrigals – among which *Stracciami pur il core*,
at least, marked a further advance – appeared soon after
Monteverdi had taken up a permanent post as viol-player at
the court of the reigning Duke of Mantua in 1591 or there
abouts. Then followed a remarkable episode which I believe
has no parallel in the career of any other great composer.

In 1595 Emperor Rudolf II (third in succession to Charles
V, mentioned on page 9) called upon Monteverdi's employer,
Duke Vincenzo of Mantua, to play his part in resisting
Ottoman encroachment on the Holy Roman Empire, for
the Turks (who sixty-five years earlier had been driven back
to the Balkans from the very gates of Vienna) were again
surging westwards to threaten the Christian dominions over
which the emperor held sway. Duke Vincenzo was a loyal
liege but he was also a keen musician; when he set out to do
his master's bidding he took singers and an orchestra along
with him. Monteverdi and the rest had to journey, perhaps

on foot, over the Brenner Pass to Innsbruck and then by heaven knows what route through Upper Austria, Bohemia, Moravia and Hungary. As a military exercise the campaign was inconclusive and possibly futile (for the Turks won a major battle and then withdrew!), and the return journey through Vienna, Graz, and then Carinthia must have been somewhat of an anti-climax. But all along, in moments of both despair and triumph, Monteverdi and his colleagues provided their Duke with the entertainment he required; they surely deserve posthumous election to honorary membership of ENSA.

A few years later Monteverdi was once more off on his travels, accompanying the Duke on an equally lengthy but this time more peaceful and no doubt more pleasurable excursion north-westwards, in the course of which they penetrated as far as Antwerp. (Meanwhile he had married Claudia Cattaneo, a singer, also employed at the ducal court; she died in 1607, after presenting him with three children.) In 1602 he realized a long-standing ambition when he was appointed choirmaster; as such he was in charge of all court music at Mantua, choral and instru mental, sacred and secular, and the salary was higher than any he had earned hitherto. This was a turning point in more ways than one, for from that date onwards one finds traces of genius as well as of talent in his compositions. The next three volumes of madrigals showed increased assur ance in technique (e.g. in *Voi pur da me*) and moreover displayed an extraordinary range of emotional expression; it is interesting to compare, for example, the languishment of *Si ch'io vorrei morire* with what his biographer Leo Schrade pertinently called the frightening intensity of *Era l'anima*. Then came his first two operas, *La favola d'Orfeo* (1607) and *L'Arianna* (1608).

Although the long history of opera is generally taken to have begun with Jacopo Peri's *Dafne*, produced in 1597 at Florence, it is worth recording that at Mantua itself, during Monteverdi's viol-playing days, the then choirmaster Orazio Vecchi had provided Duke Vincenzo with *L'Amfiparnaso*, a 'comedy with music'. *L'Amfiparnaso* consisted merely of a succession of madrigals and although *Dafne* was more serious in intent and more ambitious in conception it would be fair to say that Monteverdi's *Orfeo* established a precedent in that it was deliberately planned to combine appropriate music with stage scenes and action, the object being to forge the whole into a dramatic entity. Before discussing *Orfeo* and the works which followed it, however, space must be found to point the significance of another crucial development in the art of music-making which was taking place at the time and was to affect future generations of composers to almost as great a degree as the substitution of tonality for the modes (which has already been briefly referred to in the previous chapters).

Towards the end of the sixteenth century realization began to dawn that not even serious music need necessarily be polyphonic; that after all there was something to be said for the troubadours who had accompanied their love-songs with at the most a few simple chords on a lute. When music became a permanent feature of gracious living in royal and ducal households all over western Europe the despised travelling lutenist was supplanted by the useful resident harpsichordist – or organist. He was a boon to composers who adopted the new (or strictly speaking revived) style, for his all-round musicianship encouraged them to fit their melodies with only a bass line – hereinafter referred to as *basso continuo* or just *continuo*; the harpsichordist or organist himself had to fill in the gaps to the best of his ability, for as a rule he could rely only on shorthand indications – sometimes not even that – of the composer's intentions. (It was therefore in the early seventeenth century rather than in the jazz age that the art of vamping was first developed.)

Monteverdi took full advantage of the *basso continuo* method of composition in *Orfeo* – especially but not exclusively in the recitative passages – and presumably also in *L'Arianna*, nearly all the music of which is lost. In a pastoral version of the Orpheus legend the librettist (Alessandro Striggio) rather shabbily allotted a minor role to Eurydice, the nominal heroine, concentrating his attention on the hero, on Apollo, Pluto, Proserpine, Charon and the allegorical figures of Music and Hope – backed by a chorus of Dionysian shepherds and shepherdesses. The music – recitative, aria, chorus and ritornello (orchestral interlude) in turn – was lyrical in feeling almost throughout but nevertheless conformed admirably with the stage situation at moments of dramatic tension and bore unmistakable signs of mastery. *Orfeo* and *L'Arianna* were followed by an elaborate and in places beautiful choral work, *Vespro della beata vergine* (1610), and by the death of Monteverdi's ducal patron (1612). For a time he was unemployed but a year or so later was appointed choirmaster at St. Mark's in Venice, where he signalled his arrival by publishing yet another volume of madrigals (some of them, be it noted, with *continuo* accompaniment) which included a very fine sequence entitled *Lagrime d'amante al sepolcro dell' amata* ('A lover weeps over the tomb of his beloved'). He did not lose touch with Mantua, however, where opera was better received than it was, as yet, in Venice; for the benefit of Vincenzo's successor, Duke Francesco, he wrote the ballet-opera *Tirso e Clori,* which provided evidence of a growing realization that what the public wanted was dancing and singing rather than declamation. Recitatives were reduced to a minimum.

Living in Venice for the rest of his life – he died there in 1643 at the age of seventy-six – Monteverdi went on composing madrigals to his heart's content; among them were such gems as *Zefira torna* and *Hor che 'l ciel e la terra.* He also wrote seven or eight more works for the stage (call them operas, ballets or what-you-will); most have been lost of which by contemporary accounts *La finta pazza Licori* was pre-eminent. Still extant, however, is *L'incoronazione di Poppea* (1642) in which his genius, so far as his extant compositions permit one to judge, came to full fruition. Lyrical inspiration rivalled that of *Orfeo* (witness the lullaby 'Oblivion soave'), the successful exploitation of *musica ficta* (see page 15) out-Byrded Byrd (e.g. in the middle section of 'Pur ti miro, pur ti stringo'), and even today it is hard to resist the genuinely moving appeal of some of the final cadences – however simple they may appear on paper.

Moreover there was greater merging than hitherto of the distinctive characteristics of sung speech and spoken song: while *Poppea* admittedly contained arias, duets and recita tives, there were also moments when the composer fitted music to the text regardless of formal requirements, moments which impel the listener to ask himself: is this an aria or a monologue? is this a *parlando* duet or accompanied recitative? Such an approach to the problems of opera, then in its infancy, was so highly individualistic as to prove unacceptable to later and more prolific exponents like Handel and Mozart – and indeed has generally speaking found more favour in the twentieth century than it ever did in the late seventeenth, the eighteenth or even the nine teenth. It has only recently become realized, therefore, that in some respects Claudio Monteverdi was three hundred years ahead of his time.

CHAPTER FOUR

PURCELL

The sixteenth century was extraordinarily productive of composers, among them such important figures as Palestrina and Monteverdi from Italy, Heinrich Schütz from Saxony, Orlando di Lassus from Flanders, Tomas Luis de Victoria from Spain and the crowd of Englishman catalogued on page 13. By sad contrast the only composer of real historical significance born during the first half of the seventeenth was Jean Baptiste Lully (1632-1687, Italian by birth and French by naturalization) whose ballets and operas earned him fame and favour at the court of King Louis XIV, established major/minor tonality on a sound basis, and helped to bridge the chronological gap between the death of Monteverdi in 1643 and the advent to maturity of Henry Purcell and Alessandro Scarlatti some forty years later.

HENRY PURCELL (1659-1695) was born in Westminster and lived there all his life. There is some uncertainty about his parentage, but research by Sir Jack Westrup (Professor of Music at Oxford University) has now established beyond reasonable doubt that he was the son of Thomas Purcell and not, as was long believed, of Thomas's elder brother Henry. This Thomas was an accomplished court-musician who under the Commonwealth must have been hard put to it to earn a good living but after the Restoration became a veri table Pooh-Bah – 'gentleman of the Chapel Royal, musician for the lute, viol and voices, composer for the violins, groom of the robes, and musician-in-ordinary for the private music'. Small wonder that young Henry, with this back ground, should have found himself first a chorister at the Chapel Royal and subsequently assistant keeper of the King's instruments, organ-tuner at Westminster Abbey, and composer-in-ordinary for the violins; even greater honour was in store, for in 1679 ne was appointed *organist* at the abbey, where he officiated at two royal funerals and two coronations – and in due course was buried. Little is known of his private affairs except that he married (in 1681) and had six children of whom the three eldest died in infancy. (His wife and two of the younger children sur vived him by many years.) Although he died at the early age of thirty-six Purcell's career spanned five regimes in English history – those of Richard Cromwell, Charles II, James II, William III and Mary, William III *solus*; further more his younger brother Daniel, a well-known musician in his day, outlived both William III and Queen Anne and was thus able to welcome our first Hanoverian monarch, George I. Another curious fact worth noting is that Purcell was both preceded and followed as organist of Westminster Abbey by John Blow – best remembered for the masque (i.e. dance-opera) *Venus and Adonis*.

Apart from occasional trips to Windsor and Hampton Court during his keeper-of-the-instruments and organ-tuning days, Purcell (just because he was a Londoner, per haps) seems never to have ventured more than a mile or two from home; his reputation has travelled much further afield – and deservedly so. For one thing he was the only British-born composer to illumine to any degree that musically dim period in our island story which lasted from about 1630 until the eighteen-eighties. For another his art had in effect a wider range than that of Alessandro Scarlatti (whom we shall meet in chapter 5), since Purcell was not narrowly English in the sense that Scarlatti was if not narrowly then at least specifically Italian. Admittedly Purcell now and again drew on folk-melody and also inherited cer tain tics of part-writing from the Elizabethan madrigalists; what is of greater significance is that he imparted a cos mopolitan flavour to his music by adapting to his own purposes the frenchified Italianisms of J. B. Lully. Let it be stressed, therefore, that he was a great composer by inter national standards and not merely the greatest English composer of his day.

Yet in the theatre Purcell unquestionably showed his birthright. In only one of his stage-works – *Dido and Aeneas* – were the songs, choruses and dances linked together in the

Italian manner by recitative; all the rest (some forty-five) incorporated spoken dialogue, and indeed it is hard to draw a firm line between the few which were operas with dialogue and the many which were plays with incidental music. Whatever one calls them these productions, though often bawdy enough to satisfy prevailing tastes, could be of high literary (as well as musical) calibre. Some were adaptations of Shakespeare – *King Richard II*, *The Fairy Queen* (from *A Midsummer Night's Dream*), *Timon of Athens*, *The Tempest*; others of Beaumont and Fletcher – *Dioclesian* (from *The Prophetess*), *The Double Marriage*, *Bonduca;* John Dryden had a hand in *King Arthur* and *The Indian Queen*; Thomas Shadwell provided *Epsom Wells* and *The Libertine* and William Congreve (then in his early twenties) *The Old Bachelor* and *The Double-Dealer*. Several of Purcell's best-known songs were composed for these English dramas and comedies: e.g. 'When I am laid in earth' (*Dido and Aeneas*), 'What shall I do to show how much I love her' (*Dioclesian*), 'Nymphs and shepherds, come away' (*The Libertine*) and 'I attempt from love's sickness to fly' (*The Indian Queen*). The last three of these four, in their differing moods, are all representative of his genius. The first, Dido's lament, is something more: built on a recurring (and unusually chromatic) 'ground bass' and therefore an early example of that specialized form of composition called a passacaglia, this song is a technical miracle – as well as being (which is much more important) one of the most moving expressions of human sorrow in the whole history of music. (Another technical miracle, aesthetically less rewarding, is the canon by twofold augmentation in No. 6 of the 1683 volume of sonatas – for which see page 25.)

Purcell's sacred works – mostly anthems but also includ ing hymns and canticles – were nearly all written before he consummated his powers in opera (or something like it). They are interesting not so much for their own sake as because they provide a link between the (anglican) ecclesi astical music of the late sixteenth and early seventeenth centuries and that of the late seventeenth and early eighteenth. The anthems were all based on passages from the Old Testament (generally from the Psalms) and unlike those of pre-Restoration days tended to be in verse-plus-refrain form; in the verse sections Purcell set a fine prece dent by following both the sense and the underlying rhythm of the words and inclined to adopt a declamatory style fore shadowing Handel (see, for instance, *Lord, who can tell how how often he offendeth*), but it should be emphasized that taken as a whole his sacred music was no more scared in character than the music of his operas, secular cantatas, welcome-songs or odes – one of which, celebrating St. Cecilia's day 1692 and entitled *Hail, bright Cecilia,* was an extended (and splendid) outburst of commemoration.

Despite the unassuming charm of some four dozen little pieces for harpsichord – sarabandes, minuets, hornpipes and so on – Purcell's most noteworthy contribution to instru mental music was a set of twenty-two sonatas for two violins, cello – and a harpsichord which provided the *basso con-tinuo.* All but one incorporated four or five movements in contrasted *tempi* but they were intended to be played with out a break. (In the seventeenth century a sonata was merely music for sounding – i.e. for playing on instruments – as distinct from a cantata, music for singing. It was not until later that cantata came to mean an extended vocal or choral work with orchestral accompaniment and that the word sonata was associated with pieces for a single instru ment or two at the most, let alone with sonata-form – which will be described in due course. In the Purcell Society's editions the *continuo* of the sonatas has been realized for performance on a modern piano: in the first volume by J. A. Fuller-Maitland – with considerable restraint – and in the second by Charles Villiers Stanford – with much greater freedom.)

Some historians believe that Purcell originally planned twenty-four sonatas for this combination of instruments – one each in every minor and major key. That the first eight are paired in relatives – G minor and B flat major (two flats in the key signature), D minor and F major (one flat), A minor and C major (no sharps or flats), E minor and G major (one sharp) – is certainly suggestive, but the remaining four from the first volume, published in 1683, provide the irrelevant mixture of C minor (three flats), A major (three sharps), F minor (four flats) and D major (two sharps); of the ten in the second volume, published by his widow Frances Purcell in 1697, the first two are in B minor (the relative of D major) and E flat major (the relative of C minor), but all the rest are in keys that have already had their turn – one each in C, D and F major, D and A minor, and no less than three in G minor. Therefore Purcell can hardly be credited with having anticipated the zealous logic of J. S. Bach in his forty-eight preludes and fugues for well-tempered clavier (see page 42) or Chopin's equally consistant approach in his twenty-four preludes op. 28 (page 101). Nevertheless certain features of the key-structure of these sonatas demand comment. First: the separate movements of each sonata were all in the same key except (a) the short third movement – hardly more than a connecting passage – of no. 10 in A major, which set out on its little tour of modulation from an emphatic chord of F sharp major, and (b) the F minor adagio belonging to the F major no. 9 from the second volume (popularly known as the 'golden' sonata). Secondly: none of the minor movements finished on a major chord, although contemporary ears were already attuned to the *tierce de Picardie* (a conventional full close in the major which was really a modal survival). Thirdly and *per contra*: No. 12 in D major ended, most unexpect edly, in D minor. Leaving aside such semi-technical aspects it was in their formal construction and musical content that these sonatas of Henry Purcell paved the way for two even greater composers (see chapters 6 and 7) each of whom, at the time of Purcell's death, was ten years old.

SCARLATTI

ALESSANDRO SCARLATTI (originally Scarlata) was born at Palermo in 1660; he came of obscure Sicilian peasant stock and of his boyhood little is known. But it *is* known that by the age of twelve he was in Rome (probably living with relations and certainly studying music), that before he was eighteen he married a Roman maiden named Antonia Anzalone, that by nineteen he had produced the first of ten children and the first of a-hundred-and-twenty operas, that at twenty-four he moved south to become choirmaster of the royal chapel at Naples. He stayed at Naples until 1702, but during the next six or seven years he turned his steps northward; with Rome once more as headquarters but com posing operas wherever he went, he visited Florence, Venice, and Urbino in the eastern foothills of the Appenines (where the choirmaster at the time was his own eldest son Pietro). By 1709, however, he was back at his old post in Naples and there he remained (except for a further three-year period of Roman leave) until his death in 1725. Soon afterwards his fourth son Domenico, who had won considerable renown as an executant on the harpsichord and had already toured Portugal, left Italy to settle in Spain, where he composed many admirable keyboard pieces which today are more familiar to us than anything his father ever wrote. Neverthe less Scarlatti the elder was a more important figure in the history of musical development.

Before he completed his first opera – *Gli equivoci nel sembiante* (1679) – he had a bunch of chamber-cantatas to his credit. During the course of his career he composed some six hundred, each consisting of four or five short arias, con nected by recitative; most were written out only for soprano and *basso continuo* but some had two voice-parts and in a few others the accompaniment acknowledged the existence of violins or even flutes – although he is said to have disliked wind instruments because 'they are never in tune'. At first Scarlatti was not always sure-fingered in handling what was still a comparatively unfamiliar problem of tonality – the judging of the sense of key-structure imposed by the permanent adoption of the major and minor scales: many arias in the cantatas and early operas seemed unable to make up their minds whether they were in, say, C major or G major. This technical aspect, however, became comparatively immaterial when he presently showed that his strongest suit was melodic invention; he continued to play this hand to good advantage in both cantatas and operas – though less well in church music, a field in which he was not so prolific.

It was during his first Neapolitan period (1684-1702) that Scarlatti established the classical tradition of Italian *opera seria* with such works as *Olimpia vendicata, La Statira* and *Pirro e Demetrio*, the last-named being actually played and published in London during the composer's lifetime. In the English version of the libretto the rhyming quatrain

> Veder parmi
> un' ombra nera,
> cruda e' fiera
> minacciarmi

became the rhyming couplet

> Something bloody and unexpected
> at my bosom seems directed.

On the other hand there were scenes in *Clearco, Teodora Augustin* and *Eraclea* which were *intentionally* funny, where farce jostled impending tragedy as closely as in *Hamlet* and *Macbeth* a century earlier or (which is more to the point) in *Don Giovanni* a century later. These operas all followed a stereotyped constructional pattern: aria, recitative, duet, recitative, aria, etc., up to the formal concluding chorus, which as a rule was not so much a chorus in modern connotation as a short ensemble for the principal characters.

By contrast with Scarlatti's cantata manuscripts his operatic manuscripts contained fairly frequent melodic hints for the realization of the *basso continuo*; indeed the parts were sometimes written out in full and occasionally one meets the injunction 'tutti li stromenti d'arco senza cembalo' ('all the bowed instruments without the harpsichord').

While Scarlatti was travelling round central and northern Italy between 1702 and 1708 he composed the opera which those well qualified to judge regard as his best – *Il Mitridate Eupatore* Venice, (1707); this was unequivocally serious, with no intrusion of the *buffo* element and yet here the composer at last began to develop a flair for musical characterization, a flair which after his return to Naples in 1709 was main tained in *La principessa fedele* (1710) and *Tigrane* (1715). Since he so often demonstrated, even in *opera seria*, that he had a sense of humour, it is surprising that *Il trionfo dell' onore* (1718) was the only one of his extant operas which could be rated as a genuine *opera buffa* (comic opera). Here the composer in some respects foreshadowed the Mozart of *Figaro*, although he did little to establish the characteristics of traditional *opera buffa* in the manner in which he had earlier – in *La Statira* – established the characteristics of traditional *opera seria*. *Il trionfo dell' onore* contained no suggestion of the 'concerted finale' later evolved by his successor Leonardo Vinci (not to be confused with Leonardo *da* Vinci!); each act ended with an ensemble appropriate to the situation but it was only in a quartet from Act III ('Pensa, pensa ben') that vocal counterpoint acquired signifi cance in its context.

I have purposely refrained from cluttering the pages of this book with parenthetical or footnote references to authorities apart from occasional and acknowledged quota tions from the writings of recognized experts, but it would be churlish not to admit that even so brief a survey of Scarlatti as the present one would hardly have been possible unless a large measure of reliance could have been placed on the pioneering research of E. J. Dent, who somewhere about 1900 set himself the task of tracking down records and manuscripts all over Europe. Unfortunately he drew

blank everywhere except Berlin, Bologna, Brussels, Cam
bridge, Darmstadt, Dresden, Florence, London, Milan,
Modena, Montecassino, Munich, Naples, Oxford, Padua,
Rome, Schwerin and Vienna, but none the less he managed
to become acquainted with about one third of the hundred-
and-twenty operas which Scarlatti is known to have com
pleted, and he promptly revealed his conclusions in what
might be called the Scarlatti bible – *Alessandro Scarlatti, his
life and works,* first published in 1905 and re-issued in 1960
with factual annotations by his younger but equally erudite
and enthusiastic colleague Frank Walker. Meanwhile in
1927 Alfred Lorenz of Munich University wrote his admir
able *Alessandro Scarlattis Jugendoper,* which was teutonic-
ally thorough within its self-imposed limitations and in
corporated no less than four hundred music-type examples
from eighteen operas dated between 1679 and 1700. Yet to
most music lovers Scarlatti remains barely accessible: of the
operas only a fistful and of the chamber-cantatas no more
than a baker's dozen have been published complete, and
very few are readily available. A rhetorical question there
fore poses itself. Why have Italian scholars given more
attention to his (admittedly very gifted) son Domenico and
to his talented but relatively unimportant disciples Leonardo
Leo and Nicola Logroscino than to the father and master,
so that the world at large (which includes Italy) has to thank
Dent from Yorkshire and Walker from Hampshire and
Lorenz from Bavaria for persuading it that Alessandro
Scarlatti from Sicily was not only a great composer in his
own right but also the spiritual forerunner of an even
greater composer who hailed from Salzburg?

CHAPTER SIX

HANDEL

Five chapters having been devoted to five composers belong
ing to what may be regarded as a bygone age – or as an age
of transition – we now come to grips with the first indisput
ably great one of modern times – that is to say of the
eighteenth and nineteenth centuries and the first half of the
twentieth. (He was first by a short head, mark you, for his
illustrious contemporary who is the subject of chapter 7 was
junior by only twenty-six days.)

GEORGE FRIDERIC HANDEL – his own final choice of spelling
– was born at Halle on 23rd February 1685; his father was a
doctor (a 'barber-surgeon') and his mother, Dorothea *nee*
Taust, the daughter of a Protestant priest. One is at liberty
to shrug aside the romantic legend of a curly-headed six-
year-old being discovered late at night divinely playing the
harpsichord by moonlight in a cold attic, but the fact
remains that Handel was a child prodigy. His natural in
stincts were encouraged by his aunt Anna Taust rather than
by his parents, but eventually his father consented to music-
lessons – and even allowed him, at the age of eleven, to go
by himself to Berlin (a week's journey in those days) in
order to attend the unconventional court of Electress Sophia
Charlotte, to whom music was all that mattered. Soon after
wards young Handel was deputy-organist at Halle Cathedral
and at seventeen, although supposedly studying law at the
University, was appointed *head*-organist. A successful career
in that field looked to be open to him, but he was beginning
to feel the tug of the stage and after a year or so left the
organ-loft at Halle for the opera-house at Hamburg, where
between 1703 and 1706 he played in the orchestra and
secured the production of two operas of his own. Realization
that he had found his natural bent then drove him south,
to the land of opera; by what route or at whose expense (it
can hardly have been his own) has not been determined.

Although Handel never married (perhaps because his main pleasures, apart from music, were good food, good wine and good company) it is believed that during the three years he spent in Italy he had a love affair with a young singer; historians have been unable to agree as to which young singer it was out of the many he must have encoun tered while travelling back and forth (several times) between Venice, Florence, Rome and Naples. What is more impor tant is that in the course of his wanderings he experimented to good purpose in the chamber-cantata form recently popularized by Alessandro Scarlatti (see page 27) and also composed two more operas – *Roderigo* and *Agrippina*. By 1710, however, he was back in his native land as musical director at the court of the Elector of Hanover and was presently granted leave of absence to visit London, where he stayed for six months and produced *Rinaldo* at the Queen's Theatre, Haymarket. He loved London so much that a year or so later (he was twenty-seven at the time) he returned there, stayed on – and although still nominally on the Elector's pay-roll accepted an allowance from Queen Anne. Consequently there were some awkward moments when on Queen Anne's death in 1714 Handel's Hanoverian employer followed him across the North Sea to fill the vacant seat on the English throne. Good standing with the nobility, however, weighed in his favour, and the tem porary breach between the two Georges, king and com poser, was soon healed. Both lived in London for the rest of their lives, the former becoming British *ex officio* and the latter by naturalisation.

Over the next twenty-seven years the story of Handel is the story of his fluctuating operatic fortunes. As manager and artistic director of the King's (previously Queen's) Theatre he did far more than anyone else to establish Italian *opera seria* as a permanent feature of musical life in London. His own contribution included over thirty operas – among them such fine works as *Giulio Cesare*, *Admeto*, *Orlando*, *Alcina* and *Serse* – but up to 1730 or thereabouts he also called in the recognized composers Attilio Ariosti and Giovanni Bononcini – while he himself scoured Italy for the best singers that could be found. For a time all went well (and indeed the policy looked to be both prudent and enlightened), but without knowing it Handel was stirring up trouble. For one thing Ariosti and Bononcini, who were fifteen to twenty years his senior and had their own parti sans, were jealous and unco-operative, doing all they could to undermine their associate's personal position and pres tige. For another there was spiteful rivalry between the two famous sopranos Faustina Bordoni and Francesca Cuzzoni; this reached its climax during a gala performance of Bonon cini's *Astianatte* when (egged on by the audience) they indulged in a free fight on the stage with no holds barred and no quarter asked or given. Such goings-on under royal patronage could not pass without comment in an age which relished any form of scandal and were soon satirized by John Gay in *The Beggar's Opera* (1728, with music arranged from traditional and currently popular airs by Handel's Anglo-German contemporary John Christopher Pepusch). This witty little affair and other ballad-operas which followed it had a profound effect on contemporary taste. In the outcome the effect did not last long but it lasted long enough to imperil the future prospects of Handel's venture. With bulldog determination he continued (now alone and unassisted) along his chosen road, but from 1732 onwards he found it necessary to vary the exclusively operatic diet with oratorios like *Esther, Saul* and *Israel in Egypt*, and with what might conveniently be called can tatas – *Acis and Galatea* and *Alexander's Feast*. (The ora torios and cantatas were in English, not in Italian, and in the oratorios a very prominent share in the proceedings was allotted to the chorus; but it should be stressed that all these works were given on the stage – sometimes with stage costume and action.) In 1741 however, when financial ruin (not for the first time) stared him in the face, Handel the impresario wisely decided to cut his losses and shut up shop – and Handel the composer abandoned opera for ever.

All this while, when away from the theatre, he had produced a fair quantity of short choral works (e.g. the 'Chandos' anthems) and a large quantity of instrumental music. This included the *Water Music* and some eighty concertos (not as a rule concertos in the modern sense of the term, which implies the setting of a solo instrument or instruments against an orchestra, but merely concerted works for various instrumental combinations), nearly thirty sonatas for strings and *continuo* following the precedent of Purcell (see page 25) and several volumes of harpsichord pieces.

Although most of Handel's keyboard music belonged to his early years and looks comparatively unimportant when set beside the rest of his output, a nodding acquain tance helps one to easy familiarity with the forms of gavotte, bourree, minuet, courante, sarabande, gigue and fugue – which were exploited more subtly and to much greater purpose by his twin Johann Sebastian Bach. The first six were contemporary dance-measures; in a fugue – *fuga*, literally 'flight' – each vocal or instrumental line entered in turn with the same theme or a slightly modified answer to it ('subject' and ' countersubject'), thereby soon becoming involved in an intricate web of counterpoint. When tech nique is matched by inspiration a fugue can be one of the most exciting forms of musical expression yet devised; when inspiration is lacking it may be no more than a laborious academic exercise. Many – though not all – of Handel's and Bach's belonged to the former category.

Soon after the collapse of his operatic schemes Handel composed the most popular oratorio of all time – *Messiah* (not, please, THE *Messiah*); then, perhaps partly because he felt in need of a change of atmosphere and partly because creditors were pressing, he went to Ireland – taking the manuscript along with him. He was rapturously wel comed and the nine months he spent there helped to lighten his depression and stabilize his financial situation: *Messiah* had its world *premiere* on 13th April 1742 at the Music Hall (not music-hall) in Fishamble Street, Dublin, where, too, some of his other recent works were much better received than they had been in London. Thenceforth Handel concentrated his attention largely on oratorio, although he also produced the 'Dettingen Te Deum' and the cantata *Semele*. As already hinted, the dividing line between the sacred and the secular was not very clearly drawn in mid-eighteenth-century London and it is signifi cant that of the eight oratorios that followed *Messiah* seven were first given at Covent Garden and one at the theatre in the Haymarket which had been the scene of so many of the composer's former triumphs and disasters; it is even more significant that five at least out of the eight were masterpieces – *Samson, Belshazzar, Solomon, Theodora* and *Jephtha*. It was while he was engaged on *Jephtha* (1752) that his eyesight began to fail; presently he became totally blind. For seven years, with characteristic courage, he went on conducting his own works from memory and actually played the organ at a performance of *Messiah* on 6th April 1759. But by that time he was not only blind but also very ill; a week later, on the evening of Good Friday, he fell into a coma, and he breathed his last before the next day dawned.

The expression 'typically Handelian' is often used as a means of describing such straightforward evocations of healthy sentiment as 'For unto us a child is born', but in truth this style was only narrowly typical of Handel himself although widely typical of many contemporary composers of whom he can be seen in retrospect to have been the leader. The outstanding attribute which earned him sup remacy over his colleagues was spontaneous versatility of melodic invention. 'For unto us', let us remember, was fol lowed by 'Rejoice greatly', 'He shall feed His flock', 'Why do the nations' and 'I know that my Redeemer liveth'; therein lay an infinite variety of richness. Yet *Messiah*, taken as a whole, retains its hold on the public through its appeal to nostalgia rather than through its intrinsic merit; it is un deniably a great work but there are those who would not agree that it is any greater than *Solomon* or *Jephtha*, which indeed are better constructed, more unified in mood and therefore – from the point of view of the objective musician – more satisfying. Nor do some of Handel's other oratorios and cantatas deserve the comparative neglect which has overtaken them. Most of my readers will have had the pleasure, sometime, of hearing 'Love in her eyes sits playing', 'Let the bright Seraphim', 'Where e'er you walk' and 'Angels ever bright and fair' – but probably out of their context: few may realize that they belong respectively to *Acis and Galatea*, *Samson*, *Semele* and *Theodora*, which represent the composer at his best almost throughout. One hopes, therefore, that promoters of *Messiah* seasons may be prevailed upon to give us an occasional change of tune. When possible revivals of Handel's *operas* come under con sideration, however, there are some tricky problems to be faced.

(1) As in Scarlatti's, the space between the opening and concluding choruses of these operas is filled with a succes sion of arias and duets connected by recitative which is normally unaccompanied except by harpsichord *continuo* although here and there (cf. Scarlatti, p. 29), a string orch estra is employed. Eighteenth-century audiences did not think they had had their money's worth inside five hours, while those of the twentieth become restive after two-and-a-half; therefore when Handel's operas are given today ruth less cutting is necessary. It is impracticable to shorten the recitative to any significant extent, since this tells the story, carries on the dramatic action and indeed provides the only justification for the work being played in a theatre at all. So inevitably about fifty-per-cent of the aria/duet content has to be sacrificed, nor can the sacrifice be determined solely on musical grounds: every protagonist must be allowed a due proportion of the vocal say.

(2) In all Handel's operas at least one of the leading 'male' parts was written for a lyric soprano – or possibly a con tralto – who ranked second only to the leading soprano playing the heroine, a procedure later endorsed by Mozart in *Figaro*, Gounod in *Faust* and Strauss in *Der Rosen-kavalier*. But Handel's characters were not, as a rule, mere striplings immersed in calf-love like Cherubino, Siebel and Octavian, and one's instinct cries out for masculine representation.

(3) Then there is the problem of casting the roles which early eighteenth-century convention decreed should be

played by *castrati* (male singers who before adolescence had consented or been forced to undergo castration in order to prevent their voices from breaking); here the physical attributes of a male-impersonator would often be histrionic ally unsatisfying, the penetrating timbre of a falsetto counter-tenor vocally unsatisfying.

(4) The most logical and perhaps most sensible way out of these difficulties is to take the bull by the horns and replace all Principal Boys by tenors and all *castrati* by full-blooded baritones. This involves a spate of key-trans positions, with consequent re-arrangement not only of the accompaniments to the arias but also of the actual key-sequences in the preceding and subsequent recitative pas sages, so that the detailed effect may admittedly in places be some way from the composer's original intentions; any compromise solution, however, is unlikely to get much closer.

Enough has been said, I think, to indicate that anyone who attempts to prepare a Handel opera for present-day consumption faces no easy task, but at least he can take one comfort: so long as he recognizes that neither oboists nor those who listen to them take kindly to four- or five-minute sessions of uninterrupted reed-blowing, he will find that the *instrumental* balance, *per se*, requires little adjust ment: paradoxically it was in his stage-works rather than in his concertos that Handel proved himself an early master of what is now called orchestration, using harps, bassoons, horns, trumpets and trombones even, to obtain quite start ling colour-effects.

Handel's personal character was not untouched by the coarseness of the age in which he lived but he was generous as well as self-indulgent and too sincere, perhaps too obstinate, ever to make a thoroughgoing success of the flair for worldly opportunism with which he is sometimes credited. In any case there was no such element in his approach to his art, which was splendidly and consistently *un*-coarse. Inevitably inspiration ebbed and flowed, but for so prolific a composer the pages of tedium or triviality were comparatively rare. He occasionally played down to his public ('See the conquering hero comes' from *Judas Maccabeus* might almost be called a pot-boiler) but his music was rarely unworthy of a reputation which over the centuries has suffered very few ups and downs as generation has succeeded generation, each in turn bringing changes of taste and outlook. Englishmen, at any rate, have never swerved from allegiance to their adopted countryman George Frideric Handel and have always regarded him as an outstanding figure in the history of music. How right they have been!

CHAPTER SEVEN

BACH

During the second half of the sixteenth century and the whole of the seventeenth and eighteenth, the musical life of Thuringia (an area of central Germany roughly bor dered by the rivers Werra, Unstrut and Saale) was domin ated by the Bach family. No fewer than thirty-eight of the clan – the eldest born in 1520 and the youngest in 1759 – have earned separate articles in Grove's *Dictionary of Music and Musicians*; the first 60,000 or so words of Philip Spitta's standard but unwieldy biography of JOHANN SEBASTIAN BACH (published in 1880) were devoted to the achievements of his great-grandfather, grandfather, father, uncles and other senior relatives; three of Sebastian's own sons (Wilhelm Friedemann, Carl Philip Emmanuel and Johann Christian) distinguished themselves as composers and all-round musicians. Our present concern however is with Johann Sebastian himself – the noblest Bach of them all – who was born on 21st March 1685 at Eisenach (mid way between Cassel and Erfurt), a medium-sized town nestling in a fertile valley and overlooked by a peak known as the Wartburg (later immortalised as the scene of the song-contest in Wagner's *Tannhäuser*). Today Eisenach is primarily industrial, holds a population of some 40,000 and lies (just) on East German soil; in the seventeenth and early eighteenth centuries it was a noted centre of musical activity, activity in which almost needless to say the local branch of the Bachs played a conspicuous part. Young Sebastian probably had his first training, along with the rest, at the local choir-school, but his mother died in 1694, his father in 1695; so at the age of ten he went to live with his elder brother Johann Christoph, recently married, who was municipal choirmaster at Ohrdruf, a smaller town than Eisenach and twenty miles away to the south-east. This Christoph, besides being an organist, was an exponent of the clavichord, an instrument which outwardly resembled the harpsichord but was capable of a small measure of dynamic contrast since the strings were mechanically struck, not plucked, and if the controlling key were pressed down hard the corresponding string continued to vibrate slightly for a few seconds – although not to the same extent as on a modern piano. Sebastian quickly absorbed the technique and it was for the clavichord, as well as the harpsichord, that he later wrote some great keyboard music.

Christoph's family multiplied so rapidly that by 1700 he could no longer give hospitality to his young brother, who however was sufficiently fortunate and gifted to win a chorister's scholarship at the Benedictine school of St. Michael's at Lüneburg, which lies twenty miles south-east of Hamburg on the edge of Lüneburg Heath.[1] Bach stayed there about three years and meanwhile developed his powers as instrumentalist (organ, harpsichord, clavichord, violin) rather than as singer or composer. He returned to his home ground in 1703 and for the next four years was organist and choirmaster at Arnstadt (a mere morning's walk away from his brother at Ohrdruf); here he composed a fair quantity of organ music which owed much to the influence of the Scandinavian-born Dietrich Buxtehude, whom Bach greatly admired and indeed travelled to Lübeck to visit, thereby incurring the displeasure of his employers at Arnstadt. Then in 1707 there occurred two events of considerable importance in his career: in June he was installed as organist and choirmaster at the free imperial city of Mühlhausen (fifteen miles north of Eisenach and not to be con fused with Mülhausen – now Mulhouse – in Alsace); in October he married his second cousin Maria Barbara Bach – hoping no doubt to ensure that his children would thus be doubly well equipped to carry on the family tradition.

Bach did not stay long at Muhlhausen, for his astonish ing virtuosity on the organ was quickly noted in exalted

[1] It was here that on 7th May 1945 General Keitel signed and handed to Field-Marshal Montgomery the instrument of uncon ditional surrender of all German forces in north-west Germany, Denmark and Holland.

circles and within a year or so he was called upon to join a select musical household at the ducal court of Weimar. (He was still within easy distance of innumerable relatives.) His patron, Duke Wilhelm Ernst of Saxe-Weimar, yielded to none as a feudal overlord, but unlike many other minor potentates of his day he was deeply religious (an austere and indeed ascetic member of the 'pietest' branch of the Lutheran faith); nevertheless he enjoyed his music so long as it was serious in intent and not merely an excuse for irreverent caperings in a dissolute gavotte or licentious minuet. Bach was engaged as court-organist and director of chamber music, and it was at Weimar that over the next nine years his talent blossomed into genius; he composed the first thirty or so of his two-hundred-odd church can tatas and his mastery of at least one branch of composition – organ music – became apparent in such works as the chorale preludes of the *Little Organ Book* and the toccata and fugue in D minor. (I should prefer to call this just the toccata in D minor, because by definition a toccata is a piece of music designed to display executive rather than creative powers; if the composer chooses to round things off with a fugue, well and good, but the fugue remains *part* of the toccata, not a sequel to it. A chorale prelude was in essence an organ voluntary based on a hymn-tune but in Bach's hands became a polyphonic development of volun tary melodies of such intrinsic worth that the intrusion of the hymn-tune which was its nominal *primum mobile* some times, though not always, struck an incongruous note.)

Eventually Bach fell from ducal favour and was passed over when a vacancy occurred in the post of head choir master. The reason was a personal one: the strait-laced Duke Wilhelm Ernst had a worldly nephew – Duke Ernst August – of whom he strongly disapproved, and he was furious when he discovered that his organist was on cor dial terms with him. The composer's disappointment was short-lived however, for his new friend introduced him to Prince Leopold of Anhalt and before the end of 1717 Bach left Weimar to take charge of the more comprehensive musical establishment which Prince Leopold maintained at his court at Cothen (equidistant from Magdeburg and Leipzig). His new employer, though no less devoted a churchman than Duke Wilhelm Ernst, was far less bigoted – and indeed was a most enlightened patron of the arts. In this congenial atmosphere Bach set out to tackle instrumental music (almost for the first time) and presently produced some twenty sonatas, either for violin unaccompanied (e.g. the 'chaconne'), for cello unaccompanied, for violin and clavier (a generic term covering harpsichord, clavichord and early types of piano) or for flute and clavier; a handful of orchestral suites; the concerto in D minor for two violins with string accompaniment; above all the six 'Brandenburg' concertos – so called because they were dedicated to Christian Ludwig, Margrave of Brandenburg. Taken collectively these approximated rather more closely than did most of Handel's to the modern notion of a concerto: although nos. 3 and 6 were for strings and *continuo* only, all the rest had in addition a solo violin, nos. 2, 4 and 5 a solo flute, no. 2 a solo oboe as well, while no. 1 actually called for three solo oboes, a solo bassoon and two solo horns. In no. 5, exceptionally, the clavier-player had a specific part of his own, so that instead of being a mere filler-in he too became a soloist with a laid-down share in the concerting. (No. 1 was in four movements, no. 3 in two, the others in three, and it is interesting to note that all six began and ended in major keys; several of the middle movements, however, were in the relative minor.) Meanwhile the organ was not entirely neglected, for the 'great' preludes and fugues in A minor, C minor and G major belong to the Cothen period; but during these years Bach's output for a smaller keyboard held greater significance, including as it did the six 'French' suites and the first twenty-four of his famous 'forty-eight preludes and fugues for well-tempered clavier'. And at this juncture, I fear, there must be a brief theoretical digression.

The sound vibrations which produce musical notes of varying pitch are attuned to pitch-intervals which are very nearly but not absolutely equal: the interval between E and F, for instance, is not quite the same as that between

F and F sharp. The singers and string-players of Bach's day, who had – or should have had – complete control over their intonation, would subconsciously adjust that control when the music modulated from, say, the key of F to the key of E. But when the notes were reproduced mechanically on a key board instrument there could be no such almost imper ceptible raising or lowering of the pitch, so that a harpsi chord or clavichord perfectly in tune for the key of F would become out of tune in the key of E; as a corollary a piece composed for an instrument tuned to F could never modulate to E (nor to any but the most closely related key) without courting disaster. Bach, a traditionalist in many respects, here allied himself with the progressive party which was prepared to sacrifice 'just intonation' in favour of 'equal temperament', i.e. a division of the octave, on keyboard instruments, into twelve identical semitone-intervals. To point the fact he wrote this set of preludes and fugues, twenty-four of them, one each in every major and minor key, and all playable, without disaster, on a well-tempered clavier.

Bach's stay at Cothen, which lasted from 1717 until 1723, was extremely productive, but it was clouded by personal tragedy when his wife Maria Barbara died in 1720; she had borne him seven children of whom four still survived (among them were Wilhelm Friedemann and Carl Phillip Emmanuel). He was one of those who stood in need of a permanent feminine helpmeet, and little more than a year later he married the twenty-year-old soprano Anna Mag-dalena Wilcken. His second marriage was as happy as the first had been and the union produced thirteen more children; only six survived infancy however (among them was Johann Christian). Meanwhile Bach's patron, Prince Leopold, had himself married a lively young lady named Friederica Henrietta who evidently had little taste for music and no taste at all for the solemnity of chorale preludes, fugues and cantatas; in consequence Bach found himself rather cold-shouldered and sent in his resignation as soon as an opportunity presented itself.

During the remaining twenty-seven years of his life when

43

he was cantor of St. Thomas's church in Leipzig (and as part of his duties had to teach small boys Latin) there must have been many moments when he looked longingly back to his comparatively carefree days at Cöthen. But on the whole he seems to have settled fairly happily to a new way of life, although many tales are told of his disputes with the rector of the school, the university authorities, the Leip zig municipal council and the king of Saxony. Be that as it may, no one could cavil at the quality of the compositions which meanwhile flowed fast from his pen: the best of his church cantatas; the full-length choral works *The Passion according to St John*, the *Passion according to St Matthew*, the *Christmas Oratorio* and the *Mass in B minor* (originally conceived as a short Lutheran mass but later expanded to fit the longer Catholic liturgy); in the secular field the cantatas known as *Phoebus and Pan*, the 'Coffee' and the 'Peasant'; for the orchestra more concertos; for the organ a further set of preludes and fugues including the 'great' B minor, C major and E minor; for the clavier the six 'English' suites, the variations (thirty of them) on a theme of his pupil Johann Gottlieb Goldberg and the second volume of the 'forty-eight'. At the time of their composition however, these works made little impression on the public (one is inclined to think they might have been better received at Weimar or Eisenach, not so far away to the west in his native Thuringia), and when – like Handel – Bach was stricken by blindness no one seemed much concerned about it except his wife Anna Magdalena. His immortal soul went aloft on 28th July 1750 but the burghers of Leipzig apparently cared little, for they erected no monument to his memory and allowed his widow to die in poverty.

Although Handel and Bach were born and spent their boyhood less than a hundred miles apart they never met: the former's visits to Germany after he settled in London were few and far between, and the latter did not move further afield than Lübeck or Berlin. Bach is unlikely to have been familiar with the music of Handel's maturity and Handel almost certainly never heard a note of Bach's. So although they are inevitably and rightly regarded as twin giants it is not surprising that their music held little in common apart from the easily recognizable harmonic and contrapuntal tendencies which characterized the music of the age rather than of any individual composer. It has already been stressed that what raised Handel to a higher level than Bononcini and company was an extraordinary gift for varied and contrasted melody; at the risk of over simplification it might be added that one factor which helped to raise Bach above the level of Buxtehude was an extraordinary gift for varied and contrasted rhythm. At times the initial rhythmic impulse carries a whole move ment successfully through to its conclusion – as in the finale of the concerto in D minor for three claviers and strings, and the short chorus 'Sind Blitze, sind Donner' from the *Matthew Passion*; at others the actual counterpoint seems to spring from the interweaving of rhythmic figures rather than of melodic phrases – as in the prelude in F sharp major from the second book of the 'forty-eight' and the opening section of the 'Gloria' from the *Mass in B minor*. Bach's technique was indeed so stupendous that now and again he let it be his master rather than his servant and it cannot be denied that at times his music was in consequence more liable than Handel's to sound uninspired – even dull. On the other hand, when in serious and con templative mood (which was by no means in the church music alone) he could conjure up a spiritual endowment beyond the imaginings of his contemporary. I shall venture no further on comparative judgment; if Handel himself could have the last word he would no doubt point out that Bach never wrote an opera and that if he had it probably wouldn't have been a very good one.

The oft-quoted affirmation of Robert Schumann that 'music owes as much to Johann Sebastian Bach as Christ ianity does to its Founder' was the colourful and pardon able exaggeration of an enthusiastic champion. One might well concede, however, that the subsequent *spread* of music owes him as much as the subsequent spread of Christianity did to Saint Paul.

CHAPTER EIGHT

GLUCK

In the early eighteenth century some of the wealthiest men in the Empire (as the Holy Roman Empire had by then become simply and familiarly known) were the princes, archdukes, counts and other nobilities who owned vast tracts of land in both Bohemia and Bavaria; among the many thousand of their retainers was one Alexander Johannes Gluck. He must have been a reliable fellow for he was employed (first as huntsman and then as forester and finally as head-forester) at various widely-separated feudal estates in turn. That is how it came about that his son CHRISTOPH WILLIBALD GLUCK (1714-1787) was born at the Bavarian hamlet of Erasbach in the valley of the river Altmühl (some thirty miles west of Regensburg) and yet spent most of his youth in the woods and fields of northern Bohemia (not far from the Sudetenland which just over two hundred years later was to earn a measure of unenvi able notoriety as a political storm-centre); for a time, too, he studied music at Prague and possibly attended its university. Today therefore, Germans and Czechs and Austrians alike claim Gluck as their own: he was born on what is now West German soil and was nurtured and edu cated in what is now Czechoslovakia, but both regions were then under Habsburg – i.e. Austrian – domination. Com pilers of reference books often sit tactfully on a fence and describe him as Bohemian-German; what matters is that thanks to extensive travel he eventually became a cosmo politan European, equally at home in Leipzig, Prague, Vienna, Milan, Rome, Paris, Hamburg and Copenhagen – although not quite so much at home in London, as we shall very soon see.

At the age of twenty-two Gluck was made welcome in Vienna under the auspices of his father's employer Prince Lobkowitz but very soon he discovered a noble patron of his own – Prince Francesco Saverio Melzi, who added him to a private orchestra (in which he apparently played violin and cello indiscriminately) and presently carried him off to Italy, where he embarked upon a lengthy career as com poser with the opera *Artaserse* (Milan, 1741). This was followed by nine more operas in the next four years; they were so successful that he was invited to London, where his *Caduta de' giganti* and *Artamene* were produced in 1746 at the King's Theatre, Haymarket. This was after Handel had severed his connection with that establishment (see page 33), but *Giulio Cesare* and *Alcina* were still remem bered and to London opera-goers Gluck's offerings seemed pale by comparison – as indeed they were. Handel himself was severely critical: 'Gluck knows no more counterpoint than my cook' he asserted (being a gourmet he always chose his cooks carefully) and here he placed a shrewd finger on a weak spot, for Gluck's technique was barely adequate for the tasks which he set himself and the time was yet to come when he would prove that in opera musical technique was not all that mattered.

Dissatisfied with the manner in which he had been received in London he returned to Vienna, where two years later *Semiramide riconosciuta* brought him to the favour able notice of no less a personage than Empress Maria Theresa; thereafter he was *persona grata* in the highest social circles and in 1754 was appointed musical director at the imperial court. Meanwhile he made further tours abroad (to Italy, Germany, Denmark), composing and pro ducing operas as he went, and in 1750 married a wealthy Viennese lady named Marianne Pergin. His material future thus assured, Gluck (who never lacked initiative) felt free to indulge in experiment.

On his way from Italy to London in 1746 he had spent some time in Paris, the only western European capital where opera had partially escaped from the shackles of Italian tradition and language – thanks largely to the earnest-minded Jean Philippe Rameau (1683-1764, the most outstanding French composer of his generation) and the unassuming François Philidor (composer of *comedies a ariettes*). Gluck, who had hitherto adopted the pattern of *opera seria* inaugurated by Alessandro Scarlatti (see page 29) and subscribed to by Handel, may well have been impressed by the unconventionality of the (French) libretti which Rameau had chosen and by his unconventional treatment of them – especially in recitative passages. At all events, during the next few years he devoted some of his time to studying poetry, literature and drama, and soon came to the conclusion that what opera needed was closer integration between words and music. Very wisely, instead of rushing in where angels might have feared to tread, he felt his way carefully by first providing the Austrian court with a series of French comic operas *a la* Philidor – of which the first was *Les amours champetres* (1755) and the most successful *L'ile de Merlin* (1758). Meanwhile he made contact with an enlightened Italian writer named Raniera da Calzabigi, and between them in due course they fash ioned *Orfeo ed Eurydice*, which had its first performance at Vienna on 5th October 1762. This was a turning point not only in Gluck's career but also in the history of opera, for in *Orfeo* drama and music were fused to entity by partial elimination of the formal absurdities catalogued on pages 36/37 (paragraphs 2 and 3), by reduction to a minimum of the incongruous contrast between *recitativo secco* and florid vocalism, by granting the chorus a larger share in the proceedings than had hitherto been customary. In the next two Calzabigi/Gluck operas – *Alceste* (1767) and *Paride ed Elena* (1770) – the policy of integration was carried a stage further and in 1773 the composer was encouraged by his ex-pupil Marie Antoinette (Maria Theresa's daughter, by now dauphine of France and presently to be its queen) to set a French libretto based on Jean Racine's translation of Euripides' *Iphigenie en Aulide*. Accordingly he travelled to Paris, where not only the new work itself but also French versions of *Orfeo* and *Alceste* made a profound impression: ardent nationalists acclaimed him as a worthy successor of their own Rameau and were almost inclined to regard him as a naturalized Frenchman. On the other hand he had to face noisy opposition from the adherents of Nicola Piccinni, a talented Italian composer of conventional *opera seria* and frenchified *opera buffa*. Over the next few years the Gluckists and Piccinnists made confounded nuisances of themselves by trying to stir up trouble between the two composers, who to their credit refused to join in the acri monious debates and remained throughout on terms of cordiality, if not of mutual admiration. Gluck conclusively established his artistic supremacy with *Armide* (1777), *Iphigenie en Tauride* and *Écho et Narcisse* (both 1779); ne then returned to Vienna where he lived in extremely com fortable retirement until eight years later, when he died of a stroke at the age of seventy-three.

Despite the fact that for many years 'Che faro senza Eurydice' was accounted one of the world's best tunes, Gluck was in truth no more distinguished as a melodist than as a contrapuntist (although Piccinni never compared his rival with his *chef de cuisine*); indeed it could plausibly be argued that in the narrowest sense of the term he wasn't a great composer at all. What cannot be gainsaid is that he was a great reformer, endowed with the instinct and good sense to realize what was wrong with opera and the diligence and ability to demonstrate in practice how it could be put right. From 1790 onwards old-fashioned *opera seria* gradually fell into neglect in France, the Netherlands and Germany; it even took a back seat in Vienna. The reason was that Christoph Willibald Gluck, with *Alceste, Iphigenie en Aulide* and the others, had in effect inaugur ated a new art-form – which no-one had as yet had the brain-wave to call music drama.

CHAPTER NINE

HAYDN

JOSEPH HAYDN was born on 31st March 1732 at the village of Rohrau, thirty miles east of Vienna on the verge of that low-lying region round the Neusiedlersee (Ferto Tava) which has long been a bone of political contention between Austria and Hungary. Rohrau, although typically Hun garian in lay-out (single-storied cottages set far back from the grass-lined road), was – and is – on Austrian territory, but the border was not far away and the inhabitants were of mixed racial descent; nor were the elements exclusively Austrian and Magyar, for during the seventeenth century there had been a surge of immigrants to this indeterminate no-man's-land both from high (southern) Germany and from Croatia (now part of Yugoslavia). It is probable that two at least of Haydn's great-grandparents came from high Germany (not, let it be stressed, from Prussia) and that he also had Croatian blood in his veins; be that as it may he was Austrian by birth. Since the local landowner employed his father as a coach-repairer (later as a bailiff) and his mother as a kitchen-maid (later as a cook) he enjoyed, in the words of Hubert Parry, the advantages of a thoroughly plebeian extraction.

When he was six he was sent to live with an uncle (school- and choir-master at the nearby town of Hainburg overlook ing the Danube) who in 1740 arranged for him to enter the cathedral school of St. Stephen's, Vienna; a few years later he was joined there by his younger brother Michael.[1] They sang in the cathedral choir and meanwhile received a sound education, but Joseph's boyish exuberance continually led him into stupid pranks and as soon as his voice broke – at the unusually late age of seventeen – he was summarily dis missed under a cloud of official disapproval. During the

[1] Michael Haydn became well-known as an organist and composer; among his pupils was Carl Weber (page 77).

difficult years that followed he scraped a bare living by sing ing and playing in the streets of Vienna, but was eventually befriended by the stage comedian Joseph Kurz for whom he composed a comic opera (*The Crooked Devil*), by the versatile Niccola Porpora (composer, singer, pedagogue) for whom he acted both as valet and accompanist, and finally by two grandees named Baron von Fürnberg and Count Morzin who in turn engaged him as 'private musician'; between-whiles he augmented his meagre earnings by giving singing lessons. The excellence of Count Morzin's private music brought Haydn to the notice of Prince Anton Esterhazy, wealthiest of all wealthy Hungarian noblemen, who promptly offered him the post of assistant musical director at his court at Eisenstadt (twenty-five miles south of Vienna) with a good prospect of presently taking complete control; Haydn jumped at the chance and thereafter his livelihood was assured. In domestic affairs he was less fortunate: in 1760 he married one of his pupils, Maria Anna Keller, and for the next forty years (she died in 1800) both bitterly regretted it. Haydn, who had little experience in such matters, seems to have been trapped into marriage with a woman who had no intention of giving him wifely help or encouragement and even, by one account, used his scores for curl-papers; in course of time his frequent infideli ties (for boyish exuberance never deserted him) drove her to devote herself to good works, which according to his biographer Rosemary Hughes (with whom I cannot claim kinship) consisted mainly of 'entertaining at their house a continuous and distracting procession of clergy'.

Prince Paul Anton Esterhazy, as it happened, died a few months after Haydn took up his appointment at Eisenstadt, but his brother Nicolas (who succeeded to the title and estates) was an equally enthusiastic patron; the expected promotion to full directorship of the musical establishment coincided with the building of a magnificent new palace, known henceforth as Esterhaza, on the site of a former shooting-lodge at Süttor in the desolate marshland south east of the Neusiedlersee. Haydn's position in the household was no easy one, for his time was divided between Eisenstadt and Esterhaza, he had entire charge of a valuable collection of musical instruments and was furthermore responsible for the behaviour (both on and off duty) of a motley crowd of resident singers and players – to say noth ing of guest artists. The routine duties were indeed so onerous that at first he found it a hard struggle to fulfil the clause in his contract which stipulated that he 'should com pose at all times whatever works His Highness might require', but he soon evolved a satisfactory *modus vivendi* and over the ensuing period of years no-one could have made better use of such golden opportunities. Prior to entering the service of the Esterhazy family in 1761 he had produced *The Crooked Devil* and perhaps three dozen instrumental works including string quartets and miniature symphonies. By the time he left it in 1790 (with a generous pension) the number of his operas had grown to fifteen, of string quartets to sixty-two, of symphonies to ninety-one; five masses, forty-odd piano sonatas (the piano was by then gradually replacing both the harpsichord and the clavi chord) and a huge quantity of miscellaneous shorter works had been thrown in for good measure. Apart from a hand ful of delightful string quartets and symphonies compara tively little of this Eisenstadt/Esterhaza output is familiar to present-day listeners (of the operas not even the best – *Lo speziale* and *L'infedelta delusa* – are likely to be revived except as curiosities[1]) and Haydn is mainly remembered for his *subsequent* compositions, notably the oratorios *The Creation* and *The Seasons,* the 'Nelson' and 'Theresa' masses, the last three piano sonatas, the last dozen or so string quartets, a ninety-second symphony (celebrating a visit to Oxford where he was installed as honorary Doctor of Music) and twelve further symphonies (nos. 93-104) written in London at the behest of the concert-impresario J. P. Salomon. It was during the early seventeen-nineties that Haydn, who by that time had retired to Vienna, was welcomed in Britain (he had previously never seen the sea) and developed an attachment for the country; besides the

[1] *L'infedelta delusa* has had its first British stage-performance since these words were written.

Salomon symphonies he published six collections of Scottish and Welsh folk-song arrangements (about four hundred all told). After the turn of the century however, he virtually abandoned both travel and composition, and he died on 31st May 1809 during Vienna's occupation by the victorious troops of Napoleon Bonaparte, then well on the way to becoming master of Europe. It is pleasant to be able to record that the respect due to a musical genius overrode military etiquette: at Haydn's memorial service the guard of honour comprised a mixed detachment of French soldiery and Austrian civil guards.

Haydn lived longer than any other great composer belonging to the eighteenth century and moreover his life spanned an era of change. Born when the Turks, though the Ottoman Empire was by then in decline, still main tained a stranglehold on the Balkans and were therefore a menace to Catholic Austria from the east, he lived long enough to find his homeland prey to aggression from the west; meanwhile he survived the war of the Austrian Succession and the Seven Years' war – and like everyone else in Europe felt the impact, however indirectly, of the French Revolution. On a more peaceful level it should be noted that he was already at school when Handel wrote his *Messiah* and yet lived to hear Beethoven's *Fidelio*. In early days he was profoundly influenced by C. P. E. Bach (see page 39), talented son of a famous father and moreover largely responsible for inaugurating that astonishing mani festation of artistic ingenuity known as sonata-form, a subtle *ABAB* evolution combining the features of binary form (*AB*) and ternary form (*ABA*). Since almost every composer worthy of the name, from the mid-eighteenth century to the mid-twentieth, has at some time or other written pieces in sonata-form (or some barely-disguised modification of it) the term will crop up time and again in the ensuing pages and it will be as well to indicate, at this juncture, the essential characteristics.

A movement in sonata-form starts with an exposition of tune *A*, usually a vigorous and masculine affair, which establishes the tonic (main) key. Next comes a bridge passage, possibly based on *A,* which leads to the exposition of a contrasted and often 'feminine' tune *B* (the 'second subject') in a different but nearly-related key – e.g. G major against C major or E flat major against C minor. There follows a development section in which *A* and *B,* or frag ments of them, are tossed hither and thither in any key the composer chooses (bar the tonic) and their hidden potentialities are exploited to the best of his ability. This eventually leads back to a recapitulation of *A* (often a straightforward repetition) followed by an amended bridge passage and a recapitulation of *B,* which this time however is presented in the tonic key; sometimes a coda (tailpiece) rounds things off.

Historians have been at pains to point out that Haydn did not *invent* either the string quartet (for two violins, viola and cello) or the symphony (for a larger band in corporating both string and wind instruments); none the less he established their basic form of construction. The early quartets of his Fürnberg and Morzin days were nearly all in five movements – fast, minuet, slow, minuet, fast – but presently he discarded the second minuet, thus leaving four movements (as compared with the standard three movements of duos, trios and concertos), in one or two of which at least (an innovation) the melodic outline, rather than being a mere violin solo, was subjected to thematic development on all four instruments. As nearly as I can calculate Haydn composed forty-six string quartets for the exclusive enjoyment (initially) of his Esterhazy employers, and it will be worth while to pin-point some of their structural characteristics. (For his later quartets see chapter 11. I have also omitted from the reckoning op. 51, a set of seven single-movement 'sonatas' for the same combination of instruments transcribed from an earlier orchestral work illustrating *The Seven Words of Our Saviour on the Cross.*)

(1) The forty-six quartets all comprised four movements.

(2) Of their first movements forty-three were fast or moderately fast and in sonata-form; the other three were themes with variations, slow or moderately slow.

(3) The finale (last movement) was invariably fast; in four cases it was a fugue.

(4) One of the two middle movements was always a minuet, which in the earlier quartets was usually placed second but was later more likely to be placed third, thus predicating the traditional order of fast, slow, minuet, fast.

(5) Although the majority of the opening and closing movements were in square time (2/4, 4/4, or 2/2), there were seventeen instances of 3/8 or 6/8 and six (all in first movements) of fairly fast 3/4.

(6) Of the forty-six Esterhazy quartets only nine were 'minor' (which means, by convention, that they *started* in a minor key) and two of these nine *ended* in the major; of their eighteen middle movements eleven were in closely related major keys.

(7) In every one of the thirty-seven 'major' quartets the minuet was in the main key of the work and the other middle movement – nearly always slow – in a different but closely related one. (Students may care to note that of the thirty-seven 'other middle' movements twenty were in the subdominant major; eight in the dominant major; nine in the tonic minor; none, curiously enough, in the relative minor which nowadays one would regard as equally logical and which was adopted by Haydn himself in several of his symphonies.)

These statistics are presented not for the sake of pedantry but to make clear precisely how much his younger con temporaries – including the most illustrious among them – owed Haydn for evolving, in his Esterhazy days, such an admirable and reasonably flexible form of construction, giving opportunity for appropriately varied contrasts of form, tempo, rhythm and key. (And bear in mind that this applied not only to the string quartet but also, *mutatis mutandis*, to the symphony.) In the long run Haydn's successors were even more in his debt than were his con temporaries, for in the seventeen-nineties he himself was one of the first to escape from some of the conventions which he had earlier propounded and which by then had become generally accepted: in his full maturity a C major or even C minor opening movement, for instance, would quite possibly be followed by a slow movement in a distant key like A major or E major. His crowning achievements belong, by such tokens, to an age of greater emancipation than his early works, and discussion of them will therefore be postponed until after we have met W. A. Mozart, who was Haydn's junior by nearly a quarter of a century but unhappily died just as his friend, at fifty-nine, was taking wing for the zenith he was soon to reach.

CHAPTER TEN

MOZART

In the seventeen-fifties when Joseph Haydn, expelled from school, was still a struggling Viennese street-busker, there lived a hundred-and-fifty miles away to the west at Salzburg (on the third floor of the house now numbered 9 Getreide-gasse) a worthy musician named Leopold Mozart and his wife Anna Maria, *nee* Pertl. Of their six children only two survived for more than a few months: one was a girl, the other a boy. The girl, born in July 1751 and christened Maria Anna, was a clever child who had already learnt to play the harpsichord by the time her brother WOLFGANG AMADEUS MOZART joined the family circle on 27th January 1756. *His* aptitude for music was even more extraordinary: at the age of three his prowess on harpsichord and piano rivalled that of his seven-year-old sister, and he started to compose when he was five. The pieces Wolfgang wrote in those days were short and simple, but so far from resemb ling the jejune efforts of most infantile composers they were competent little affairs and would hardly be out of place in say the Papageno scenes of *The Magic Flute*, which belonged to his last year on earth.

Presently Leopold Mozart resigned the permanent post which he held at the court of the archbishop of Salzburg (Sigismund von Schrattenbach) in order to exploit – and who shall blame him? – the precocity of his children. From 1762 until 1766 he exhibited them in turn at Munich, Vienna, Brussels, Paris, London, the Hague, Berne, Zurich – and between-whiles at many other centres of musical culture in western Europe. Everywhere they went, and above all in Paris, the Mozart prodigies were acclaimed and feted. When they returned to Salzburg 'sister Nannerl' had become a mature young lady of fourteen and Wolfgang an oncoming adolescent of ten. Having already completed many instrumental and choral works which demonstrated

57

instinctive ability, amounting to genius, in melodic con
struction, in harmony, even in counterpoint and orchestra
tion, he was now determined to tackle opera; after a year or
so in Vienna (where he composed *La finta semplice* and
Bastien und Bastienne) his father took him for a grand tour
of Italy (*Mitridate* and *Lucia Silla*).[1] This was followed,
after a short stay at home, by return visits to Vienna and
northern Italy (and the composition of *La finta giardiniera,*
the most accomplished of his teen-age operas). By this time,
however, Leopold Mozart had re-entered the service of the
church and the new archbishop (Hieronymus von Col-
loredo) held strong views on absenteeism; consequently
when in 1777 Wolfgang, never a time-waster, set out from
Salzburg for a second visit to Paris it was his mother and
not his father who accompanied him. They broke their
journey at Mannheim where he fell in love with Aloysia
Weber, daughter of a well-known local musician and herself
a promising soprano singer. His feelings appeared to be
reciprocated but there was no formal engagement.

Thus far Mozart's career, despite occasional disappoint
ments and difficulties, had on the whole been astonishingly
successful; his character had remained unspoilt because he
was inwardly content in the knowledge that success had
been achieved through hard work and merit. This happy
state of affairs was too good to last: in Paris the fickle
public which fifteen years earlier had been so eager to
applaud an infant phenomenon was now indifferent;
Mozart's sole new compositions of any importance were
the charming ballet *Les petits riens* and the 'Paris' sym
phony, and he soon found himself in desperate financial
straits. Moreover for the first time in his life he was brought
face to face with personal tragedy when his devoted mother
fell ill and died. A few months later, on borrowed money,
he turned his back on Paris for ever and rejoined the
Webers – who meanwhile had moved their home to
Munich. Here he learnt that Aloysia had just run away

[1] Nannerl was left behind; she later married into the nobility and
eventually outlived not only her husband and her brother but also
Beethoven, Weber and Schubert.

with an actor; this crowning blow finally shattered his hopes and his nerves, and it was a thoroughly wretched and disillusioned young musician who slunk back to Salzburg early in 1779. He was only twenty-three but already the wheel of fortune had revolved through a full cycle.

Leopold Mozart helped to restore his son's self-respect by securing him a permanent job as organist at the court of his own employer, Archbishop Hieronymus. This appoint ment gave Wolfgang a chance to settle down, and rather more than a year later he completed his most ambitious opera yet – *Idomeneo*. The libretto was inept, but it had the practical advantage of having been written by a clerical colleague at the ecclesiastical court and his new employer viewed the first production at Munich with such favour that he summoned its composer to join him, not at his palace in Salzburg, but at the more modest establishment which he maintained in Vienna. Here Mozart took his meals in the servants' hall. 'The two valets', he wrote to his father, 'sit at the head of the table, and I have the honour to be placed above the cooks; during dinner there is a good deal of coarse silly joking, but not with me, for I do not speak a word but what I am obliged, and that with the greatest circumspection'. Not being sufficiently well-educated to appreciate the prevailing niceties of social precedence, Mozart complained of his treatment to his lordship's high steward, but the interview had a hurtful ending for accord ing to the historian Otto Jahn the high steward literally kicked him out. ('[Dann] warf er ihn mit einem Fusstritt zur Tür hinaus.') Fortunately however – and largely through the agency of Christian Gottlob Stephanie, a man-of-the-theatre who had an *entree* to court circles – Mozart's talents were soon brought to the notice of none other than Emperor Joseph II, who was keenly interested in music and saw no reason why operas should nearly always be settings of *Italian* words. Mozart was therefore encouraged to embark upon a *German* opera – to be neither too light nor too heavy – and forthwith produced *Die Entfuhrung aus dem Serail* (libretto by Stephanie) which had its first per formance in July 1782. Although very well received – by aged Gluck, among others – it failed to break down the long-standing tradition that Italian was the language of opera and indeed is itself more generally known (except in German-speaking countries) as *Il Seraglio*.

After his hasty departure from the archiepiscopal house hold Mozart had gone to live with his old friends the Webers – now settled in Vienna – and had transferred his affections to Aloysia's younger sister Constanze. A few weeks after the successful production of his new opera (whose heroine was named after her) they became man and wife. Leopold Mozart was furious, for he had always regarded the Weber family with disapproval – and in truth they were a very easy-going and bohemian crowd. When the wedding took place he relented to the extent of sending a conventional message of good wishes, but the closely sympathetic relationship between father and son was severed. (Leopold, who died five years later, was in many ways a tyrannical parent, but he deserves credit for having done all in his power to promote contemporary world-wide recognition of the incomparable genius whom he had begotten.) Constanze, now Mrs. Mozart, was in almost every respect the exact opposite of Mrs. Haydn: she was devoted to her husband and genuinely anxious to further his success but far too scatterbrained (and possibly, be it whispered, too intemperate) ever to make a good housewife. Consequently Mozart's marriage, unlike Haydn's, paid reasonable dividends – but it showed little capital apprecia tion: except when professional engagements took him away from Vienna (to Salzburg, Berlin, Leipzig, Dresden, Prague) he led a disordered existence in frowsy and un comfortable lodgings. An occasional guest was Haydn – when up in town from Eisenstadt or Esterhaza; the two men very properly formed a mutual admiration society, and with Constanze's enthusiasm outweighing her other short comings Mozart set out to produce his finest masterpieces.

Every musician owes a debt of gratitude to the Austrian bibliographer Ludwig von Kochel, who in the early eighteen-sixties compiled a comprehensive catalogue of Mozart's works (revised in 1937 by Alfred Einstein). The

'Kochel numbers' are invaluable for identifying pieces with no specific title and are in reasonably accurate chrono logical sequence. Mozart's output during the first eight years or so of his married life comprised roughly K.390 to K.565 inclusive, and if any student runs his eye down that list he will agree, I think, that it includes most of the works in which the composer touched the heights of supremacy that have assured him of immortality. Here is a selection.

(a) The 'Linz' and 'Prague' symphonies (K.425 and 504) where Mozart came strongly under the influence of Haydn and which at the time of their composition were unsur passed for beauty of melody, clarity of expression and technical assurance.

(b) The Fantasy in C minor (K.475) which was the summit-point of his music for keyboard alone and was notable for some astonishingly daring harmonic sequences.

(c) No less than sixteen piano concertos which are all so excellent that it would be invidious to single out any as pre eminent; yet at grievous personal risk I venture to suggest that K.453, 466, 467, 488, 491 and 503 are the pick of the bunch.

(d) The so-called 'Haydn set' of six string quartets all of which approach perfection; the superb string quintet in G minor (K.516, five movements) which achieves it; six trios for violin, cello and piano of almost equal merit.

(e) The captivating orchestral serenade entitled *Eine kleine Nachtmusik* (K.525).

(f) The operas *The Impresario* (one act), *The Marriage of Figaro, Don Giovanni* and *Cosi fan tutte*. (*Figaro*, if played in the right spirit and judiciously cut in Act IV, is the best *opera buffa* ever written – with *Cosi fan tutte* as runner-up. That *Don Giovanni* is often regarded nowadays as an *opera seria* should not blind one to the fact that it was dubbed by its composer as a *dramma giocoso*. Although Mozart was not insensitive to Gluck, all these operas ad hered, in general, to Italian tradition.)

(g) *The Mass in C minor* which established new standards of artistry for the late eighteenth century in liturgical music.

(h) Three works which remain supreme examples of

classical symphony: K.543 in E flat major, K.550 in G minor and K.551 in C major (the 'Jupiter'), where Mozart improved upon Haydn's manner with an intensity of feeling which the elder man had never (so far) been able to express.

All these superb compositions (in which his astonishing flair for creating, developing and instrumenting melodies of great beauty reached its apex) belonged to the period 1782-90, when Mozart was enjoying fairly good health, but as time went on he became increasingly subject to neurosis. By the summer of 1791 – when Haydn was in England and Constanze had gone to the country to recuperate from illness – he was engaged simultaneously on the clarinet concerto K.622 (a completely carefree composition), *La Clemenza di Tito* (an operatic *piece d'occasion*) and *The Magic Flute,* which was the brain-child of a clever and unscrupulous impresario named Emanuel Schikaneder whose pantomimic libretto appealed to the composer (con tradictorily both a practising Catholic and a practising Freemason). Planned, like *Die Entfuhrung,* as a *Singspiel* – an opera written in German and incorporating dialogue – *The Magic Flute* contained some of Mozart's most sublime music (as well as some of his most naive) but all along he was obsessed with a feeling of frustration; presently the taut threads began to snap and he fell prey to morbid depression. When he received a mysterious commission to compose a Requiem from a tall dark stranger (who later turned out to be little more than a leg-puller) he was con vinced that this was to be his *own* Requiem. And so it proved: on 5th December 1791, with the Requiem still in complete, he died in a fit of delirium. There was an element of pathos about it all: old and true friends like his father and Haydn were either dead or far away; new fair-weather friends like Schikaneder and his associates proved broken reeds; Constanze, hysterical with grief, was incapable of coping with the emergency. So Wolfgang Amadeus Mozart, the greatest composer of his generation and perhaps of all time, received a pauper's burial: to this day his grave is unidentified. His memorial lies in his music – the finest memorial anyone could wish for.

CHAPTER ELEVEN

HAYDN again

In December 1790 Mozart had taken a somewhat emotional farewell of JOSEPH HAYDN on the eve of the Haydn's depar ture for London. Mozart seems to have had a presentiment that they would never meet again, but this was before his own shadows so suddenly and so grievously lengthened: having as yet no premonition that he himself would be dead within a year his sole misgiving was on behalf of his aging friend who had never previously ventured abroad and might not be able, perhaps, to stand the strain of all that tiring travel. He underestimated the strength of Haydn's constitution, for in the event this was only the first of two long visits which the latter paid to Britain where he was lionized, spent three years all told and produced – apart from many smaller pieces – twelve splendid symphonies. (The popular English numbering of the Salo mon symphonies as 1 to 12 is confusing, since the composer had previously completed ninety-two. Moreover it goes astray in chronological detail: to correspond with the correct sequence – 93 to 104 inclusive – they must be placed by their English numbering in the following order: 5, 6, 9, 10, 7, 8, 3, 11, 4, 12, 1, 2. This has led to widespread mis understanding; an unwary broadcaster has been known to announce Haydn's one-hundred-and-fourth – and last – symphony as his second.)

Among these twelve glorious works every music lover has of course his own favourites. Mine are nos. 100, 103 (the 'Drumroll') and 104 (the 'London'), because I feel that they display more consistently than the others a perfection of utterance associated with Haydn at his best. These three, and possibly nos. 94 (the 'Surprise'), 98 and 101 (the 'Clock'), are great enough to rank alongside any of Mozart's symphonies except the unparalleled E flat major, G minor and 'Jupiter' (K. 543, 550, 551). Yet it must be emphasized that in every one of the twelve Haydn some where showed indebtedness to Mozart, perhaps especially in the perky minuet of no. 94, in the magnificent *adagio cantabile* of no. 98 where he plumbed unwonted depths of feeling, in the surprising modulations of the *adagio* introduction to no. 99, in the naïvely contrapuntal finale of no. 103. On the other hand the sheer jollity of the first movements of nos. 94 and 101 and the finales of nos. 97, 98 and 100 was pre-eminently Haydnesque and owed nothing to anyone.

Uninhibited jollity (the boyish exuberance which led him into scrapes at school) was one of Haydn's most endearing traits, and it cropped up as frequently in his string quartets as in his symphonies. Indeed in his Esterhazy days he had not always lived up to the tenet which inspired Thomas Dunhill's solemn dictum in *Chamber Music* (1913) that 'there is absolutely no excuse for setting forth music to be played by four trained and sensitive musicians which could as well be interpreted by the average fiddlers of a restaurant or beer-garden'. But the six quartets of ops. 71 and 74 (composed in Vienna between his two London visits) and the eight of ops. 76 and 77 (composed after the second visit there) show that by that time Haydn was in agreement with Dunhill that 'there is a certain dignity to be upheld in dealing with the string-quartet form'. Admittedly light-heartedness is the key-note of the whole of op. 74 no. 2 and of many single movements from nearly all the other thirteen, but dignified would be an appropriate epithet to apply to op. 76 nos. 3 and 5 and op. 77 no. 2. In these quartets and the piano trios of the same decade – notably that in D major usually called no. 6 – one feels that Haydn was not only consolidating what he had learnt from Mozart but was already beginning to teach Beethoven. (Here I use the word 'teach' to imply example rather than precept, although Haydn did actually give Beethoven a few lessons in composition when the latter settled in Vienna in 1792 – see page 71.)

The oratorios *The Creation* and *The Seasons* were composed during the late seventeen-nineties to libretti by Baron

Gottfried van Swieten (Dutch by birth, Viennese by adoption, diplomat by calling, *litterateur* and musician by inclination). Van Swieten's *Creation* was based on his own German version of Milton's *Paradise Lost*; *The Seasons* on his own German version of a less well-known poem by the Scottish writer James Thomson (who flourished during the first half of the eighteenth century). Perhaps *The Seasons* should really rank as a cantata rather than an oratorio, for parts of it are distinctly earthy and it is only at the very end that religion comes into the picture; so far as Haydn is concerned it was a rather uneven production which surprisingly showed this sunny composer to best advantage in the winter freeze-up, where the steady tempo and persistent semi-quaver accompaniment of 'Let the wheel move gaily' set a precedent for many later spinning-songs – e.g. Schubert's *Gretchen am Spinnrade* (see page 82) and the opening chorus of Act II from Wagner's *Flying Dutchman*. *The Creation* on the other hand was an oratorio *par excellence* and moreover a landmark in the history of the genre, for it bridged the gap between Handel's *Messiah* (1742, see page 34) and Mendelssohn's *Elijah* (1846, page 90). In this country *The Creation* is still usually given in van Swieten's own re-translation from German back to (very teutonic) English, since a scholarly and in many respects acceptable revision of the text by A. H. Fox-Strangways and Steuart Wilson (1930) has been slow to make headway against such lovable absurdities of phraseology as 'Cheerful roaring stands the tawny lion' and 'In long dimensions creeps with sinuous trace the worm'; nor are traditionalists convinced that 'The fields are dressed in living green' marks worthwhile improvement on the more familiar 'With verdure clad the fields appear'. The *musical* creation, from the first open octave of the 'Representation of Chaos' (which, thank goodness, is not a representation of 'chaos') to the last bar of the final fugal chorus, suggests that the heavens were telling Haydn his every move, and rationalists should not scoff when they read that 'he knelt down every day and prayed God to strengthen him for his work'. Let them recall, if they wish, that the humorously descriptive orchestral treatment of the roaring lion and the creeping worm caused the composer a few moments of spiritual unease and drove him to expose his simple philosophy in one short sentence.

I hope that God will not be angry if I am irrespressibly cheerful in my worship of Him.

A reference to irrespressible cheerfulness reminds one that in the mid-eighteenth century it was still assumed that the primary purpose of music was to entertain. Joseph Haydn remained to the end an entertainer; in an era of artistic *Sturm und Drang* he was blessedly unaware of any moral obligation to espouse a cause or join a noble army, being content merely to find out musical tunes. As a com poser of great music which typified this strictly classical approach he stood in sharp contrast to such notable reformers – in their respective fields – as Gluck, Goethe, Schiller and Beethoven, for he was concerned not so much with making the world better as with making it happier.

CHAPTER TWELVE

BEETHOVEN

When I was a small boy the master who had to correct my fortnightly 'essays' used to insist that they should stress only the best features of the subject under discussion, skirt round any defects and avoid deleterious comparisons. But I think I was as unconvinced then as I am now that an essayist should necessarily be an advocate. The putting forward of all points *pro* to the exclusion of those *con* has a proper function in any mutual exchange of views between the knowledgeable few, but when standing alone is liable to produce a false impression on the uninitiated many, who may never hear the other side of the argument and cannot be expected to read between the lines or recognise the significance of what counsel for the defence has (purposely) left unsaid. The reputations of many painters, poets, authors and composers have on balance lost more than they have gained through such well-intentioned but unthinking advocacy, often misinterpreted as implying adulation and thereby laying itself open to superficial counter-attack.

No great composer has suffered more in this respect than LUDWIG VAN BEETHOVEN. It would be a relatively simple matter to put his enemies to flight and his detractors to shame, did one not simultaneously face the task of saving him from friends blind to his weaknesses and from champions determined to ignore them. Since friends and champions have included such honoured figures as George Grove and Donald Tovey the rescue operation is a delicate one, and it is with trepidation that I propound the theory that both these distinguished essayists followed too closely the precepts of my old English master. Grove was a very trustworthy biographer but some of his more pompous pronouncements on his idol's music should not be taken too seriously. Every student is in debt to Tovey for his six classic volumes of *Essays in Musical Analysis* (nearly all based on extended programme-notes for the Reid orchestral concerts in Edinburgh which he conducted from 1914 until his death in 1940) and in programme-notes he was often justified in eschewing deleterious comparisons; indeed it is fascinating to observe the forensic skill with which he conscientiously made out a good case for composers with whom he was temperamentally out of sympathy – Tchaikovsky, for example. But his warmth of feeling for Beethoven led him to become a skirter-round and even to declare (in another book) that 'what Beethoven does I accept as evidence' – which was surely tantamount to saying that he was prepared to find everyone else out of step. Now although Beethoven was honoured during his life-time and on his death, he became a puzzle to the immediately succeeding generation and it needed the fervent propaganda of Berlioz and Liszt to spread his fame round the continent in the eighteen-fifties and -sixties; in Britain it was not until the George Grove days of the late nineteenth century that he was deified and it became blasphemy not to fall down and pay homage. When the twentieth century was under way the inevitable reaction set in and the *avant-garde* began to denounce him as nothing more than a sacred cow of the Victorians. Fortunately vituperation of this sort, understandable enough in the prevailing climate of musical opinion, caused broad-minded scholars to realize that a detached approach was overdue. In 1913 Ernest Walker, a staunch admirer of all that was best in Beethoven, went so far as to admit that 'compared with many of the great composers his output is distinctly unequal'; one work was castigated for its 'uncouth inconsequence'. (The quotations are taken from his informative little book on Beethoven in the *Music of the Masters* series.) Walker, though a traditionalist, was a wise and upright judge. His high-pitched verbal comments on a more recent and briefer assessment by my colleague Norman Suckling (incorporated in his valuable study of guess whom – Gabriel Fauré!) might not be entirely unsympathetic; it would be only a friendly bone that he had to pick with the French painter Jean Renoir who observed that 'Beethoven is positively indecent the way he tells us about himself; he doesn't spare us either the pain in his heart or the pain in his stomach'. (Although Renoir's metaphor was blunt he here scored a shrewd and palpable hit, hammering home that Beethoven, instead of emulating say Bach or Mozart as an objective observer of human emotions, forced his own emotions on a world which was at first too stunned to accept the proposition that he was a superman – and later too stunned to reject it.) Despite the fair-minded Walkers, the sceptical Sucklings and the outspoken Renoirs, many people regard Beethoven as the greatest composer that ever lived – and there can be no complaint about that so long as they don't hold the opinion merely because they have been told to. He was in any case the greatest born between 1756 and 1797 and more over was endowed with definable attributes which set him apart from any predecessor or contemporary – and which must be noted right away.

Beethoven is the first composer we have met who might be described as a rebel, for his career was spent in a struggle not only against poverty and ill-health (common enough adversaries) but also against anything that he rated as unjust in politics or unworthy in art. This outlook drove him to choose an unusual *modus operandi*: in his sketch books (mercifully preserved) one can trace in detail how preliminary jottings-down of a few notes led eventually to the emergence of the finally polished article. They have a further and less technical interest since they make it clear that some of his finest works, so far from being spon taneous inspirations of the moment, had gradually evolved in his mind, and on paper, over many years. From the outset of the tonal era until Beethoven's day nearly all music held a measure of predictability: every phrase, every bar, sometimes even every note, was an explicit thread in the tapestry; with composers of the Bach/Mozart calibre there was often a *perfection* of seeming inevitability where any alternative phrase or bar or even note would have been unthinkable. Beethoven's was a different sort of perfection and inevitability had little to do with it. His sketch books show that the goal was reached through a slow and painful process of conscious striving; as Romain Rolland put it in *Beethoven the Creator* (1928), 'once he takes hold upon an idea, he never lets it go until he possesses it wholly'. Con sequently his music is rarely predictable in the sense that one might apply the term – without any disapprobation – to much of Bach's or Mozart's; indeed one of Beethoven's out standing characteristics is his *un*predictability. Bolts from the blue like the 'irrelevant roaring C sharp' (Tovey's phrase) in the finale of the eighth symphony have been and no doubt will continue to be interpreted according to taste as strokes of genius, as good jokes, as bad jokes, or as attacks of indigestion. But whatever else they may have been they were unquestionably part of the essence of Beet hoven – which had nothing in common with the essence of Bach. Nor for that matter had it as much in common with the essence of Brahms as has sometimes been made out: the grouping together of these composers as the three B's was merely a convenient and rather inept analogy favoured by the pious 'Brahmins' of the eighteen-eighties (see page 150). No; Beethoven was emphatically not a middleman between Bach and Brahms. On the contrary, he was the propagator of an entirely new line of descent leading through Berlioz and Liszt to Wagner, all of whom were tarred with the same revolutionary brush and adopted much the same approach to the problems of musical com position – with (as we shall see later) varying degrees of success.

Beethoven was partly Flemish by ancestry (please note that he was Ludwig van, not Ludwig von) but for fifty years or so before his birth his grandfather and father had earned their keep by playing or singing at the court of the Elector of Cologne and it was at Bonn (515 – now 20 – Bonnstrasse) that he first saw the light of day on 16th December 1770. Few composers were less addicted to travel: during his teens (when he displayed extraordinary ability as a pianist, particularly in extemporisation) he never left his native Rhineland except for a trip to Vienna in 1787; when he went there again in 1792 he realized that the Austrian capital was his spiritual home – and for the rest of his life he lived either there or at nearby Mödling on the edge of the Wienerwald. Somewhat unprepossessing in appearance and brusque in behaviour, Beethoven was no ladies' man and although he fell in love once or twice he remained a bachelor. For practical purposes, therefore, the record of his life is the record of his music.

He did not take seriously to composition until he settled in Vienna, where for a time he studied with Haydn and others but was an awkward pupil: he was already in his twenties and when he did not see eye to eye with his teachers he adopted an attitude of aggressive self-assurance: formal lessons were soon abandoned by mutual consent and he came to rely not so much on tuition as on intuition. During the nine years 1792 to 1800 inclusive he composed eleven piano sonatas (the best of which were op. 10 no. 3 and op. 13, the 'Pathetique'), the concert-aria *Adelaide* (a fine song, splendidly representative of this early period), four violin sonatas of no more than average merit, two piano concertos each of which held their charm but neither of which was remarkable, six string quartets, one symphony and a host of less important pieces. The quartets (op. 18) were stylistically in the Haydn manner but in all but one of them Beethoven replaced the traditional minuet with a faster 'scherzo' – literally 'joke'. (In no. 4, which did incorporate a minuet, the fugal second movement was *entitled* a scherzo.) His first symphony, too, owed much to Haydn: it is so pleasant to listen to – and in the third move ment (designated a minuet but actually a scherzo) presages such mastery – that it may be captious to point out that it would rarely have been played during the last hundred-and-fifty years had it been written in a moment of exceptional inspiration (as it possibly might have been, apart from the scherzo) by some talented but less well-known contemporary like Johann Schenk or Adalbert Gyrowetz.

It was during the next nine years (1801-1809) that *unser echter Beethoven* emerged, the Beethoven who was to stimulate Grove to panegyrics and goad Renoir to fury; the Beethoven of the 'Waldstein' sonata with its frightening prestissimo octave passages; of the 'Kreutzer' sonata demanding unprecedented virtuosity on the part of the violinist; of the 'Rasumovsky' string quartets which imparted a new look to chamber music; of the 'Eroica' symphony with the calculated false entry at the start of the recapitulation in its first movement and the quixotic open ing to its last; of the solitary violin concerto where surpris ing prominence was given to the kettledrums (with an effect so poetic in the context that not even a Renoir could cavil); of the opera *Fidelio* the like of which had never before been seen on any stage. Yet recognition of the genius which Beet hoven demonstrated during this period does not – or should not – depend solely upon his capacity for puzzling or shocking people, for in retrospect it can be seen that he was often in more confident mood when *not* doing so. The 'Waldstein' is undeniably a fine sonata, but nowadays many musicians (outside the ranks of professional pianists) prefer the more serene op. 28, the more ardent op. 57 (the 'appassionata') and the more descriptive op. 81a ('Les adieux, l'absence et le retour'). To say that the 'Kreutzer' is with one exception (op. 96) the most satisfying of Beethoven's ten violin sonatas might be a backhanded compliment to its composer, for in eight out of the ten he was not at his best. The three 'Rasumovsky' quartets of op. 59 are great beyond doubt, but no greater than the suavely beautiful op. 74 – nor than the two well-contrasted and more conventional piano trios of op. 70. There is no accounting for taste and I have to confess that personally I find the much-admired 'Eroica' symphony, no. 3, apart from its superb scherzo, less attractive than nos. 2, 4 and 6 (all of which have their short comings but by comparison are underrated) and certainly not in the same class as the equally famous and popular no. 5 – despite its rather weak and noisy finale. The violin concerto, magnificent up to a point, is also marred I feel by its last movement, in which Beethoven, trying to emulate Haydn at his brightest, slips perilously near banality. *Fidelio* is unique in conception and contains some wonderfully impressive scenes, but taken as a whole it is not really a very good opera in the accepted sense of the term; fortunately Beethoven provided it with no less than four overtures – all

of them excellent. The fourth – known as the *Fidelio* over
ture – was written for a revival some eight years after the
original production; thanks to its forthright breeziness it is
admirably suited to the theatre, but in the concert-hall it
yields pride of place to the three earlier 'Leonora' overtures
– whose slightly varying orchestral treatment of Florestan's
lovely aria 'In des Lebens Frühlingstagen' must be of
absorbing interest to students of technical empiricism.
(*Leonora no.* 3 must be awarded the palm but the others
run very close.) Two out of the three piano concertos dating
from these years – the romantic no. 4 in G major and the
more vigorous but equally expressive no. 5 in E flat major
(the 'Emperor') – leave an impression of utter spontaneity;
in the concerto field these inspired and perfectly-propor
tioned works have rarely been surpassed.

Beethoven, as a social rebel, was enraged that the
musicians of his day had to depend for their livelihood upon
feudal, political or ecclesiastical patronage; on principle he
had no time for Gluck's empresses, Haydn's princes or
Mozart's archbishops. Yet he had to live in the world into
which he had been born and during his early days in
Vienna had not been too proud to accept pecuniary assist
ance from Prince Charles Lichnowsky, Baron Pasquati and
Count Browne – three noblemen whose names would be for
gotten had they not befriended a struggling composer who
later achieved greatness. In 1809 three other notabilities –
Prince Lobkowitz (descended from the one mentioned on
page 46), Prince Kinsky and Archduke Rudolf of Habsburg
– clubbed together to provide him with an annuity; in the
event devaluation of currency (an inescapable phenomenon
even in those days) played havoc with their good intentions
but nevertheless he was thereby enabled to maintain him
self well above starvation level. Unfortunately he had other
troubles to face which no patron, however wealthy or well-
disposed, could alleviate. One was the onset of deafness and
buzzing in the ears, first noticeable about 1798 and from
1812 onwards an increasing cause of distress and frustration
– although it is doubtful how far the unsatisfactory instru
mental balance of his middle period choral and orchestral

works should be ascribed thereto since he had never been immune from such miscalculations. The other cross he had to bear was guardianship of his scapegrace young nephew Karl, whose delinquencies brought dishonour on the family name and were a continual source of worry and expense. It is not surprising, therefore, that Beethoven's third nine-year period in Vienna (1810-18) was less prolific than those which preceded it – but what it lacked in quantity it made up in quality. In their respective categories the 'Hammerklavier' sonata op. 106, the string quartet op. 95, the violin sonata op. 96, the song-cycle *An die ferne Geliebte* and symphony no. 7 maintained throughout a level of excellence compar able with that of the 'Leonora' overtures and the two great piano concertos. Symphony no. 8 and the two cello sonatas of op. 102 were less consistent.

To the last nine years of Beethoven's life (1819-27), when his deafness and his nephew were driving him nearly frantic, belong the *Mass in D major* and symphony no. 9 – which between them took four years to complete and were not finished until 1823 – and five string quartets (ops. 127, 130, 131, 132 and 135) all dated between 1824 and 1826. The mass has its moments of beauty, notably the marvellous 'Et incarnatus' section where Beethoven catches the spirit of Palestrina; but in the double fugue 'Et vitam venturi sæculi' – as in the choral finale of the ninth symphony – imagina tive enthusiasm demands an excess of lung-power and agility on the part of the singers and an excess of intellectual concentration on the part of the audience. However both the first movement of the ninth symphony and its scherzo (placed second and not, as usual, third) are arrestingly vital; the slow movement, too, with its alternations of mood and key, is wonderfully effective. Yet for all its calm dignity it is not so deeply expressive as the 'cavatina' from the string quartet op. 130 or the *lento* from op. 135, both of which remain rare examples of music which bridges the gap be tween earth and heaven: listening to these sublime strains might surely bring comfort and hope to an anxious soul at the dread moment when it is about to pass from the measurable known to the limitless unknown.

The elusive characteristics of late Beethoven, however, are seldom so easily communicable; taken as a whole the last quartets make heavy going, and even listeners who manage to negotiate the awkward aesthetic obstacles of the *Mass in D major* and the finale of the ninth symphony have to ride rough-shod over such stumbling-blocks as the second movement (*vivace*) of op. 135. *Pace* Donald Tovey, what Beethoven does here one is not prepared to accept as evid ence. There are those who find beauty even in ugliness, but ugly music remains ugly no matter who put his name to it. Rather therefore than pay the customary lip-service to these extraordinary works (for their mysterious profundity, ethereal grandeur, inspired anticipation of the methods of Bela Bartok, etc.) let us recognize and accept the fact that they are predominantly rough-edged and excuse it by recal ling that they were put to paper at a time when Beethoven had become *stone*-deaf: it is significant that alongside pass ages of almost divine beauty (as in the two slow movements already referred to) are some which in theory ought to sound well but in practice don't; others which are so frag mentary in construction that they look (and sound) as though they were preliminary sketches for an orchestral composition on a larger scale. One is driven to assume that many of the shadowy ideas surging through a mind still active but by now out of touch with the world of familiar hearing were beyond interpretation in any known instru mental medium, that the eagerly searching spirit of Ludwig van Beethoven was already in tune with the infinite, that his inspiration was no longer adjustable to a language of earthly comprehension.

Release from mortal shackles came on 26th May 1827; at the moment of his passing a violent thunderstorm was raging which can be seen in retrospect as symbolizing the tremendous impact of this remarkable composer upon generations of musicians as yet unborn. Take him for all in all he was a great genius; it is improbable that we shall look upon his like again.

WEBER

As recorded in chapter 10, W. A. Mozart married Constanze Weber who came of a musical family. Constanze's uncle Franz Anton Weber did not attend the wedding, but he was very proud of the connection and conceived an ambition to emulate Mozart's father Leopold as the parental propagandist of a famous composer. Unfortunately the omens were unfavourable: although he claimed noble ancestry and added a 'von' to his name to which he was not entitled, he had for many years been a rather disreputable soldier of fortune, twice married but never settled down; by the time he wooed and won his second wife he had found no more remunerative occupation than that of arranging concerts in the small municipality of Eutin, twenty miles north of Lübeck in an isolated part of the grand duchy of Oldenburg. Today the region is incorporated in the West German province of Schleswig-Holstein, and although Eutin lies on the new direct rail and road link between Hamburg and Copenhagen via the Puttgarden-Rødyhavn ferry the only people who stop off there are commercial travellers (or should they be called sales-representatives?) and a few music lovers who think it worth their while to cast an eye on 26 Lübeckerstrasse, birthplace of CARL MARIA VON WEBER (1786-1826). His birthplace, yes; his home, no. Before he had learnt to walk (and incidentally he never learnt to run, for he was born with a diseased hip-joint) his father recruited a band of actors and musicians – among them several older children by his first wife – and for the next eight or nine years the family travelled all over Germany, entertaining the public at small theatres and playgrounds. Franz was delighted when little Carl showed musical ability and he did what he could, according to his lights and the circumstances in which he was placed, to foster him as a prodigy *a la* Mozart. In 1796, having taught the ten-year-old all he knew, he abandoned a roaming life and found semi-perman ent jobs in turn at Salzburg, Munich, Freiberg and Chem nitz (now Karlmarxstadt), where the resident professors of music were better qualified than himself to complete the education of a budding genius. (One of them, at Salzburg, was Joseph Haydn's brother Michael – see page 50.)

By Mozart standards Weber's talents were slow to come to fruition; nevertheless his operas *The Forest Maiden* and *Peter Schmoll*, composed between the ages of thirteen and fifteen, were played with fair success, the former at Freiberg in 1800 and the latter at Augsburg in 1803. In 1804 he was appointed conductor at Breslau but he was unsuited for the post by reason of youth and inexperience, and furthermore incurred local notoriety by leading a promiscuous life and running up a pile of debts; two years later he was asked to leave. After fulfilling an even shorter-lived engagement of a similar nature he joined the household of King Frederick of Wurttemberg where his duties were largely secretarial and only partly concerned with music-making. The court at Stuttgart was one of the most dissolute in Europe (which is saying plenty) and while Weber was completing another opera, *Silvana*, he indulged in extravagance and dissipation to such an extent that he got into trouble with the police and was thrown in jail; although ultimately acquitted of the criminal misdemeanour with which he was charged, his unsavoury reputation led to banishment from the kingdom. This humiliating experience had a salutary effect on the young ne'er-do-well: thereafter he stayed for a year or more with some good friends at Mannheim, where he wrote an amusing one-act comic opera – *Abu Hassan* – and turned over a new leaf by developing his talents as a pianist to such excellent purpose that he was presently able to set out on an extended concert tour of Prussia, Saxony, Bavaria, Swit zerland and Austria. On a visit to Prague in 1813 he agreed to take over the artistic directorship of the opera-house, which had fallen on evil days and urgently needed an infusion of new blood; he took the task seriously and within three years put the Bohemian capital back on the musical map, but his wayward temperament still occasionally led

77

him to indiscreet behaviour both within and without the theatre walls and eventually involved him in a dispute with the management. Since by now Weber had earned considerable distinction not only as an administrator and an executant but also as a composer of attractive piano, vocal and choral music – and though still burdened with debts was in a slightly less parlous financial position than formerly – he felt justified in taking a firm attitude. Instead of waiting to be pushed out (as he had been from Breslau) or kicked out (as he had been from Stuttgart) he sent in his resignation; as a final gesture of defiance he filched Prague's most popular operatic soubrette – Caroline Brandt – and married her.

In 1817 Weber was placed in charge of German opera at the Dresden court theatre. The post was no sinecure: as a true German he constantly found himself at loggerheads with his Italian colleague the conductor Francesco Morlacchi and furthermore was mistrusted by his employer King Frederick Augustus of Saxony who was an ardent francophile. (Curiously enough, so was Caroline Brandt; but husband and wife did not allow political differences to disturb the domestic scene and on the whole their marriage was a happy one.) Weber's next four operas, *Der Freischütz*, *Preciosa*, *Euryanthe* and *Oberon*, were all composed between 1820 and 1825 either at Dresden or at his country retreat at Hosterwitz on the banks of the Elbe six miles upstream from the city: significantly however they were first produced not as 'his' theatre but in Berlin, Vienna or London. *Der Freischütz* stands head and shoulders above any other German opera dated between 1805 (*Fidelio*, see page 72) and 1845 (*Tannhäuser*, page 116). *Preciosa* was little more than a play which incorporated an overture and a few songs and ensembles. For *Euryanthe* – the only one of his operas in which accompanied recitative replaced the traditional dialogue of the *Singspiel* – Weber wrote some fine and original music but the libretto was preposterous. By this time, too, he was reaping the wild oats he had sown so freely in youth and became consumptive; nevertheless he put all he knew into *Oberon*, and after its completion went to

London for the first performance. *Oberon* had been specially written for Covent Garden and aroused great interest. On the opening night the composer received an ovation, but at later performances, partly because of atrocious weather, neither attendance nor reception came up to expectations. Disappointment and the British climate between them sabotaged Weber's failing health, and hasty preparations were made for his return to Dresden; before they could be put into operation he died in his sleep at the home of his English host, the organist and conductor George Smart.

At his best Weber coupled melodic inspiration and technical skill almost worthy of Mozart with a flair for capturing in music the comfortable sentimentality so dear to the hearts of his countrymen – yet only in some of his comparatively unfamiliar works did he sink to the maudlin or commonplace. To *Der Freischütz* – and to his other mature operas when librettists allowed him – he brought not only an admirable sense of 'theatre' but also a romantic atmosphere which was very much to the taste of German audiences: the wolf's glen of *Der Freischütz* and the fairy land of *Oberon* were territories hitherto almost unexplored. Away from the stage he composed two dozen or so orchestral and choral works and scores of songs and piano pieces: one is always ready to welcome the 'Concertstück' for piano and orchestra or *Invitation to the Dance* (written for piano but more often heard in Berlioz' brilliant orchestral arrangement). Nevertheless the memory of Carl Weber deserves to be honoured mainly for his German operas: along with Beethoven's *Fidelio* they effectively bridged the gap between the *Entführung* and *Magic Flute* of his cousin-by-marriage and the music dramas of Richard Wagner (which will come up for discussion in chapter 20).

CHAPTER FOURTEEN

SCHUBERT

Of our eight great composers whose names are closely associated with Vienna (Gluck, Haydn, Mozart, Beethoven, Schubert, Bruckner, Brahms, Mahler) the only one born there was FRANZ SCHUBERT. Today his birthplace – 54 Nuss-dorfstrasse, ten minutes walk from the Franz Josef Bahn-hof – is a museum in the care of the municipality: very appropriately so, for Schubert never left his native city except for occasional brief trips to the Wienerwald and two visits to nearby Hungary, where in his early days he was engaged to give lessons to the children of Count Johann Esterhazy. (The estate of this branch of the Esterhazy family lay in what is now Czechoslovakian territory, twenty miles north of Esztergom.)

Schubert's mother, who came from Silesia, was like Haydn's mother a professional cook; his father, from Moravia, was a schoolmaster with a taste for music. Franz – born 31st January 1797 – learnt the violin and piano as a small boy and at the age of eleven entered a choristers' seminary, where he soon took to composition. At seven teen he became a junior teacher in his father's school, but after a year of striving to inculcate the three R's into the thick-heads of the bottom form he abandoned scholastic duties and adopted a more congenial if less secure manner of life, spending the rest of his youth – that is to say the rest of his mortal career – in the company of like-minded bohemians who cultivated wine, women and song in the traditional Viennese fashion. Johann Mayrhofer, one of the steadier of these friends and many of whose poems Schu bert set to music, left it on record that 'his character was a mixture of tenderness and coarseness, sensuality and can dour' – probably a shrewd appraisal. The leader of the set was Franz von Schober, a wealthy dilettante who genuinely admired Schubert's genius and generously looked after his material welfare. Schober also wrote the words which inspired the lovely song *An die Musik*, but in the long run Schubert lost more than he gained from association with this rich young man and his dissolute companions. That he was often encouraged to have a little too much to drink was neither here nor there, but it was a serious matter when in 1822 he contracted syphilis; thereafter his plump, be spectacled, untidy little figure – now crowned by a wig – was more grotesque than ever. If he had had thoughts of marriage (and evidence of any deep-felt attachment is very scanty) he now put them aside, but nothing deterred him from composing until he succumbed six years later to an attack of typhoid. He died at the age of thirty-one on 19th November 1828, only nineteen years after Haydn (who was sixty-five years his senior) and barely nineteen months after Beethoven.

Schubert's industry was prodigious: his earliest known composition dates from 1810 – when he was thirteen – and during the eighteen years that remained to him he com pleted eight operas or operettas (three others were left un finished), incidental music for two plays, forty-five cantatas or liturgical settings including six masses, nearly a hundred short vocal ensembles, thirty-five orchestral pieces including seven symphonies (two others were left unfinished), forty chamber-works at least half of which were in four move ments, over two-hundred-and-fifty pieces for piano solo or duet including twenty-four sonatas, and about six hundred songs. A comparatively small proportion of this huge output was published or even performed during his lifetime; it was posterity, not the composer, who reaped the benefit.

His faults – how few beside his virtues! – were mainly those of inexperience and youthful exuberance, traceable to the fact that he never grew to know himself. The furious pace at which he lived left little opportunity for introspec tion: he never indulged, like Beethoven, in painstaking struggles to achieve perfection; he must have realized sub consciously that time was short and that he must make full use of it. Small wonder that hundreds out of the thousands of tunes he wrote were undistinguished, since everything

welling up inside him had to find immediate outward ex
pression; small wonder that despite his brilliant technique
in detail many of his more ambitious efforts (not all) are
open to criticism on the ground of structural defects, per
functory orchestration or excessive prolixity, since no sooner
had he finished a work than inspiration was already hard
at it elsewhere. (The 'heavenly length' of his compositions
in sonata-form was due not only to repetition but also to
the vast quantity of material which he crammed into the
'second subject'; it was probably Schubert who was prim
arily responsible for driving musicologists to substitute
the term 'second group of subjects'. It should also be noted.
in passing, that the key-relationship between the various
subjects sometimes marked a departure from traditional
practice.) Yet Schubert never worked carelessly: he often
wrote three or four songs in a single day (or night), but some
of his best are among them and they show no signs of
hurried execution; no sooner had he completed the first
movement of his ninth symphony than he decided that
in its most frequently recurring phrase the second G (the
fourth note of the *allegro*) should be replaced by D, where
upon he meticulously and neatly made all the hundreds of
necessary corrections to the manuscript.

Combining in balanced proportions the outlook of the
classic, the romantic and the impressionist, Schubert was a
classic in so far as he recognized that the main purpose of
music was to entertain, a romantic in so far as he was a com
poser of subjective moods, an impressionist in so far as he
could conjure up atmosphere by the simplest of means (the
spinning-wheel of *Gretchen am Spinnrade*, the galloping
horse-hoofs of *The Erl King*, the babbling brook of
Wohin?, the ghostly tread of *Der Doppelganger*). And he
was one of very few composers, even among the greatest,
who recognized the over-riding importance of beauty of
sound: he nearly always chose the right medium for ex
pression and in that respect went astray only in the early
string quartets and piano duets, where one feels that he
had an orchestra at the back of his mind. It is significant
that the *Grand Duo* was probably sketched in the first

place as a symphony; it was orchestrated long after his death by Joseph Joachim (who is remembered as an out standing violinist but was also no mean composer).

Not all Schubert's stage-works were played during his life-time and few have ever been revived: they lack the dramatic cohesion which is essential to opera or even operetta, for he was singularly undiscriminating in his choice of either plots or librettists. The earlier pieces, dated 1814-19 and mostly in one act, hold little interest except as curiosities. As for the rest, a few items from *Alfonso and Estrella* (1822) might be rescued from their surroundings – notably the duet 'Von Fels und Wald umringen' where the charming wood-wind commentaries show him in charac teristically good form – and there are some impressive choral scenes in *Fierrabras* (1823). Yet worth-while medals can be awarded only to the incidental music for *Rosamunde*, whose delightful entr'actes are supreme examples of light orchestral music and have already outlived by nearly a century-and-a-half the paltry drama which they decorated and enlivened in 1823. At one time Schubert took the theatre very seriously but successive failures caused his interest to wane: for instance he did not bother to com plete the *Alfonso and Estrella* overture until after the opera had been produced and used it instead for *Rosamunde*: he later allocated to that work an overture which had previously done duty for *The Magic Harp* (1820).

If the theatre did not as a rule stimulate Schubert to give of his best, neither did the church. Much of the sacred music of his teens and early twenties – which included the first four masses – was second-rate. The fifth mass (A flat major, 1822) was more accomplished but incongruously lighthearted: the 'Gloria', for instance, which began and ended with something like a *perpetuum mobile* on the first and second violins in unison, was well-constructed but hardly in keeping with the solemnity of the text. Perhaps only in the 'Gloria' of his sixth and last mass (E flat major, 1828), which incorporated a stupendous fugue and a very moving 'Agnus Dei' section, did he come within striking distance of achieving distinction as an ecclesiastical composer. There is even less to enthuse about in the secular cantatas and vocal ensembles: they were no doubt admir ably in place at family reunions or convivial drinking-parties, but in general they were unrepresentative and it was probably fortuitous that they included occasional gems like the unaccompanied male choruses *Sehnsucht* (no con nection with several songs similarly entitled) and *Ruhe, schönstes Glück der Erde*.

Turning to the symphonies we find ourselves in a dif ferent world, although not yet in a world where Schubert's genius always found full expression: symphonic develop ment did not come altogether naturally to this child of nature. Nos. 1 to 5 – of which 3, 4 and 5 still hold a place in the standard repertory – were written before he was twenty. The first four were for the most part in the Haydn/Mozart manner, although each opened with a slow introduction owing something to Beethoven and ended with a finale which, by contrast, suggested Rossini. In no. 5 there was no slow introduction and not much Beethoven: Mozart raised his head in the second movement and Haydn replaced Rossini (to great advantage) in the finale, but it would be fair to say that this excellent little work brought Schubert to the fore as a symphonic composer in his own right. No. 6 was less spontaneous and more diffuse; it should be noted, however, that the third movement was a scherzo – not (as in nos. 1 to 5) a minuet or *Landler* – and was incidentally the high-spot.

In 1821 Schubert sketched a symphony no. 7; it was evidently complete in his mind since a manuscript exists which – although presenting only the bare outlines – covers all four movements. The British composer J. F. Barnett (in 1883) and the Austrian conductor Felix Weingartner (in 1934) each filled in the gaps to the best of his ability and thereby helped to confirm the impression that the first three movements marked a further advance in symphonic responsibility, but Schubert himself set no. 7 aside for no. 8, the 'Unfinished'. This is one of the best loved pieces of music ever written, and if for that reason anybody should take it upon himself to disparage it as hackneyed one might rejoin 'then for heaven's sake give us some more hackneys': more sheer beauty is packed into this half-symphony than is contained in nine out of ten completed ones by any other composer no matter how illustrious and furthermore, mark you, the first movement is unusually concise. While several melodies from no. 5 are reminiscent – and worthy – of Haydn or Mozart, the oboe/clarinet unison which at the eleventh bar of no. 8 floats above the delicately vibrating violins and violas (not all conductors, alas, succeed in realizing the delicacy), the haunting second subject allocated to the cellos (and astonishingly punctual in making its appearance), the miraculous modulations at the end of the second movement – these are reminiscent of no one and worthy of Schubert alone. It has never been conclusively established why no. 8 remained unfinished but Schubert left a clue with his sketch for a scherzo: it held out little prospect that the third movement would attain the same perfection as the two which preceded it, and perhaps he did right to leave well alone. Symphony no. 9 (often incorrectly called no. 7) was composed during the last year of his life. To distinguish it from no. 6, which is in the same key, it is known as the 'great' C major – an equivocal caption, since although no. 9 certainly outshines no. 6 it has little claim to stand alongside the greater masterpieces of Haydn, Mozart or Beethoven. Here Schubert's enthusiasm perhaps outran his discretion: the *pianissimo* trombone entry at the end of the exposition in the first movement, although not precisely an oasis in a desert, is a miraculous flowering from comparatively unproductive soil; and neither the cultured panache of the *andante* nor the initial vigour of the scherzo nor the whirling energy of the finale can disguise the fact that all three hold their *longueurs*. (It must be confessed, however, that a superlatively fine performance under the direction of a dedicated interpreter like Sir Adrian Boult nearly persuades one to the contrary.)

Chamber music has been the Achilles heel of many composers, for it is a medium in which the closest attention must continually be paid to a very delicately regulated instrumental balance. It has already been hinted that Schubert's early string quartets (1811-16) were less than satisfying because the approach was orchestral, but between 1820 and 1828 he produced five of the best pieces of chamber-music ever written – the quartet-movement in C minor, the complete quartets in A minor, D minor and G major, and the string quintet in C major. Here he gave each instrument full opportunity to display its expressive powers, while at the same time using his technique to ensure that the overall effect was exactly what he wanted. The opening of the A minor quartet, for instance, is perfect *string quartet* music; half its magic would be lost if it were played on a string *orchestra*.

Although Schubert was rarely successful in combining the piano with other instruments (neither the violin sonatas nor the piano trios nor even the 'Trout' quintet represent him at his best and it is significant that he never wrote a concerto) some of his most attractive music is contained in the piano solos and duets. To strum through the solo sonatas is a practicable and enjoyable way of discovering for oneself how he progressed from immaturity to great ness: the first few are unremarkable; the last four (G major, C minor, A major, B flat major) justify comparison with Beethoven. But to appreciate Schubert's extraordinary key-sensitivity, resource in modulation and freedom from con ventional trammels one need only turn to a shorter and more familiar piano piece – the popular impromptu op. 90 no. 4. Very typically, this hovers to such an extent between A flat minor and A flat major that it is impossible to declare with certainty to which of the two keys it properly belongs; in the middle section, which sets out confidently in C sharp minor, everything is comparatively straightforward until the theme is recapitulated in C sharp *major* and extended by four bars of surprising – and beautiful – modulation.

Schubert's symphonies, string quartets and piano sonatas, when taken in sequence, provide ample evidence of the steady growth of his powers; had he written nothing else one might have been tempted to propound a theory that the classical composer of 1811-15 eventually became the romantic composer of 1822-28. His songs however refute this hypothesis, suggesting, rather, that he was a romantic or impressionist from the word go: of the four instances of impressionism cited on page 82 *Gretchen am Spinnrade* was written at seventeen, *The Erl King* at eighteen. Many of them are particularly suited for domestic music-making, for they are grateful to sing and the accompaniments are usually within the capabilities of a competent amateur pianist. Nearly all are technically impeccable; moreover Schubert often imparts an individual touch to the simplest strophic measure: in *Heidenroslein* for instance, or in *Ungeduld* – of which the melody should be examined in its entirety, since it is not only perfectly proportioned (like so many of the others), rising to a superb climax at just the right moment, but also incorporates an intriguing rhythmic ambiguity (2/4 – 3/4). He was catholic in his choice of col laborators: there were some forty-five of them all told, including Shakespeare, Goethe, Schiller and a host of his own contemporaries, many of whom were personal friends. He found himself particularly *en rapport* with Heinrich Heine and with Wilhelm Müller, a minor but not negligible poet who wrote verses for the two splendid song-cycles *Die schone Mullerin and Die Winterreise*. (Müller, nine months younger than the composer, had an even shorter life, pre deceasing him by a year.)

Schubert's six hundred songs cover a vast range of emo tion: there are hymns to nature (*An die Nachtigall, Frühlingsglaube, Im Abendroth, Am Meer*); there are musical poems evoking the tender coquetry, the hopes, fears and disappointments of young love (*Geheimes, Who is Sylvia?, Mein, Die Post*); there are outbursts of deep passion or suffering (*An Schwager Kronos, Die junge Nonne, Die Stadt*); there are songs descriptive of resignation or spiritual peace (*Litanei, Du bist die Ruh', Der Leiermann*). Not all the six hundred are masterpieces, but it is astonishing how many of them are; indeed Franz Schu bert's contributions to any collection of the world's best songs would surely outnumber all the rest put together – a fair indication of his supremacy.

CHAPTER FIFTEEN

MENDELSSOHN

Almost alone among great composers FELIX MENDELSSOHN underwent no struggle to achieve fame or fortune. Born in 1809 in the outskirts of Hamburg and brought up in Berlin, he was the son of Abraham Mendelssohn, a wealthy banker who was better placed than the impecunious Franz Weber (see page 76) to attend to the requirements of a child prodigy in the Mozart class. Whereas in boyhood Carl Weber had picked up hints from strolling musicians, young Felix Mendelssohn was sent to the most expensive teachers in Berlin and Paris – and moreover was supplied by his fond parents with a private orchestra which he could con duct whenever he wished; he was soon composing sonatas, symphonies, cantatas, operas even, some of which are still preserved in manuscript. As it turned out many were com petent little works deserving recognition on their merits, and when at seventeen Mendelssohn startled everyone with the *Midsummer Night's Dream* overture even the sternest moralist had to admit that he had used his worldly advant ages to excellent purpose.

He was never obliged, as was Weber, to seek regular employment. Indeed when pressed to accept resident director ships he often declined them, and the only permanent post which he filled for any length of time was that of conductor of the Leipzig Gewandhaus concerts; as a rule he preferred to indulge in the extensive travel which he could well afford. Not that he was ever idle; far from it: he helped to rescue the name of J. S. Bach from oblivion by reviving that great master's works all over Germany, and furthermore com posed, played and conducted his own music wherever he went, whether it was Austria, Switzerland, Italy, France or Britain—to which he paid no less than ten visits and where he found himself completely at home. He toured the remoter parts of Scotland and Wales and was enchanted with their scenery; as for London, he compared it favourably with Naples ('it is indescribably beautiful when the roses of Piccadilly gleam in the sunshine'); he even went so far as to write that he was 'delighted' with Birmingham: no wonder our countrymen hailed him as a genius. But the strain of con tinual wayfaring in all sorts of weather – by crowded stage coach, bumpy post-chaise, tossing channel-boat – eventually undermined a constitution which had never been robust and he died in 1847 (at Leipzig) at the age of thirty-eight.

Apart from being a composer Mendelssohn was a man of letters, a classical scholar, a brilliant linguist and a painter of considerable ability. Jewish by race and German-Protest ant by religion, he cherished family affection and was particularly devoted to his elder sister Fanny, an accom plished pianist who married the artist William Hensel. Instinct drove him to play down his wealth and avoid any show of extravagance, and although friendly by nature and lionized wherever he went his character remained unspoilt; by contrast with many of his colleagues he was the epitome of upper-middle-class respectability. In 1837 he married Cecile Jeanrenaud, eighteen-year-old daughter of a Lutheran minister from the Swiss-Jura village of Motiers in the val de Travers (canton Neuchatel); she proved a good wife – and he a good husband. But although excessive popularity never corrupted the man it tended to demoralize the com poser: success came so easily that in course of time he lost the power of discrimination, and since his intuition was less sure than Weber's he slipped more frequently into melodic triviality and the facile use of harmonic cliches; he knew that his admirers were not interested in unconventional modulations (*a la* Schubert) or surprising strokes of dynamic originality (Beethoven) – and he was careful not to offend their susceptibilities. It was not so much that he prostituted his talent in return for public recognition as that he let it develop along lines which ran parallel with contemporary require ments; he did not sin against the Holy Ghost, but he sinned sufficiently to incur some measure of retrospective disapproval.

Mendelssohn's technique was admirable (few composers before or since have better understood an orchestra), and professional *expertise* was apparent even in such early works as the *Rondo capriccioso* for piano (1824), the string octet (also 1824) and the *Midsummer Night's Dream* overture (1826). This youthful masterpiece was later surpassed only by the *Hebrides* overture (of which more presently), and so far as orchestral pieces are concerned was matched only by the *Midsummer Night's* scherzo and nocturne (composed sixteen years after the overture), the 'Italian' symphony, and possibly by the 'Scottish' symphony and the violin concerto – which is still the standby of every virtuoso violinist. (Neither of the piano concertos is of comparable merit.)

For about eighty years Mendelssohn's *Elijah* (first produced at Birmingham in 1846) was almost as regular a feature of a British music-festival as Handel's *Messiah*. Recently it has failed to stay the course, but despite a tendency to squareness in the part-writing it is certainly the most satisfying of his choral works. 'Is not his word like a fire?' remains a fine piece of declamation, the lyrical charm of 'For the mountains shall depart' is still apparent, and our grandfathers were not far off the mark when they acclaimed the conclusion of Part I ('Thanks be to God') as the most stirring climax in all oratorio. Of the string quartets perhaps only that in E minor exploited the medium to advantage – and few people would suggest that Mendelssohn was an outstanding song-writer. On the other hand much of his piano music, if judged by appropriate standards, is excellent. The *Songs without Words* are admittedly uneven in quality, but it would be unfair to dismiss them out of hand as pretty trifles; not all of them are trifling and I see no objection to prettiness – in moderation. The *Variations serieuses* display unexpected authority in a specialized field, and the prelude and fugue in E minor (op. 35 no. 1) – closing with a chorale in E major – is masterly. (The keys of E minor and E major often brought out the best in Mendelssohn; it is no coincidence that of the self-contained works which I have singled out for praise about half are in either one or the other – or a mixture of both.)

That Mendelssohn is normally assigned to the romantic school of composers is largely because he appeals to cosy sentiment; he was not a romantic in the true sense of the term, since he always – or nearly always – preserved a classic sense of detachment. One rarely if ever comes across a sub jective expression of emotion such as one often finds in Schubert (especially in the songs), and the attempts to evoke atmosphere *a la* Weber usually have a touch of artificiality about them – not that they are necessarily for that reason any the less effective in their context. The fairy music from *A Midsummer Night's Dream* is captivating, but it suggests not so much fairies as a well-drilled troupe of dainty ballerinas; Bottom, when translated to Eeyore, is not written down an ass – he is a stage comedian wearing an ass's head. Yet elsewhere Mendelssohn proved that besides being a classic (a romantically-inclined classic, if you insist) he was also a superb impressionist. Nobody who, like the composer himself, has been to Fingal's Cave on the isle of Staffa (off the west coast of Mull) – and few of those who haven't – could deny that the *Hebrides* overture, while perfectly fit ting the concept of sonata-form, was at the same time the first great tone-picture in music and therefore a landmark in the history of the art; not even Wagner or Debussy later surpassed its imagery – the eternal swell of the ocean, the surging of the waves round the rocks, the intermittent calm and storm, the cry of the sea-birds overhead. (Mendelssohn exploited the same flair, though less consistently, in the concert-overture *Calm Sea and Prosperous Voyage*, which is a finer work than the more familiar *Ruy Blas*.)

A crowd of Mendelssohn's compositions – including the oratorio *St. Paul*, *Walpurgisnacht*, the *Hymn of Praise* and the 'Reformation' symphony (all highly esteemed in the nineteenth century) are already as good as dead; in course of time *Elijah*, too, may sink into further and undeserved oblivion and pianists no longer think it worth while to expend their energies on the *Rondo capriccioso* or the *Songs without Words*; even the enchanting *Midsummer Night's Dream* music may eventually find itself out of favour in the brave new world of Benjamin Britten. But for the sake of the *Hebrides* overture, if of nothing else, the name of Felix Mendelssohn will surely be honoured so long as man kind remains capable of recognizing consummate artistry.

CHAPTER SIXTEEN

BERLIOZ

HECTOR BERLIOZ (1803-69), the greatest French composer of his generation (whether by birth or adoption), was rather more than five years older than Mendelssohn and therefore, were birth-date the sole criterion, would be entitled to chronological precedence. But his powers were compara tively slow to develop; all but one of his best-known works were dated long after Mendelssohn had lost that first fine careless rapture – and in any case he outlived his con temporary by more than twenty years.

Berlioz was born at La Cote St. Andre, an attractively situated but rather poky little town on the marches of Lyonnais and Dauphine. (His birthplace is now the Musee Berlioz, 69 rue de la Republique, which guards many private letters as well as the manuscript scores of *Benvenuto Cellini* and *L'Enfance du Christ*.)[1] We have it on the authority of the composer himself, whose humour was dry, that he came into the world quite naturally, unheralded by any of the signs which in poetic ages preceded the advent of remarkable personages. His father was a physician, a man of culture and well esteemed in La Cote St. Andre where for a time he held the office of mayor; broadminded, with no strong doctrinal beliefs of his own, he did not demur when his wife, a devout churchwoman, insisted that their children be brought up as Catholics. The splendour of the church ritual appealed to Hector and he never forsook the faith – although in later life he found himself in general sympathy with his father's live-and-let-live attitude towards religion. Sent to Paris at the age of eighteen to study medicine, his first sight of a dissecting laboratory so repelled him that he

[1] Motorists on their way to the *cote d'azur* should note that La Cote St. Andre lies on the N 518, which winds its way from Lyon to Die (Drome) through the lovely region of Vercors and is a more spectacular and less frequented route than the direct N 75 through Grenoble.

abandoned forthwith a half-hearted attempt to follow in parental footsteps and turned aside to music – which Berlioz *pere* had encouraged as a hobby but viewed with suspicion as a profession. To the credit of both father and son neither forfeited mutual respect during the difficult years when Berlioz *fils* was striving, on a meagre financial allowance, to justify his choice of career.

His musical aspirations derived mainly from a youthful veneration for Gluck; he visited the library of the Paris Conservatoire (open to all), copied out the score of *Orfeo* (see page 48), studied it at his leisure and wrote a modelled cantata which he showed to J. F. Lesueur (an enlightened professor of composition), who was genuinely impressed but had to point out many technical defects. Berlioz was unable to secure immediate admission to the Conservatoire because his impetuously insubordinate behaviour in its library had permanently estranged its director Luigi Cherubini (Italian-born composer of *The Water Carrier* and *Anacreon*, who had settled permanently in Paris in 1788), but he studied privately with Lesueur and others and meanwhile composed exuberantly in a garret. Recognition eluded him, but much of this early outpouring was re-furbished later – a form of economy which he never ceased to practise. One work that does survive intact from this period is the sonata-form overture to an unfinished opera, *Les Francs juges*; the second subject has a disarming lilt characteristic not only of Berlioz in his most genial mood but also of Beethoven and Schumann in theirs, recalling the second subject from the finale of Beethoven's symphony no. 1 and foreshadowing the second subject from the finale of Schumann's no. 4.

When at last in 1826 Berlioz (to use his own phrase) cracked the barriers of the Conservatoire, he immediately entered for the Prix de Rome.[1] But he went the wrong way about it: instead of adhering to the (admittedly antiquated) regulations he asserted self-confidence by disregarding them and thereby alienated the examiners. He eventually won the

[1] The Prix de Rome was awarded annually by the French Academy of Fine Arts for the best student-composition of the year; it entitled the recipient to a period of free study in Rome.

prize at his fifth attempt, in 1830, with a work which for once fulfilled academic requirements without exhibiting any disturbing symptoms of alien influence. (Beethoven and Weber were still looked upon by everyone in Paris – except Berlioz – as dangerous foreign revolutionaries.) Meanwhile an intense admiration for Goethe led to a setting of *Eight Scenes from Faust,* which brought a first small measure of material success. Goethe soon yielded place to Shakespeare, and Berlioz fell violently in love at a distance with Ophelia as personified by Harriet Smithson, Irish member of a visit ing theatrical company from Britain. The emotional fluctua tions of this (as yet) entirely one-sided affair prompted completion of the *Symphonie fantastique* ('Episode de la vie d'un artiste'), a very personal and therefore romantic expression of youthful fervour followed by disillusionment, and by any standard a remarkable composition for a twenty-six-year-old. Descriptive rather than impressionistic, it dis played many features commonly associated with typical Berlioz: loose construction, a puckish and Beethoven-like addiction to the unexpected, attractive but often inconse quential flights of melodic fancy, crude-at-first-glance harmony (with an apparent obsession for chords in 'root position'), flimsy counterpoint, a brilliant battery of orchestration. (W. H. Hadow, who did much to inculcate appreciation of music in Britain, once wrote that 'the harmony, counterpoint and form which Berlioz learnt from the best teachers in Paris are very frequently defective, while his most indisputable title to immortality lies in the orchestration, for which he had no master at all'. Hadow was right to stress the paradox, but one regrets that he did not on mature consideration cross out the words 'his most indisputable title' and substitute 'one of his titles'.) A good deal of the *Symphonie fantastique* was written before Berlioz had so much as heard of Harriet Smithson, but passion impelled him to set himself a precedent by announc ing a programme. I reproduce it (condensed), because apart from programmatic interest it provides a key to the com poser's temperament, and in the enigmatic words of Donald Tovey (for whom see page 67) 'only very silly people take

Berlioz seriously but they are not so silly as the people who don't'.

A young musician of morbid sensitivity is in love; he has the strangest of dreams wherein his sentiments are translated into musical ideas. The Beloved has become a Melody – an *idee fixe* – which he hears everywhere. First he remembers the volcanic love which she instantly inspired. Next he meets her in the tumult of a ball. But when he goes to the country [even a Berlioz symphony must have a slow movement] the gentle sound of the wind in the trees gives a new calm to his turbulent heart. Presently, however, he dreams that he has killed her in a fit of jealousy, that he is condemned to death and led to the scaffold; finally that he is at a Witches' Sabbath, where the Melody of the Beloved is transformed into a vulgar dance-tune.

By the time the symphony was completed Berlioz had found a more tangible mistress than Ophelia in the young pianist Marie Moke, who accepted his loving farewells before he set out for Rome in February 1831; in April she married a fellow-pianist, Camille Pleyel.[1] Apart from a *crise de nerfs* when he learnt of Marie's perfidy (which sent him scurrying to Nice – and then back), Berlioz' stay in Rome passed without incident. He satisfied the authorities of the Conservatoire by periodically sending them watered-down versions of back-dated works and meanwhile ran riot in the concert-overtures *Rob Roy* and *King Lear* (Shakespeare again, one notes) and in *Lelio* (a sequel to the *Symphonie fantastique* which had all the faults and few of the virtues of its predecessor). Of greater artistic merit was a fine setting of Victor Hugo's poem *Le Captive*, later revised and expanded as a concert-aria.

Still devoted to his father, Berlioz broke his return

[1] This good lady seems to have had a *penchant* for illustrious composers. Once Chopin, while on holiday, lent his Paris flat to Liszt; he returned earlier than expected and found that his tenant had installed Madame Pleyel alongside.

journey from Rome at La Cote St. Andre and did not reach Paris until November 1832, when almost immediately he had a chance social encounter with his Ophelia, Harriet Smithson. On the instant love revived – and was recipro cated; within three months they were betrothed, within a year they were married, within two years they were parents of a son. For Berlioz all this meant hard work since his actress wife, now past her prime, made no contribution to the family budget. To augment his income he took to regular journalism (pungent articles on music in the Paris press); four of his major compositions date from the same period. First came the symphony *Harold in Italy*, vaguely based on Byron's *Childe Harold*: the virtuoso violinist Niccolo Paganini, who was a very good friend to Berlioz, had recently acquired a Stradivarius viola and urged a prominent solo part for that normally neglected instru ment; for its benefit the composer retrieved a few tunes from discarded earlier works, including one which in *Rob Roy* had been allotted (more appropriately) to the cor anglais. Next: the Requiem (where the valour of a gigantic chorus and orchestra could hardly help outrunning the discretion imposed by such items as the beautiful 'Sanctus'), and the spirited but in places rather pretentious opera *Benvenuto Cellini* (which is remembered for its overture and an orchestral transcription known nowadays as *Le Carnaval romain*). These were followed by yet another pro grammatic symphony, *Romeo and Juliet* (incorporating voices); it was characteristically disjointed but here and there the music caught to perfection the spirit of the words, notably in the passage inspired by

Good night; good night; parting is such sweet sorrow
That I shall say good night till it be morrow.

Meanwhile Berlioz' own connubial bliss had faded away in scenes of personal recrimination, and from 1840 onwards he often escaped from Paris and conjugal ties in the com pany of a pretty but untrained soprano named Marie Recio. Over the next fifteen years he established his reputation abroad: still unappreciated in France, he and his music were acclaimed in Britain, Belgium, Germany, Austria, Hungary and Russia, although the distressing vocal in adequacy of his endearing young charmer was a constant source of embarrassment. During this period of travel and consolidation (consolidation of two separate urges) Berlioz wrote the concert-overture *Le Corsair* (dedicated to the music critic of *The Times*), the cantata *The Damnation of Faust* (which incorporated the original *Eight Scenes* and from which the dance of the sylphs and the Racockzy march were promptly popularized in Britain by the con ductor Charles Halle) and the oratorio *L'Enfance du Christ*. Perhaps because the approach was here more austere than usual, *L'Enfance* was better received in Paris than most of his works, but the nervous excitement of his disposition was once again mirrored in the incongruous variations of style, which ranged from the calm loveliness of a duet for Mary and Joseph at Bethlehem to the picturesque exoticism of a cabbalistic dance (in 7/4 time).

All this while Berlioz had honourably provided financial support for Harriet; when she died in 1854 he made an honest woman of Marie Recio and started work on a new five-act opera, *The Trojans*, which took four years to com plete; production difficulties were immense and only part of it was played during his lifetime. Just as the *Symphonie fantastique* holds the quintessence of youthful Berlioz so *The Trojans* represents his full maturity. One is conscious of the same vivid imagination and flashes of brilliance often coupled with the same diffuseness and gaucherie, but despite some weak threads the tapestry as a whole is woven with greater assurance and the choral sections (as in *Faust*) show uncommon mastery. Those who enjoy the Trojans' march and the Royal Hunt and Storm (who doesn't?) should also take note of passages where a subtle touch of poignant sound is added to melodies which on paper may look undistinguished.

While struggling vainly to secure a complete production of *The Trojans* Berlioz wrote a cheerful but uneven light opera, *Beatrice and Benedict*, a final tribute at the shrine of his beloved Shakespeare (*Much Ado about Nothing*).

Thereafter he concentrated on literary work – notably his memoirs – but when his second wife died in 1862 he began to age prematurely. He visited La Cote St. Andre for the last time and had a romantic meeting with a sweetheart of his adolescence, but he was already a sick man and the death of his son Louis (a sea-captain) at Havana in 1867 was a crippling blow; he himself died two years later.

Berlioz has always been a controversial figure. Of recent years his most ardent protagonist has been the erudite American musicologist Jacques Barzun whose factual conclusions, based on exhaustive research, may certainly be regarded as definitive. Other biographers, including his compatriot Adolphe Boschot, while commenting with appreciative discernment on many aspects of his work have by my interpretation of their writings been more concerned with debunking him. Boschot himself has in turn been effectively debunked by Barzun, but it would be fair to agree with the former's comment that Hector Berlioz refuses to fit into any familiar category, a refusal that surely might have been expected from such a disconcertingly unconventional genius.

CHAPTER SEVENTEEN

CHOPIN

FREDERIC CHOPIN was born at the village of Zelazowa Wola, near Warsaw; whether the date was 1809 (as some authori ties maintain) or 1810 (officially accepted) matters little. What does matter is that his father, although bred in Lorraine (which had close historic ties with Poland), had been a Polish citizen since 1787 and earned a fair living as private tutor to the sons and daughters of the nobility; that his mother, gentle and well-educated, was one-hundred-per cent Polish; that he himself was Polish not only by birth and upbringing but also by outlook and temperament. A child prodigy, he earned public recognition at the age of eight both as pianist and composer, and his choice of career was never in doubt. After a course of study in War saw with Joseph Ellsner — an honoured figure in Polish musical history – he presented himself in Vienna where he played his own compositions to appreciative audiences. That was in 1829. A year later he was back there again, purpose fully *en route* for Italy. But Italy, like Poland, was in the throes of political upheaval and perforce his second visit to Vienna lasted longer than intended. Eventually he aban doned the idea of going south and instead made for Paris, which he reached by way of Munich and Stuttgart in the autumn of 1831.

In Paris Chopin soon established his reputation as a brilliant pianist, a tactful mentor to the young hopefuls of the aristocracy – and an *emigre* composer with out-of-ordinary ability. Though handicapped by a frail constitu tion he also undertook several concert tours in Germany and one in Britain; everywhere he went his pale and interesting good looks and charming manners captivated the ladies, but his only serious love affair at the time – with a fellow-Pole, Marie Wodzinska – was terminated by mutual agreement in 1837. The same year, however, saw his first meeting with a remarkable woman who had been christened Aurore Dupin and had married a dull provincial named Casimir Dudevant by whom she had two children; she is known to posterity by her pseudonym as an authoress, George Sand. Having for a time lived openly with the poet Alfred de Musset, she now took Chopin under her wing and carried him off to spend the winter of 1838/39 in Majorca. As it happened he was in an even poorer state of health than usual and the trip was not an unqualified success, but thereafter he was a constant guest at her country-house at Nohant (Indre), where he could relax in quietude and carry on with his composing; consequently he soon came to regard Nohant as his home. (The chateau and its grounds, today no less gloomy and derelict than most of their kind, adjoin the N 143 twenty miles south of Chateauroux and three miles north of La Chatre.) It is acknowledged by all that George Sand was a generous patron and Chopin a grateful *protege* with whom she had much in common; few will agree with the good people who have convinced themselves that this close friendship, which lasted for ten years, depended solely upon a shared enthusiasm for intellectual pursuits. Be that as it may, the permanent cuckoo eventually became a source of embarrassment even in this most unconventional of nests, and the regime finally broke itself on a violent family quarrel in which George Sand sided with her son Maurice (who had always resented the intruder) against Chopin and her daughter Solange (with whom he had remained on cordial terms). Frustrated and depressed, he paid another visit to Britain, where he stayed for seven months and despite the onset of tuberculosis gave four concerts; in the autumn of 1848 he returned to Paris too ill to make any further public appearance and he died there a year later.

Apart from two concertos, both belonging to his early Warsaw days, all Chopin's works of any importance were written for piano alone: it will be convenient to refer to them in generic groups, identifying individual pieces, when mentioned, by *opus* numbers. These indicate sequence of publication rather than of composition, but a rough guide would assign ops. 1-22 to the Warsaw-Vienna period of 1825-31, ops. 23-34 to the Paris period of 1832-38, ops. 35-65 to the Nohant period of 1839-47. (Ops. 66-74 are posthumous publications, their composition-dates ranging from 1825 on wards.) It must be stressed that this division of Chopin's active career into three periods is purely for the sake of easy chronological reference and has little if any stylistic signifi cance. One has heard the view expressed that he 'was at his best in the polonaises and mazurkas which belonged to Poland, while his later and more popular *salon* works were tainted with Parisian mannerisms and affection'. This is nonsense. All the well-known polonaises and at least two thirds of the mazurkas were composed after Chopin reached Paris, while many of the more popular *salon* works date from before he ever set foot there – among them the in escapable nocture in E flat major op. 9 no. 2, the luscious *etude* in E major op. 10 no. 3 (nowadays incorporated in the ballet *Les Sylphides*), the big waltz in E flat major op. 18, and the unique slow waltz in A minor published later as op. 34 no. 2. Even in the twenty-four preludes op 28 – one in every major and minor key and which taken collectively may perhaps convey a superficial impression of conven tionality – there are fewer signs of Parisian mannerisms and affectation than of Slav influence. (See especially nos. 2, 4, 12, 18 and 22.)

Emphasis on his consistency must not be taken to imply that Chopin the artist stood still, that op. 65 showed no advance on op. 1; nevertheless the progressive development of his powers was largely a matter of technique rather than of style. As befitted an outstanding exponent of lyrical romanticism in music he had an inborn flair for varied melody – graceful, passionate, rhapsodic; to this in due course was added a sense of harmonic colour-contrast beyond contemporary imaginings (glance through the chromatic sequences of the mazurka in A flat major op. 59 no. 2) and a growing realization that brilliant pianism should cease to be mere decoration and become welded to the melodic scheme; the *leggierissimo* passages of the scherzo in C sharp minor op. 39, for example, were an integral part of the whole conception. Furthermore from about 1835 onwards Chopin tackled larger forms with greater assurance. Admittedly he never completed a wholly satisfying sonata (for even op. 35 in B flat minor, funeral march and all, was thrown off balance by the brevity of its demoniac finale), but he was at his best in the scherzo in B flat minor op. 31, the *ballade* in A flat major op. 47, the fantasy in F minor op. 49 and the polonaise-fantasy in A flat major op. 61 – all of which are much more massive in scale than their titles would suggest. Nevertheless Frederic Chopin also deserves our heart-felt gratitude for bringing us perfection in miniature (e.g. the preludes op. 28 nos. 7 and 20), as well as for raising the modest mazurka and ball-room waltz to a level of artistry hitherto undreamt of.

CHAPTER EIGHTEEN

SCHUMANN

Both Berlioz and Chopin were among those who demon
strated, in their different ways, that a secondary feature
distinguishing romantic from classical music was a ten
dency to reflect more closely the personality of its composer.
The unquestionably romantic music of ROBERT SCHUMANN
was an exception which neither proved nor disproved the
generalization. The man, despite a fund of good nature, was
unsociable and wayward, liable to fits of depression and
even to mental instability; it is true that his music was
always good-natured, but it was rarely wayward and never
depressing or unstable. One hesitates to hail him as he
himself hailed Chopin – 'hats off, gentlemen, a genius!' –
but he had immense talent which he used to splendid
purpose.

This most unreliable of men and most reliable of com
posers was born in 1810 at Zwickau (equidistant from
Weimar, Leipzig and Dresden), today an industrial centre
with a population of nearly 100,000 but then a typical
Saxon market-town with perhaps one-twentieth that number
of inhabitants. His father was a publisher and bookseller,
and although Robert showed precocity in music he was also
an avid reader of Goethe and Schiller – as well as of E. T. A.
Hoffman and Jean Paul (J. P. F. Richter), who took romanti
cism in literature to a level of extravagant fantasy. On the
death of his father (who had encouraged artistic ambitions)
his mother (who hadn't) sent him to study law at Leipzig,
where he attended a few lectures but spent most of his time
hob-nobbing with musical friends who gave him lessons in
harmony, counterpoint, piano-playing – and wine-bibbing;
one of his mentors was Friedrich Wieck, whose pretty nine-
year-old daughter Clara, he noticed, was a very promising
young pianist. Presently, however, Schumann decided he
was getting nowhere; so did the university authorities, who

readily agreed that his student's registration should be transferred to Heidelberg. His intention was to study law and music side by side, but bouts of drunkenness soon made him unpopular even in that traditionally free-and-easy academy and he was eventually dismissed on the ground that he had not paid his fees. Back, then, to Leipzig, where having thrown away his legal books and permanently injured two fingers in a foolish scientific experiment, Schumann finally abandoned all hope of becoming either a barrister or a concert pianist and devoted himself entirely to composition and journalism. (It was at this stage that he founded *Die neue Zeitschrift,* which under his editorship continued for many years to print pithy comment, both pertinent and impertinent, on contemporary personalities and events in the musical world.) In due course, after a short-lived engagement to one Ernestine von Fricken, he became seriously enamoured of Clara Wieck (who alone was able to wean him from alcoholic excess), but his old piano-teacher did not fancy him as a son-in-law and the wedding was postponed until she was on the verge of attaining the age of twenty-one.

Up to now Schumann had composed only piano music: notably the very original *Carnaval* ('Scenes mignonnes sur quatres notes'), the more conventional but equally attractive *Études symphoniques,* and many shorter but by no means trivial pieces published under collective titles like *Fantasie-stucke* and *Noveletten.* His bride, however, urged him to seek new pastures, and the next four years were given over in turn to songs, orchestral works, chamber music, and oratorio. In 1840, the first year of their married life, Schumann completed the song-cycles *Frauenliebe und Leben* and *Dichterliebe;* in 1841 two symphonies (the second of which was afterwards revised and is now known as no. 4), *Overture, Scherzo and Finale* (in effect a symphony in three movements) and a fantasia for piano and orchestra (later expanded as a full-length concerto); in 1842 half-a-dozen miscellaneous chamber works with or without piano; in 1843 *Paradise and the Peri.*

Thanks largely to conjugal understanding and devotion

this was the happiest and most placid phase of Schumann's career. Unfortunately over the next six years or so the physical and mental strain of visits to Berlin, Vienna, St. Petersburg and elsewhere (giving concerts at which Clara played divinely and he himself demonstrated his incom petence as a conductor) caused a succession of nervous breakdowns. Nevertheless he composed two more symphonies (nos. 2 and 3), a concerto for cello and another for four horns, incidental music for Byron's *Manfred* and Goethe's *Faust,* the opera *Genoveva,* and some further piano pieces including two admirable collections dedicated to youthful executants (our old friend 'The Merry Peasant', etc). Most of these works were penned at Dresden, where the Schumanns maintained a *pied-a-terre* during their travels, but in 1850 they settled in Dusseldorf. Here they lived very quietly, for by that time Schumann had become a psychiatric case; his later compositions – apart perhaps from two violin sonatas – were unrepresentative. After an unsuccessful attempt to commit suicide he was placed at his own request in a private asylum in the outskirts of Bonn; it was there that in 1856 he died in the arms of his beloved Clara – who for forty long years of widowhood continued to play and teach the piano and remained her husband's most faithful champion.

Although Schumann studied music with many respected professors of the art in Zwickau, Leipzig and Heidelberg, there was only one master to whom he owed and owned life long allegiance – J. S. Bach. He had little time for Haydn; not a great deal, in his secret heart, for Mozart or even Beet hoven (although his music often showed traces of Beet hoven's influence): all three, he felt, had chosen to follow easy but ultimately unrewarding byways rather than march boldly forward along the hard high road which Bach had signposted. This apparently intolerant attitude should not be ascribed to bigotry; in the eighteen-thirties and forties Bach was generally shrugged aside as an academic pedant, and Schumann was one of the few who strove (along with Mendelssohn) to force recognition of his true greatness – and to implement it. Admittedly there is not much outward resemblance between, say, the 'forty-eight' and the *Fantasiestucke*, but Schumann was a throw back to Bach in so far as he adopted the same approach to music's formal problems and furthermore he was capable of evoking Bach-like clarity in contemporary mood: although he rarely exploited counterpoint *per se* his pianistic effects, unlike Chopin's, often derived from a cunning flair for treating snatches of melody 'canonically'. Another characteristic feature of his music was a specialized form of syncopation; the rhythm is sometimes cross to the eye rather than the ear – there are passages in the finale of the piano concerto where the poor conductor always looks as though he couldn't keep time with the orchestra – but there is no mistaking the aural impact in (for instance) the 'Davidsbundler March' from *Carnaval*.

It has often been said that Schumann appears to better advantage in the recital room (or even *salon*) than in the concert hall, a tenable proposition since undeniably there are some exquisite gems amongst his songs and piano pieces while many of the larger works are clumsily fashioned – and inexpertly orchestrated. Yet in truth the point at issue is one of medium rather than of scale: the insensitivity of his scoring for strings and wood-wind, due mainly to his lack of interest in the aesthetic or technical potentialities of any instrument save the piano (which he loved and understood), matters relatively little when the piano itself is the principal centre of attraction. Partly if not wholly for that reason the string quartets are less satisfying than the piano trios, the piano quartet and the (splendid) piano quintet; and although *Paradise and the Peri, Manfred* and *Genoveva* contain some good music and the symphonies some excel lent music most of us, if allowed only one Schumann disc on our desert island, would plump for the piano concerto – which in any case is a masterpiece in its own right. Although conceived, as we have already noted, in two separate spasms, it is better balanced than Schumann's other works of comparable proportions and is more com pact and unified than any of the symphonies, each of which (despite the unifying finale of no. 4) compels admiration not so much *qua* symphony as for sake of certain individual movements: the sonata-form finale of no. 1, for instance, where the sombre development section contrasts so well with the light-hearted Mendelssohn-like melodies of the exposition; the expressive *adagio* (better orchestrated than usual) from no. 2; the stirring *allegro* which opens no. 3; the vigorous scherzo from no. 4.

It is arguable whether Schumann's claim to immortality depends upon an instinct for the miniature amounting to genius (in summing up one cannot, after all, escape the word) or upon an unbounded talent which found expression in almost every branch of composition: it is certain that the claim, be it in little or big, is firmly established, and even those for whom German romanticism spells anathema should not grudge him praise for having been, in his day, a manly and at the same time poetic interpreter of its characteristics. Robert Schumann had his failings and his failures, but he never courted easy popularity or wrote a bar of music that marked conscious withdrawal from the highest standards of artistic integrity.

CHAPTER NINETEEN

LISZT

The versatile FRANZ LISZT – for tidy-minded historians an even more disturbing character than Berlioz – came from that Austro-Hungarian borderland where Joseph Haydn had spent much of his life (see chapter 9). He was born in 1811 at Dobrjan, ten miles south of Sopron in the extreme west of Hungary, where his father was employed as bailiff by Prince Nicolas Esterhazy, son of Haydn's patron. (The village now lies in the Austrian province of Burgenland and is called Raiding.) As a small boy he demonstrated such musical ability that his parents took him to Vienna, some fifty miles away, for they decided that there – and there alone – could his talent be brought to fruition. Their confidence in him was justified: at the age of twelve he started a long and successful career as pianist – and a long but more chequered career as composer.

From 1823 till 1837 Liszt lived in Paris and from 1848 till 1861 he was director of the Weimar court opera-house, but throughout his life he was continually on the move. A succession of concert tours – spread intermittently over half a century and bewildering to follow in detail – led him to every European country except Sweden and Norway: his virtuosity was acclaimed with equal fervour in Constantinople and Kiev, Lisbon and Liege, Milan and Manchester, Hanover and Heligoland. During the course of his travels he became acquainted with nearly every musician of contemporary importance as well as with some who belonged to previous or subsequent generations: for instance he met Beethoven, forty-one years his senior, at Vienna in 1823; he met a promising young Norwegian named Edvard Grieg, thirty-two years his junior, at Rome in 1869; he met the eighteen-year-old Isaac Albeniz (from Spain) at Budapest in 1878. He was on particularly friendly terms with Berlioz, Chopin and Schumann, to all three of whom – and to many others – he gave practical help by transcribing, playing or conducting their works and by arranging concerts at which they could play or conduct their own. Generosity to fellow-artists was indeed Liszt's most endearing personal charac teristic; among his favourite *proteges* were Peter Cornelius (the underrated composer of *The Barber of Bagdad*), Joachim Raff (now only remembered, poor fellow, for a cavatina) and Richard Wagner (who eventually became his son-in-law, see page 118). During his declining years Liszt suffered from dropsy, but it was of pneumonia that he died – rather suddenly – while attending the Bayreuth Festival of 1886. (For Bayreuth see page 117.)

No account of Liszt's career would be complete without a reference to what Eric Blom – in the admirably laconic style which he adopted throughout the strictly factual *Everyman's Dictionary of Music* – called 'his 2 great and innumerable minor love affairs'. A footnote on page 95 has already drawn attention to a minor one; the 2 great were with the golden-haired Countess Marie d'Agoult (which lasted from 1834 till 1844 and produced three children) and the cigar-smoking Princess Caroline Sayn-Wittgenstein (1847 till 1863). The second of these protracted *liaisons* might have led to marriage had not Pope Pius IX (to Liszt's secret relief) refused in 1861 to sanction Caroline's divorce. As it happened her husband died three years later, but by that time her lover had chosen to immerse himself in religious mysticism; after two years devoted to study and meditation he received the tonsure as a lay priest – and thereupon resumed his roving. Ernest Newman in *The Man Liszt* (1934) once and for all dispelled the myth that he was a romantic *galant* who treated his mistresses with unfailing chivalry and renounced the pleasures of the flesh on becoming an *abbe*.

Most of Liszt's original compositions for piano – some three hundred pieces all told – were written between the ages of twenty and fifty and fall into three groups: the Chopinesque; the Hungarian; the truly Lisztian. The source of inspiration for the bulk of his waltzes, mazurkas, *etudes* and *consolations* (in effect nocturnes) was obvious, but only now and again – e.g. in the *etude de concert* in D flat major and the *consolation* in the same key – did he capture the poetic sensibility of his Polish contemporary. On the other hand his only piano sonata (in B minor) was original in conception (it is played without a break) and more satisfy ing than any of Chopin's. He took great interest in the gipsy music of his native land, but not even in the vigorous Hungarian rhapsodies (among which it would be snobbish to disparage the ever-popular No. 2) did he fully exploit its essential characteristics: an Italian flavour was apt to over whelm the Magyar. More truly Lisztian, or so one would like to believe, were the short pieces published under such collective titles as *Apparitions*, *Harmonies poetiques et religieuses*, and *Annees de pelerinages*; the third volume of the *Annees*, belonging exceptionally to his sixties, displayed a flair for impressionism (e.g. in 'Les Jeux d'eaux a la villa d'Este') which hitherto had often been clouded by flashy showmanship. It is interesting to note that the famous *Liebestraum* (the third of a set of three) started life as a song – 'O lieb', so lang du lieben kannst'; as a song-writer Liszt was rarely at his best, although a handful of Victor Hugo settings – notably *Enfant, si j'etais roi* – were un affectedly charming.

Until he was about forty-five Liszt, although a conductor, was curiously insensitive to orchestral values; he was actu ally driven to call in outside help when orchestrating the first few of his dozen or so symphonic poems. Confined to one movement, these were more consistent in style and less diffuse than the *Symphonie fantastique* and *Harold in Italy* of Berlioz (which provided programmatic precedents) but hardly matched them in spontaneity of inspiration; *Les Preludes* (1848, revised 1854) is the most familiar, but *Hamlet* (1858) is more concise and contains finer music. Liszt's most noteworthy orchestral work, however, was the full-length *Faust* symphony – character-pictures of Faust, Gretchen and Mephistopheles – dated 1857; here his des criptive powers reached their summit-point. The two piano concertos came comparatively early (although each was later revised); the emphatic opening of the first (in E flat major) can still make an audience sit up and take notice but both works are uneven: there are passages of dignity and indeed of beauty, but the brilliance of the treatment (with Liszt a matter of theme-transformation rather than symphonic development) cannot hide the poverty of much of the material. A shorter piece for piano and orchestra (strings only), the posthumously-published *Malediction*, probably written when he was about thirty, incorporated some startling harmonic progressions typifying a life-long struggle to prove himself an innovator which reached its climax in the self-conscious modernity of the *Via Crucis* (1879) for four soloists, choir and organ. Among his sacred works this does not rank so high as the impressive and indeed masterly oratorio *Christus* (1867), where he cut his coat in accordance with his cloth and showed that he was not the mountebank some of his harsher critics have made him out to be; honourable mention should also be made of the admirable setting of Psalm XIII for tenor, chorus and orchestra (1859), with its unexpected initial juxtaposition of the common chords of C major and G sharp minor.

Finally a word about Liszt's piano transcriptions. Although virtuosity was their motivation it would be unfair to dismiss them as mere show-pieces, for he had an extra ordinary knack of interpreting for his own instrument the more diversified expositions of abler composers: one feels that Mozart, for instance, would have enjoyed the para phrase of *Don Giovanni*, Schubert the wordless *Winterreise*. To attempt a piano-solo reduction of Beethoven's symphonies may have been presumptuous; in the outcome it was not only a stupendous technical achievement but moreover focussed public attention on their greatness, at the time not fully recognized. And furthermore, where lesser composers were concerned, the Liszt version often transcended the original in artistry.

By all accounts Liszt was the finest pianist of his age; unfortunately he could leave no tape-recordings and so his prowess in that field must remain a legend. As a man he deserves to be remembered not so much for his exploits as a lady-killer as for the goodwill he showed to contemporary musicians with fewer worldly advantages. In Franz Liszt the composer there burned a flame of genius: though often flickering, it nevertheless shone brightly enough to light the stairway to the master-musicians' gallery.

CHAPTER TWENTY

WAGNER

RICHARD WAGNER (1813-1883), who rode the seas of nine teenth-century music with a stormy bluster worthy of any flying Dutchman, was the ninth child of Johanna Wagner, *nee* Patz, whose husband, an actuary at the Leipzig police court, died in a typhoid epidemic which swept the city after the crushing defeat there of Napoleon's army by the Prussians and Russians in October 1813. On his death she took her children (Richard was six months old at the time) to Dresden, where Ludwig Geyer, a well-established singer and actor, generously assumed responsibility for their up bringing. Johanna married him in 1815 and soon afterwards presented him with a daughter, Cacilie. Cacilie Geyer (or Cacilie Avenarius as she became when she married a book-publisher) will not reappear in this narrative, but it is worth noting that throughout his life Wagner remained on affectionate terms with his half-sister – if indeed she was no more than a *half*-sister: research has revealed good grounds for belief that Geyer, who for many years had been a close friend of the family, was also responsible for Richard himself. (The available evidence has been set forth fully and fairly by the indispensable Ernest Newman in his monu mental *Life of Richard Wagner,* Vol. I pages 17-24, Vol. II pages 560-5, Vol. III pages 524-8 and Vol. IV page 597 foot note 9). There was always a touch of irony in the thought that a police servant had fathered such an uncompromising rebel against authority – in politics, art and morals.

Any attempt to assess Wagner's true worth as an artist continually finds itself up against the problem as to how far his work reflected a half-digested intake of the writings of the teutonic philosophiser Arthur Schopenhauer, for he aimed at being an author and a poet as well as a composer (he wrote all his own libretti) and even when his music apparently illustrated to near-perfection a straightforward dramatic situation he had to expound the inner meaning in characteristic jargon.

(a) In Elsa I saw my desired antithesis to Lohengrin – yet not so absolute an antithesis as that which is included in his general nature and forms the necessarily longed-for complement. Elsa is the Unconscious, the Undeliberate, into which Lohengrin's conscious, deliberate being yearns to be redeemed; but his *yearning*, again, is itself the unconscious, undeliberate necessity in Lohengrin, whereby he feels himself akin to Elsa's being. (*A Communication to my Friends*, 1851.)

(b) The necessity of prolonging beyond the point of change the subjection to the tie that binds Wotan to Fricka – a tie resulting from an involuntary illusion of love, the duty of maintaining at all costs the relation into which they have entered, and so placing themselves in hopeless opposition to the universal law of change and renewal, which governs the world of phenomena – these are the conditions which bring the pair of them to a state of torment and lovelessness. (Letter to August Röckel, dated 25th January 1854.[1])

(c) The grand concordance of all sterling Myths, as thrust upon me by my studies, had sharpened my eyesight for the wondrous variations standing out amid this harmony. Such a one confronted me with fascinating clearness in the relation of Tristan to Isolde as compared with that of Siegfried to Brynhilde. Just as in languages the transmutation of a single sound forms two apparently quite diverse words, so here, by a similar transmutation or shifting of the Time-motive, two seemingly unlike relations had sprung from the same mythic factor. Their intrinsic parity consists in this: both Tristan and Siegfried, in bondage to an illusion which makes this deed of theirs unfree, woo for another their eternally pre-destined

[1] Röckel was a close associate of Wagner's (both in music and politics) at the time of the 1849 revolution (see page 117); they remained friends until 1868, when Wagner accused Röckel of trying to make mischief between himself and his by then established mistress, Cosima von Bülow (page 118).

bride, and in the false relation hence arising find their doom. (*Epilogue to* The Ring of the Nibelung, 1871.)

Perhaps all one really gathers from (*a*) is that Elsa was a romantically minded young lady and Lohengrin a very romantic lover, from (*b*) that Wotan was an adulterous husband and Fricka a nagging wife, from (*c*) that Wagner was not too happy about having used the same plot twice over. I shall not argue the points further; for present purposes I prefer to confine myself to a condensed summary of his career and brief comment on the *musical* content of his operas – or music dramas.

For the first twenty years of his life Wagner did not stray further than eighty miles or so from Dresden; his time was divided between Dresden itself, Eisleben (nearby), Prague, and his birth-place Leipzig. Brought up in a household whose bread and butter depended upon opera and drama and where he was left largely to his own devices, he at first concentrated youthful attention on the theatre's literary side (Sophocles, Dante, Shakespeare, Schiller) and took little serious interest in music until he was about fifteen. At that age he discovered Mozart, Beethoven and Weber, and thereafter there was no holding him. All other studies were put aside; during the next four years he composed a piano sonata and a handful of concert-overtures and started work on two operas – *The Wedding* (which he did not finish) and *The Fairies* (which he did finish but which was never performed during his lifetime). In 1833, at the age of twenty, he was appointed chorus-master at the Würzburg opera-house and in 1834 musical director of a recently inaugurated municipal theatre at Magdeburg. He joined the Magdeburg company at Lauchstadt (a small watering-place near Halle where it was giving a summer season) and promptly fell in love with the leading lady, Minna Planer. When the venture foundered for want of support the two young people went to look for work in the Baltic port of Konigsberg – where in 1836 they were married. Meanwhile Wagner had completed another opera (*The Novice of Palermo*) but he was heavily in debt and his bride, appalled at the prospect of unrelieved poverty and insecurity, soon became the mistress of a local business worthy who could afford to indulge her extrava gant tastes. Wagner threatened divorce, but when Minna was discarded by her wealthy lover he took her back rather than let her go on the streets. It was a rewarding gesture: over a long period of years she showed her gratitude – and, let one add, some nobility of character – by sharing with equanimity the uncertain fortunes of a husband whose budding genius can have been but small compensation for his profligacy. Privation was the order – privation aggra vated by travel: from Königsberg to Riga; from Riga by sea to London and thence via Boulogne to Paris (where they continually had to shift their lodgings because they rarely paid any rent); from Paris back to Dresden, where in 1842 Wagner at last found regular employment as deputy con ductor at the opera-house.

During three unhappy years in Paris he had composed *Rienzi* (here and there showing prophetic signs of origin ality), *The Flying Dutchman* (nearly all the best of which was incorporated in the overture, a fine piece of tone-paint ing which owed something to Mendelssohn's *Hebrides,* see page 91) and the very effective *Faust* overture (intended as the first movement of a symphony). Settled once again in Dresden, with a reasonable stipend, he was able to tackle composition in better heart. There he completed *Tann-hauser* (1845) and *Lohengrin* (1847) which presently, thanks to the patronage of Franz Liszt, brought him to the notice of a wide public; both operas are still deservedly popular although it can now be seen that neither marked such an advance on *Euryanthe* or *The Huguenots* as some ardent Wagnerites would have us believe. (For Weber's *Euryanthe* see page 78. *The Huguenots* was a typical grand opera by Jakob Meyerbeer, a German composer who settled in Paris in 1825 and six years later had a sensational success with *Robert the Devil*; he befriended Wagner in Paris and later received contumely in return.) It is true that Weber's flair for atmosphere was brought neatly up to date in the *Tann-hauser* overture and Venusberg scene, and that in the duet between Ortrud and Frederick in Act II of *Lohengrin* the

Meyerbeer convention was pushed aside when the orchestra was allowed to play its part in the unfolding of the drama; but although these two operas do indeed hold moments of rare beauty one is continually oppressed by the monotonous rhythmic background: relief from 2/2 or 4/4 time comes only in the pilgrims' chorus from *Tannhauser* and the ensemble 'Mein Herr und Gott, nun ruf' ich dich' from Act I of *Lohengrin*. (Wagner eventually outgrew this weakness: many of the lyrical passages in *The Ring* and *The Mastersingers* are in flowing 9/8 time, and it is significant that for the 1861 'Paris version' of *Tannhauser* – see page 120 – he recast some 4/4 choral sections in 3/4.)

Back in 1830, as a rioting Leipzig student, Wagner had had his first brush with the police. When in 1849 he was faced with imprisonment as an active political revolutionary (his friend Rockel – see page 114, footnote – paid that penalty), he fled ignominiously from Dresden with a forged passport and sought asylum in Switzerland. For many years thereafter his career again became picaresque: he was always moving on, sometimes to fulfil professional engagements but as often as not to escape imminent arrest as a dangerous mutineer against governmental authority or as an accomplished bilker of importunate creditors. It would take too much time and space to recount his travels in chronological and topographical detail; suffice to record that being barred from his native Saxony he was mostly resident in tolerant Switzerland where he continued to compose, while also visiting (among other cities) London, Paris, Bordeaux, Venice, Vienna, Budapest, Prague, St Petersburg and – from 1864 onwards – Munich. At Munich (and at the royal retreat at Starnberg on the nearby Wurmsee) he was a frequent guest of young King Ludwig II of Bavaria, to whose personal interest and financial support he owed the privilege and satisfaction – on his fifty-ninth birthday – of laying the foundation-stone of the Festival Theatre at Bayreuth (about thirty miles north-east of Nuremberg) which has ever since been consecrated to performances of his works.

Meanwhile in the domestic world chaos reigned and poor

117

Minna's patience was sorely tried. Her position became well-nigh intolerable during Wagner's typically passionate but more-than-usually protracted love affair with Mathilde Wesendonck (wife of one of his most sympathetic admirers), but the final break did not come until about 1864 when he entered into a permanent *liaison* with Cosima von Bülow, the illegitimate daughter of his life-long patron Franz Liszt by Countess Marie d'Agoult (see page 109) and the wife of his good friend the conductor Hans von Bülow. When Minna died two years later Wagner established himself with Cosima in idyllic surroundings at Triebschen on Lake Lucerne and he married her in 1870 as soon as von Bülow obtained a divorce. (Their villa, now a museum full of interesting relics, should not be missed by any music lover who finds himself in Lucerne: it is barely two miles from the town centre.) They stayed at Triebschen until 1873 when they moved to Bayreuth – the villa Wahnfried – but from 1876 onwards they spent much of their time in Italy. With Cosima by his side – and thanks to King Ludwig a fairly full purse – Wagner found travel less exhausting than it had been with Minna thirty-five years before: there was no despair, no privation; southern sunshine and good living were objectives both attainable and attained. In September 1882 they took root in Venice where he died the following February, aged sixty-nine.

Before being driven from Dresden in 1849 Wagner had written the libretto of a projected music drama entitled *The Death of Siegfried*: several years later he made it the starting or rather finishing point of the mighty tetralogy which we now know as *The Ring of the Nibelung*. By 1856 he had completed both words and music of the first two sections, *The Rhinegold* and *The Valkyrie,* and had began work on the third, *Siegfried*: at that stage, prompted by Mathilde Wesendonck, he slipped aside to *Tristan and Isolde* (1857-9). It was not until after he had also written and composed that great operatic comedy *The Master-singers of Nuremberg* (1862-7) tnat he returned to his Nibelung: *Siegfried* was eventually finished in 1869 and *The Dusk of the Gods* in 1871; the forging of *The Ring* had thus taken him nearly a quarter of a century. *Parsifal*, a sublime hotch-potch of esoteric Christianity, mediaeval legend, eroticism and pantomime magic, occupied him from 1877 until 1882.

The Ring, Tristan, The Mastersingers and *Parsifal* belong to a different world from Wagner's earlier operas, which broadly adhered to the convention of separate arias and ensembles connected by recitative or something like it (though the composer was careful to explain that no single passage in *Lohengrin* was strictly speaking a recitative.) The structure of his later music dramas, by contrast, depended almost entirely upon the interlinking of significant *Leit motive* (guiding themes), each of which represented or suggested a place, a person, a particular aspect of a person's character, or some abstract idea. Though a risky method of musical composition and apt to invite irreverent lampoon ing, one is almost persuaded of its rightness by Wagner's masterly treatment of literally scores of *Leitmotive;* at times they undergo symphonic development, at others they are recapitulated at a climax in a different context or in new guise – often with overwhelming effect. For instance: one of the great moments in Act III of *The Valkyrie* is Sieglinde's ecstatic outburst when she learns from Bryn-hilde's lips that the child in her womb is destined to be the mightiest hero in the world (Siegfried), but nothing more is heard of this noble theme until Act III of *The Dusk of the Gods*, where it reappears, transfigured, in the course of Brynhilde's final lament, and from the words 'Das Feuer, das mich verbrennt' onwards dominates the scene. This *Motiv* is said to typify 'Siegfried as redeemer', but listeners should not concern themselves too much with the *Motiv*-ticketing of erudite analysts. It scarcely matters how one labels a certain magical passage from the love duet in *Tristan* (at the change of key-signature marked *immer mehr ruhig*): what matters a lot is that when Tristan lies close to death, anxiously awaiting the ship that brings Isolde to Britanny, its recollection weaves itself in and out of his feverish dreams with a poignancy that almost tears human heart-strings asunder, and that when the ship at last arrives and Isolde hurries to his side the same theme acquires new urgency (in 5 4 time) as the dying man, with a sudden access of strength born of delirious excitement, raises himself from his couch and staggers forward to embrace her. There is no more moving scene in all opera; Wagner – Wagner in his prime – alone could have contrived it.

Aside from his more massive achievements there are two minor works which deserve appreciative comment – the 'Venusberg music' and the *Siegfried Idyll*. The former was written for a Paris production of *Tannhäuser* in 1861 (ostensibly to provide the ballet-girls of the Opera with a chance to show their paces and their charms); by that time Wagner's matured artistic perception enabled him to give added point to several of the already suggestive themes, and it would not be going too far to say that this gorgeous bacchanale excites one by the vivid imagery of its self-evident attempt to portray in music the physical sensations of sexual intercourse. The *Siegfried Idyll*, an orchestral piece composed in 1870 as a surprise birthday offering for Cosima and a tribute to their son Siegfried (then eighteen months old), is largely but not entirely based on tunes drawn from Act III of *Siegfried*: lasting only about fifteen minutes and scored with unusual restraint for single wood wind, horn, trumpet and strings, this of all the jewels in Wagner's crown is the smallest – and perhaps the brightest.

Today there is a widespread impression (not only widespread but inescapable, since apart from anything else his ostentatious *Kaisermarsch* celebrated the foundation of the German Empire in 1871) that despite Wagner's having been during much of his life *persona non grata* in his fatherland his work, taken as a whole, had a pan-German quality which later well served Nazi propaganda. The phase may pass, for Wagner the poet is dead, Wagner the philosopher is dead, Wagner the conceivable stimulator of an abhorrent regime is dead – or so we hope. Still very much alive, although possibly receiving fewer enconiums than hitherto, is the extraordinarily talented and ambitious schemer who conceived and created *Lohengrin, The Ring, The Master-*

singers and the rest as entities. Unquestionably immortal is the consummate artist who clothed with exquisite music the rapture of Elsa and her anonymous bridegroom, the unconsciously incestuous passion of Sieglinde and Sieg-mund, the warm humanity of Hans Sachs. Purists maintain that it is unfair to Wagner's memory to present purple patches from his music dramas at orchestral concerts, though all but the most hidebound admit the suitability of the overtures and a few interludes like 'Siegfried's Journey to the Rhine' (which is a magnificent piece of music but in the opera-house merely serves to keep the audience inter ested while the scene-shifters are noisily dismantling the Valkyries' rock and setting up the hall of the Gibichungs). Many of us would go further, believing that Wagner was in the broadest sense of the term a *symphonic* composer, at his best when concentrating on the music and away from his best when giving equal rein to literary or philosophic urges. In the great works of his full maturity the exposition and development of the all-important *Leitmotive* is almost entirely orchestral and the singers, who should be the true unfolders of the saga, are left at a disadvantage; far too often for comfort the vocal line – which is dramatically essential – fits the pattern awkwardly and thereby becomes musically redundant. Then there are those long meta physical discourses: to assert that King Mark and Gurne-manz are crashing bores might involve excommunication from the diminishing band of perfect Wagnerites but devotees, even, go so far as to concede that there *are* patches of tedium in *Tristan* and *Parsifal* – to say nothing of *The Ring*. The eminent philosopher Friedrich Nietzsche once wrote that he loathed Wagner's music but could no longer listen to any other: less inhibited folk might affirm that they like Wagner's music but prefer it in small doses. One therefore feels free to put forward the proposition that as a composer Richard Wagner often wrought better than he knew: that thanks to his incomparable musical genius his sound-pictures do not require the simultaneous visible enactments which he himself regarded as essential for their understanding but which in practice nearly always fall short of one's imaginings. While good performances of *Tannhäuser, Parsifal, Tristan, The Mastersingers* and *The Ring* remain unforgettable experiences, let us be thankful that if we wish to do so we can relax in a concert-hall or by our own fireside and there (with closed eyes, perhaps) savour to the full the sensuous delights of the Venusberg or the searing anguish of Amfortas's spear-wound, share the last mortal longings of dying Tristan, dance with a jolly crowd of youngsters in the streets of sixteenth-century Nuremberg or march with the gods into Valhalla.

CHAPTER TWENTY-ONE

VERDI

In the age which had witnessed the bright flowering of
Weber, Schubert and Mendelssohn, *bel canto* opera had
been kept alive in Italy – very much alive – by Gioacchino
Rossini, Gaetano Donizetti and Vincenzo Bellini, all of
whom at times touched the heights. Bellini perhaps had
greater potential than the other two but he died young and
his output was small. Rossini and Donizetti were better
equipped technically, more liable to lapse into triviality –
and far more prolific. (It may be significant that each was
outstandingly successful in *opera buffa* – witness *The Barber
of Seville* and *Don Pasquale*.) Next in line of succession
came GIUSEPPE VERDI. Had he died like Bellini at thirty-
four, his name might now be forgotten. Had he died like
Donizetti at fifty, he might be remembered only as one
who carried on the existing custom of conventional Italian
opera and perhaps here and there improved on it. Had he
died at the traditional three-score-and-ten, an age by which
Rossini was dead in all but the purely physical sense, he
might have earned his chapter in this book – but only just.
In the event the gods, though they loved Verdi dearly,
refrained from calling him home in youth – that is to say
at thirty-four, fifty or seventy; it was when he produced his
two finest works between the ages of seventy and eighty that
he raised himself alongside Wagner, who was the elder by
five months and had already been dead for three years by
the time his twin established himself as a giant of compar
able magnitude, a giant demanding comparable attention.

After the defeat of Napoleon at the battle of Leipzig,
from which baby Wagner emerged unscathed but officially
an orphan (see page 113), Austrian and Russian troops were
sent to occupy the Napoleonic kingdom of Italy, an area
covering (roughly) the regions now known as Lombardy,
Venetia and Emilia-Romagna; during the course of the

operation a marauding band of undisciplined soldiers massacred half the population of the hamlet Roncole – two miles south-east of Busseto and about midway between Parma and Cremona (birthplace of Monteverdi). Among those who escaped were the tavern-and-store-keeper Carlo Verdi, his wife Luigia and their few-months-old son Giuseppe – who had been born 10th October 1813. The Congress of Vienna (1815) left them citizens of the duchy of Parma, *de jure* an independent state but *de facto* under Austrian domination, like Lombardy, until forty-five years later. For the peasants of Roncole life was hard, and weekly services in the village church provided their sole respite from the laborious task of wringing a bare livelihood from the soil; Carlo Verdi as a licensed victualler supplying their necessities may have been slightly better off than his neigh bours, and for Giuseppe the church meant only one thing – music. He was no infant prodigy but by the age of twelve had proved himself a capable organist; since he was also a sensible and intelligent lad his parents sent him to school at nearby Busseto where he came under the notice of Antonio Barezzi, a prosperous wine-merchant who was also a keen amateur musician. Thanks to his help and encouragement young Verdi soon became a prominent figure in the musical life of the little town: he conducted the brass band (for whose benefit he tried his hand at composition) and from time to time deputised for the organist and choirmaster Ferdinando Provesi. It was Provesi who had charge of his musical education; he was an unconventional preceptor and instilled, also, a profound distrust of clericalism. Between the ages of eighteen and twenty, with a local grant and an allowance from Barezzi, Verdi continued his studies in Milan (about sixty miles away); he was adjudged too old to enter the Conservatoire, but found an excellent private teacher in Vincenzo Lavigna, senior accompanist at the Scala Theatre.

By the autumn of 1834 he was back in Busseto, where eighteen months later he married Margherita Barezzi – daughter of his benefactor – and became choirmaster in succession to Provesi, although the ecclesiastical authorities insisted upon having as organist a rival candidate for the two posts (normally combined) whose religious orthodoxy was less suspect. Verdi relinquished this equivocal appointment in 1838 and returned to Milan where Bartolomeo Merelli, director of the Scala, engaged him to compose an *opera seria* and an *opera buffa*. *Oberto* (1839 and serious) was well received but *Un giorno di regno* (1840 and comic) was an utter failure. Hereabouts, too, Verdi's career was clouded by personal tragedy: his elder child Virginia had died in infancy; the same fate overtook his little son Romano while *Oberto* was in rehearsal; to crown all his wife died of meningitis while he was at work on *Un giorno di regno*. By the time his twenty-seventh birthday came round, therefore, he was alone in the world and in deep despair, but with characteristic resolution he soon pulled himself together: in 1842 *Nabucco* set him on the road to international fame and by 1848 not only Milan but also Venice, Rome, Naples, Florence, London, Paris and Trieste had each in turn welcomed a Verdi *premiere*. With part of his rapidly growing fortune he bought an estate at Sant' Agata just north of Busseto. Having had the villa – almost a *castello* – completely re-furbished and the surrounding farmland cleared of rubbish he took possession three years later and apart from holidays and occasional visits to Milan, Rome and other Italian cities (as well as to Paris and London) he stayed there for the rest of his life. (Like his birthplace five miles away on the other side of Busseto, the 'villa Verdi' at Sant' Agata is now a national monument in the care of the Italian Ministry of Fine Arts.)

By this time Verdi had recaptured domestic happiness. In his early Milan days he had been friendly with Giuseppina ('Peppina') Strepponi, a fine singer and actress from the Scala; when they met again in Paris in 1847 she became his inseparable companion and she remained so until her death forty years later. Despite the wagging of busy tongues and the occasional misgivings of 'Peppina' (a devout Catholic), Verdi with his sturdily independent outlook for long opposed any civil or religious binding of a union which had been entered into freel and with full recognition of its implications. When Barezzi, his generous patron and father of his late wife, not unnaturally made inquiries, Verdi replied with dignity.

I have nothing to hide. In my house there lives a lady, free, independent, like myself a lover of the country, the possessor of a private fortune which places her beyond the reach of need. Neither of us have to account for our actions to anybody. I will say this, however: in my house she is entitled to the deference due to myself – nay, more. On no consideration whatever must this be forgotten, for her conduct and her character give her a special claim to the consideration which she never fails to show to others.

Neither Verdi nor Peppina ever disclosed to the world why it was that in 1859, after twelve years of 'living in sin', they decided to bow to common usage; it is perhaps significant, however, that they chose to be married not at Busseto but at the village of Collonges on the Savoy/Switzerland border, while they were spending a summer holiday at Geneva.

I shall not list all Verdi's operas, since more than half have fallen into a comparative obscurity from which, in some cases at least, it might be unkind to rescue them. (Many of the earlier ones were full of tendencious political allusions which landed him in trouble with the Austrian censors; he was an ardent supporter of Cavour and the *risorgimento* and in 1861, after the liberation and unification of Italy, became for four years a member of parliament – an unusual side-line for a composer.) To my mind there is scant justification for enthusing over the output of his twenties and early thirties: admittedly an unquenchable flow of spontaneous melody was already apparent, but apart from a healthy vigour not untouched by vulgarity *Nabucco, Ernani, Macbeth* and the rest made little real advance on the cult of *bel canto* opera as practised by Rossini in *Tancredi* and *Semiramide*, Bellini in *La Sonnambula* and *Norma*, Donizetti in *Lucia di Lammermoor* and *La Favorita*. (In *Macbeth* as we know it today Act II opens with a fine soprano aria 'La luce langue' which would be well in place in *Aida*, but this is not part of the original, having been composed in 1865 as substitution for the commonplace 'Trionfai! securi alfine'.)

The next group (1850-67) includes some more distinctive works which taken by and large show greater initiative than their forerunners. In *Rigoletto* (surprisingly dated as early as 1851) uninhibited and eminently singable tunes are again in evidence, but one is also conscious of a growing power of musical characterisation (as in the masterly quartet 'Bella figlia dell' amore') and of a tendency to break away from conventional design ('Pari siamo'). Its successors *Il trovatore* (despite some stirring moments) and *La traviata* (for all its captivating bravura) appear slightly retrograde by compari son, although both have always been able to attract capacity audiences on a Sunday night in Italy or even on a Saturday night in Britain. That *Simon Boccanegra, Un ballo in maschera* and *La forza del destino* did not immediately acquire equal popularity may have been due to *dramatic* weaknesses. Verdi certainly did the best he could with rather unpromising material by continuing and developing the *Rigoletto* approach; moreover the music allotted to the page Oscar in *Un ballo* displayed a delicacy which was as unexpected as it was welcome, and the comic friar Melitone in *La forza* gave the composer a chance to prove, almost for the first time, that he could incorporate a sense of humour alongside a sense of drama. Unfortunately all three works suffered from faulty construction. So did *Don Carlos* (based on Schiller and written for the Paris Opera) in which Verdi made a brave attempt to reconcile his own manner with the methods of Meyerbeer (see page 116); in the event only a few numbers – notably the final duet – held the qualities which his legionary admirers had by then come to expect.

Although *Boccanegra, La forza* and *Don Carlos* were later revised to good purpose (and thereby perhaps achieved greatness without having been born great), neither they nor *Un ballo in maschera* (which has had a measure of greatness thrust upon it by distinguished interpreters of its leading roles) have ever found as secure a place in the repertory as the last opera of Verdi's youth which he completed in 1871 when a mere fifty-seven. Of all grand operas *Aida* might be called the grandest; here Verdi flirted with *Leitmotive* (and in the prelude combined two in counterpoint), but whatever was said at the time Wagner's influence was in no other respect observable: vocal melody, lyrical melody, was still the order of the day, although there was more variety than hitherto in the orchestral accompaniments where tum-tum and arpeggios were on the way out. Perhaps the most striking feature of *Aida*, however, was a new assurance in harmony, the emergence indeed of a recognisable and individual harmonic style. Students should examine in particular Amonasro's appeal 'Ma tu Re, tu signore possente' from the second-act finale, where the consecutive 'six-four' chords in the seventh bar look so startling on paper and yet sound so perfectly right in performance. They should also consider the contrasted effects of the frequent straightforward transitions from minor to major. (In this respect Verdi certainly learnt something from Schubert – see page 86.) In the trio from the first scene there is a wonderful moment where coinciding with a change of key from E minor to E major Aida's voice joins the others and floats above them in a *cantabile*; the same hovering of tonality acquires a bitter-sweet taste in the last few bars of 'Ritorna vincitor' and adds an appropriately exotic flavour to 'O ciel azzure'. Two-and-a-half years later Verdi used the same device again at the beginning of the Requiem; here the sudden shift from A minor to A major is neither bitter sweet nor exotic – just sublimely beautiful.

This Requiem (dedicated to the memory of the author and poet Alessandro Manzoni whom Verdi much admired) was paradoxically the first unquestionable masterpiece of a composer whose name is always associated with opera. That Verdi, an unbeliever, should have been at the top of his form in an extended piece of church music is perhaps no more surprising than that a century-and-a-half pre viously J. S. Bach, a staunch Lutheran, should have excelled himself in a mass acceptable to Catholics: it was simply that Verdi – like Bach – found the traditional liturgy the only possible vehicle for a burden of self-expression. Admittedly much of the music of the Requiem was in the mood of *Aida* and such outbursts as the 'Dies irae' were unconventionally dramatic; yet there was nothing *theatrical* about this remarkable work, which leaves one with the conviction that it was composed in a spirit of profound reverence.

After the Requiem (if one disregards revisions of two earlier operas) Verdi wrote nothing at all until *Otello*, produced in 1886; *Falstaff* followed in 1893. Both libretti were splendid adaptations of Shakespeare (*Othello* and *The Merry Wives of Windsor*) by Verdi's friend and fellow composer Arrigi Boito, who deserves high praise for having given his elder and more illustrious colleague the opportunity to crown his career with a two-fold triumph. What is so astonishing is that throughout twelve years of silence Verdi's latent powers had evidently been developing subconsciously: *Otello* marked an advance on *Aida* which could have been no greater had the gap between them been filled with half a dozen operas, each a finer work of art than the one which preceded it. Thus despite superficial appearance to the contrary *Otello* and *Falstaff* stand in direct line of succession from *Oberto* through *Rigoletto*, *La forza del destino* and *Aida*; let it be stressed at once that there is nothing Wagnerian about them. (Apart from *Falstaff's* other unique attributes its six scenes last on average only about twenty minutes each and it is one of the few operas ever written that leaves one regretting that all is over so soon.) During his eighties Verdi composed four short choral pieces of which two at least, the *Ave Maria* based on an 'enigmatic scale' and the *Laudi alle Vergine Maria* (words by Dante), possess a singular loveliness; they should be played now and again. (So should the attractive string quartet, dated 1873.) After the death of his beloved Peppina in 1897 Verdi knew the loneliness of old age; in the autumn of 1900 he was taken from Sant' Agata to a comfortable hotel in Milan, where he breathed his last on 27th January 1901.

'I am not a very learned composer but I am a very experienced one,' was Verdi's self-assessment. In truth his learning was far from negligible (witness the fugues in the Requiem) and instinct rather than experience dictated that even in his last two operas the orchestra should be the servant and not (as in Wagner's music dramas) the master of the singers. But it was experience which eventually drove him to abandon the old operatic formula of stylized arias and ensembles – even as amended by Gluck – in favour of a more homogeneous framework and so enabled him to con trive (for example) the unconventional but exquisite love duet which ends Act I of *Otello*. Experience, too, brought in its train a new sense of artistic values: *Otello* and *Falstaff* were entirely free from the vulgarity which had reared its head frequently in his early operas – occasionally in *Trovatore* and even *Aida*. Experience moreover led to the superb musical delineations of Iago's villainy, Pistol and Bardolph's roguery, the swagger of Sir John Falstaff himself. What other composer could so perfectly have portrayed cor pulence as Verdi did in *Falstaff* Act I scene 1 at the words 'sul fianco baldo, sul gran torace, sul maschio pie, sul fusto saldo, erto capace'? Note, too, the difference between his treatment of the jealous raging of the Moor, ending in tragedy, and his treatment (except perhaps in one short scene) of the jealous raging of the comic butt Master Ford. By contrast he had a curious habit – which only a genius could have exploited to such good purpose – of applying the same technical process to achieve varied emotional effects. An instance has already been cited, on page 128, con cerning *Aida* and the Requiem. In that same passage from the Requiem there is also a characteristic chromatic move ment in one of the inner parts, a tic which reappears not only at a moment of deep pathos in *Otello* (Act III, nine teenth bar after letter I) but also at a moment of teasing charm in *Falstaff* (Act II scene 2, fifth bar after figure 41).

I shall not presume to pass judgment on whether *Otello* is a greater masterpiece than *Tristan and Isolde* or *Falstaff* than *The Mastersingers*; too much depends upon the listener's temperament. Yet since in the previous chapter the mature Wagner did not escape criticism it is only fair that the mature Verdi should also be brought under the microscope. While *Otello* is never boring – as *Tristan* is in places for any but the most ardent devotee – a sensitive musician cannot fail to notice that nearly all the terrific climaxes are built on a chord which he views with sus picion (the diminished seventh) and that there are a few – a very few – passages where the composer's melodic inspira tion seems to desert him. Of *Falstaff* it might be said that here Verdi's melodic inspiration was almost *too* overpower ing: the delightful little tunes follow one another so rapidly that sometimes there is hardly time to make their acquaintance. But criticism on this score would be criticism run wild, for such fluency was really a sign not of weakness but of strength, providing further evidence of the integrity with which the composer faced every problem as it presented itself. One is left with a single rhetorical speculation: would not Verdi have done better to have scored *Falstaff* for a smaller orchestra?

The humble innkeeper's son from Roncole who became a national figure in politics and an international figure in music had his personal shortcomings like everyone else: he was evidently somewhat of a domestic tyrant and in moods of depression was notoriously liable to become a naughty schoolboy and growl at all around him like a sore-headed bear. But his collaborator Boito was on the mark in recording that in every moral and social sense Giuseppe Verdi was a true Christian. On his death at the age of eighty-seven the world lost a great composer – and a great man.

CHAPTER TWENTY-TWO

BIZET[1]

Eighteen of our thirty-five great composers spent the whole or a large part of their working lives in either London, Vienna or Paris, but among the eighteen the only born Londoner was Henry Purcell, the only born Viennese Franz Schubert and the only born Parisian GEORGES BIZET, who drew his first breath of Montmartre air at 26 rue de la Tour d'Auvergne on 25th October 1838. His father (a hairdresser turned singing-teacher) came from Rouen and his mother from Cambrai, and so the point can be made that Bizet, remembered above all else for his evocations of the sun drenched south, was in fact a French *northerner*.

Both parents encouraged a youthful aptitude for music, and at the age of ten he was enrolled at the Paris Con servatoire where in due course he became a pupil of Jacques Francois Halevy (composer of the fine opera *La Juive*) – whose daughter Genevieve he was to marry in 1869. At seventeen Bizet wrote a symphony, at eighteen two operettas – *La Maison du docteur* and *Le Docteur Miracle* – the second of which tied for first place in a competition organ ized by Jacques Offenbach (uncrowned king in that realm) and thereby secured public representation. Soon afterwards, at the second attempt, he won the coveted Prix de Rome (see page 93, footnote); while in Italy he composed, along side some conventional student pieces, a third and more ambitious operetta – *Don Procopio* – but this did not as he had hoped and expected earn a renewal of the prize and before the end of 1860 he was back in Paris. During the next ten years he worked hard but spasmodically (in truth

[1] Bizet was younger than either Franck, Bruckner, Brahms or Borodin, who are allotted chapters 23-26 inclusive. I have given him chronological precedence because it was not until after his death at the early age of thirty-six that any of the other four reached full maturity.

he was never a very steady character), spending much of his time making piano transcriptions for the publishing firm of Choudens et Cie. The only really significant compositions belonging to this period were the operas *The Pearl Fishers* (1864) and *The Fair Maid of Perth* (1867), each of which incorporated tunes lifted from *Don Procopio*. (This was a justifiable procedure on the composer's part, seeing that the earlier work had made no headway; it was neither played nor published until thirty years after his death.)

Of all the music which Bizet composed during his teens and twenties nothing is more attractive than the very early symphony in C major which was rescued from oblivion when it had its first performance (under the baton of Felix Weingartner) at Basle in 1935; since then it has made friends all over the world. Although this charming work owed something to an almost unknown symphony by Charles Gounod (who for many years was a very good friend) its primary instigator was Franz Schubert – witness the uninterrupted flow of melody and the tendency to longwindedness in the two middle movements. Bizet's symphony should not be taken as a model, for although the eager young student carefully adhered to convention (sonata-form for the first movement, etc.) he was no master of thematic development. Nor does one find many traces of typical Bizet, except perhaps in the second movement where the pseudo-oriental colouring presages *Djamileh*. But there is an abundance of tunes (which is what really matters), most of them very good, some fairly good, none bad. This spontaneous and unsymphonic symphony was certainly a remarkable achievement for a seventeen-year-old.

Of the three operettas (all early) *Don Procopio* is the best; in some respects it is Italian *opera buffa* rather than French *opera bouffe*, but one can trace here and there the emergence of an individual style. In the more serious and more renowned *Pearl Fishers* and *Fair Maid of Perth* Bizet tried too conscientiously to emulate the ideals of his friend Gounod as exemplified in *Sapho* and *Romeo and Juliet*. *The Pearl Fishers*, a work of considerable technical accomplishment, is marred in places by a barely successful attempt

133

to capture an asiatic atmosphere, but it retains considerable popularity in France and elsewhere at the expense of *The Fair Maid*, which has no specifically Caledonian pretensions and deserves occasional presentation.

At the outbreak of the Franco-Prussian war in 1870 many Paris musicians did themselves little credit as citizens: there seems to have been a scramble to get on board the next train for Bordeaux or the next *paquebot* from Calais to Dover as quickly as possible. All the more credit there fore to Bizet, who promptly enlisted in the National Guard (roughly corresponding to our own Home Guard during the second world war).[1] This did not involve service in the field but it did involve long hours of routine training and sentry duty, especially (as events turned out) during the siege of Paris and the ultimate Prussian occupation. Nor was the part-time composer and part-time militiaman free from domestic worry, for Genevieve Bizet, *nee* Halevy, had a domineering and possessive mother and was herself some what neurotic; she was hardly attuned to cope with an easy going husband who seems to have indulged in casual promiscuity as a matter of course. On a woman of her temperament the hardships of the siege perhaps pressed deeper than on housewives more accustomed to privation. At any rate Bizet wrote to Ernest Guiraud (who was later to compose recitatives for insertion in *Carmen*) that 'a kind friend brought us a few horse-bones which we shall share; every night, however, Genevieve dreams of chicken and lobster; for myself I dream that we are all at Naples, living in a charming villa under a purely artistic government com posed of people like Michaelangelo and Shakespeare'.

By the time things had returned to something like normal Bizet, now in failing health, must have realized subcon sciously (like Schubert before him) that not many years were left to him, for he concentrated much harder on composition than before the war. Within little more than three years he completed (apart from a fair quantity of comparatively unimportant works) the set of piano pieces entitled *Children's Games*, the symphonic suite *Roma*

[1] Another honourable patriot was Gabriel Fauré (see page 188).

(based on the earlier *Souvenirs de Rome* of 1868), the one-act opera *Djamileh*, comprehensive incidental music for Alphonse Daudet's play *L'Arlesienne*, the concert-overture *La Patrie* – and finally *Carmen*. *Roma* is uninspiring and *La Patrie* rather dull; many of the *Children's Games*, on the other hand, are charming, though taken as a whole they are perhaps not so attractive as the *Dix pieces pittoresques* of Bizet's younger contemporary Emmanuel Chabrier, with which they have certain features in common; *Djamileh* – based on the same poem by Alfred de Musset as was Edouard Lalo's *Namouna* – was Bizet's best opera so far, but its compromises with exoticism have militated against wide popularity. With *L'Arlesienne* and *Carmen* however he came into his own; it would hardly be an exaggeration to say that each outshone anything that the talented Lalo, Gounod and Chabrier had ever written or were ever to write.

When travelling from Paris to Rome in the winter of 1857/58 Bizet had arrived on Christmas Day at Avignon, which at that time was the terminus of the PLM railway. From Avignon to Toulon, his next objective, was a mere eighty miles by road and I find it hard to believe that the young composer, had he so wished, could not have covered that distance by stage-coach in a day or so. Instead he took *four* days, following a circuitous route which enabled him to visit (among other famous antiquities of Provence) the *maison carree* at Nîmes, the chateau at Tarascon and the Roman theatre at Arles. Like many others before and since he succumbed to the fascination of the region – and it was probably his nostalgic recollections of that journey which encouraged and inspired him, fourteen years later, to com pose music for *L'Arlesienne*, all of whose scenes are set either in the town itself or in the surrounding countryside. Bizet, although only here and there using traditional dance tunes (e.g. in the farandole), was completely successful in capturing the authentic Provençal atmosphere. Moreover the orchestration was brilliantly original throughout – and not just because he used a saxophone, either: look, for instance, at the *andantino* section of the prelude, where the cellos play a *legato* version of the vigorous main theme against a sonorous horn counterpoint while two bassoons scamper all over the place with *staccato* triplets. As for the 'adagietto' (actually marked *adagio* in the score, and only thirty-four bars long), one admirer of Bizet, at least, finds it a perfect – and moving – example of what Ernest New man once called the small poem in music. (Most listeners are familiar with *L'Arlesienne* through two popular orches tral suites. The first of these was transcribed by the com poser himself and played during his lifetime; 'suite no. 2' was arranged by Guiraud after Bizet's death and includes excerpts from both *L'Arlesienne* and *The Fair Maid of Perth*.)

Among regular opera-goers there are some queer fish. On the one hand is a hard core which interests itself in opera to the exclusion of all else in music and is ready to undergo considerable discomfort in order to attent *any* performance of (say) *Il trovatore* or *Tannhauser* without ever having realized, apparently, that Verdi wrote a superb Requiem and Wagner the incomparable *Siegfried Idyll*.[1] Then there are those whose taste is so uncatholic that they resent Rossini's *Barber of Seville* because it isn't Mozart's *Marriage of Figaro*, Weber's *Freischütz* because it isn't Beethoven's *Fidelio*, Richard Strauss's *Rosenkavalier* because it isn't Johann Strauss's *Fledermaus*. (Or vice versa.) Yet all these good people, I think, would agree with the rest of us that Bizet's *Carmen* is one of the seven operatic wonders of the

[1] Somewhere about 1930, while standing in the gallery queue at Covent Garden for a performance of *Don Giovanni*, I got into con versation with my neighbour who turned out to be just such an opera 'fan'. Inevitably the talk turned on Mozart and it was soon clear that he knew his *Figaro*, *Don Giovanni* and *Magic Flute* from A to Z. When I briefly referred to the 'Jupiter' he interjected 'What's that? An opera called *Jupiter*?' Somewhat taken aback I explained as tactfully as I could that the 'Jupiter' was not an opera but a symphony. 'Oh,' came the reply, 'I've never heard a symphony; I thought it was only Bach and Handel who wrote anything of the sort.' At that moment the doors opened and we surged forward to the diminutive box-office; after climbing those interminable stairs I was cowardly enough to seat myself on a bench as far away from him as possible.

world. (Devotees of Mozart, Beethoven, Weber, Rossini, Wagner, Verdi, the Strausses, Puccini and who-you-will are at liberty to argue to their heart's content about which are the other six.)

For *Carmen* Henri Meilhac and Ludovic Halevy (Bizet's cousin-by-marriage), whose names had previously been asso ciated only with operetta, between them forged a very good libretto out of Prosper Merimee's short story — which incidentally is worth reading for its own sake. Bizet took full advantage and gave the world a galaxy of good tunes, inevitably not all of the very highest quality but all appro priate in their context. In their different ways the seguidilla, the quintet, the 'card trio', Micaela's aria 'Je dis que rien ne m'epouvante', these – and not these alone – entitle their composer to world-wide recognition as a master of his craft, yet true genius is equally in evidence in the musical treat ment of the drama as a whole, the steady progression through situations which though clearly dangerous are at first sight not likely to prove fatal but which lead ultimately to the tragedy which throughout the course of the last act is seen to be inevitable.

It has never been conclusively established whether the cool reception at first accorded to *Carmen* was due to the reluctance of the Parisian public to accept a virago as an operatic heroine or to the antagonism of a pressure-group of musicians who for one reason or another cherished a measure of animosity against the composer; possibly it was a bit of both. However that may be Bizet was greatly dis tressed and about a year later he died – on 3rd June 1875. Not of a broken heart, for such a phenomenon is unknown to medical science; his worthy doctor reported, no doubt with pathological accuracy, that 'he succumbed to a cardiac complication of articular rheumatism'.

Bizet worked subjectively and can therefore be accounted a romantic, but his subjectivity was less personal, less indi vidual, than that of, say, Berlioz. He was one of those (Wagner perhaps was another) who rather than interpret the mood or *milieu* in which they found themselves at the time – as Berlioz had in the *Symphonie fantastique* – preferred to interpret (and were at their best when doing so) the mood or *milieu* in which they would have *wished* to find themselves. Therein lies the explanation of the apparent paradox pointed in this chapter's first paragraph. Georges Bizet the man was a Parisian to his fingertips; his finest music, by contrast, belonged to those lands of southern sun shine and song of which he used to dream during the care worn days and nights when his native city lay blockaded and besieged.

CHAPTER TWENTY-THREE

FRANCK

CESAR FRANCK (1822-90) was born in Liege (at 13 rue St. Pierre, within a stone's-throw of the Prince-Bishops' Palace), but like his fellow-townsman Andre Gretry eighty years earlier he left his native Belgium while still a youngster and spent most of his life in Paris. It is no good pretending, however, that he was French by anything but naturalization and adoption, and indeed he was only just Belgian, for his father came from the indeterminate borderland west of Aachen and his mother was German by birth. Cesar showed youthful precocity as a pianist and did well at the Paris Conservatoire but then disappointed his parents (who had great ambitions on his behalf) by declining to follow in the steps of Franz Liszt as a virtuoso. He again disappointed them by marrying Felicite Saillot, daughter of an actor and actress, and yet again by adopting the unglamorous career of organist and teacher of music.

Franck even pursued the smooth tenor of his way – although inevitably losing a few pupils – during the siege of Paris and the *commune*. Meanwhile he had produced a fair quantity of instrumental and choral music superficially comparable in style and quality with that of his colleague Gounod (whose achievements in those fields are often underrated), but it was only when at the age of fifty he was appointed a professor at the Conservatoire that his compositions began to make an impact. Since his reputation depends almost entirely upon the piano pieces, chamber-music and orchestral works which he wrote during the eighteen years that remained to him it is perhaps both unfair and inaccurate to dub him – as disparagers are wont to – as an organ-loft composer.

Yet one can see the disparager's point of view, for Franck's music does display features which one tends to associate with composers who spend their working lives in the service

of the Church: sincerity of approach, thickness of instru
mental texture and an addiction to square-cut rhythmic
figures (although this last never became such an obsession
as it did with his fellow organist Anton Bruckner whom we
shall meet in the next chapter). What eventually set Franck
apart from Gounod and the younger Jules Massenet (with
whom also he had certain characteristics in common) was an
extremely individual exploitation of chromatic harmonies
which in his day could be interpreted as a genuine attempt
to widen the musical horizon but in which later generations
have found evidence of mannered artificiality: many of us
have to make a conscious effort to put ourselves in the right
frame of mind before we can appreciate Franck as he
deserves to be appreciated – but the effort brings worth
while rewards.

The oratorio *Les Beatitudes* (completed in 1879) and three
symphonic poems – *Les Éolides* (1876), *Le Chasseur maudit*
(1882) and *Les Djinns* (1884) – were not altogether success
ful, mainly because Franck's style, unlike Bizet's, was so
personal that it allowed little scope for musical characteriza
tion; *Les Djinns* was the most typical, and noteworthy for
incorporating a part for solo piano not so much for the sake
of virtuosity as to provide tone-contrast with the orchestral
forces. The fact remains that the works which hold Franck's
quintessence number precisely seven: in order of composi
tion they were

a piano quintet (1879)
Prelude, chorale and fugue for piano (1884)
Symphonic Variations for piano and orchestra (1885)
a violin sonata (1886)
Prelude, aria and finale for piano (1887)
a symphony (1888)
a string quartet (1889).

All adhered to classical formulae, though the quintet and
the symphony were each in three movements rather than
the four which might have been expected; for a composer
who adopted a highly-flavoured harmonic idiom such
restraint was particularly appropriate – and commendable.

The piano quintet (in F minor), make no mistake about

it, is a fine piece of work. It admittedly has weaknesses: the first movement is both diffuse and disjointed, and when the second, after setting out confidently in A minor, suddenly jumps back in its fifth bar to the F minor of the first move ment – a curious case of key-insensitivity – both composer and listener are momentarily thrown off balance. But there is far more to be said on the credit side of the ledger: except here and there in the finale, where an orchestra seems called for, the quintet combination is expertly handled; the first movement, for all its faults of construc tion, rises at one moment to a joyous climax and then dies away in a subtly contrived anti-climax of despondency; the D flat major section of the slow movement (marked *dolcissimo ma cantabile*) takes one to a world of ethereality; the finale, despite its naïvities of despair, admirably rounds off a work which is predominantly gloomy in mood but which an objective critic will place among the three best piano quin tets ever written. Nor is this a backhanded compliment: although piano quintets are not three a penny, seven of our thirty-five great composers between them provided eight, and there have been others of considerable merit – notably one by Franck's junior contemporary Camille Saint-Saens.

Saint-Saens (as tantalizing a musicologist as he was a composer) complained of the *Prelude, chorale and fugue* that the chorale wasn't a chorale and the fugue wasn't a fugue. (He could hardly deny Franck the right to call the first movement a prelude.) His criticism was justified only from the narrowest academic standpoint, for here Franck (like Mendelssohn before him) merely adapted eighteenth-century convention to fit nineteenth-century practice. Never theless the companion piece *Prelude, aria and finale* is more immediately attractive: the prelude is splendidly masculine and virile; the aria is delightfully feminine and yielding; the finale, though the least satisfying of the three move ments, is at least lively – and thematically unifying.

The *Symphonic Variations* (in F sharp minor) are based (*a*) on two short phrases of four bars each and (*b*) on a more extended theme which does not emerge in concise form until about a quarter of the way through. The second of the two initial four-bar phrases one was taught in youth to identify with the words 'get your hair cut', and in all seriousness the bearing-in-mind of this unromantic precept is more helpful than any laborious analysis in enabling one to appreciate the artistry of the work – e.g. in the extra ordinarily poetic passage which leads from a beautiful F sharp major variation – marked *molto più lento* – to the sparkling finale. This finale, incidentally, sweeps aside sultry hot-house chromaticism in as exhilarating an open-air dis play of brilliantine as any barber could wish for; students should take special note of bars 385-99, where wood-wind players and violinists in turn get their hair cut – in 4/4 time – while the pianist provides a whirling spin-drier accompaniment that might derive from a Chopin waltz or the last movement of Schumann's piano concerto.

The lovely violin sonata was dedicated to the eminent virtuoso Eugene Ysaye – another native of Liege – and stands rather apart from the rest of Franck's representative compositions for in none of the others does one find such a continuous flow of limpid melody. Spontaneous lyricism is apparent not only in the undulating 9/8 of the first move ment and the unconventional 'recitative-fantasia' which does duty as the third (slow) movement but also in the turbulent *allegro* (placed second) – where the violin often seems to be giving added point to what the piano has to say – and in the graceful finale where both the placid theme and its canonic treatment recall Schumann once again.

By comparison Franck's symphony (in D minor) is dis appointing. The first movement, which in most symphonies is expected to set a standard for the whole, shows him in a rather poor and artificial light which even an ingenious adaptation of sonata-form fails to brighten. The second movement however, whose middle section is a discreetly abbreviated scherzo, is most attractive; at the risk of enrag ing Franck devotees I suggest that it might sometimes be rescued from its surroundings and played all by itself as an orchestral intermezzo. As for the third and last movement, that perceptive critic Martin Cooper, champion of all that is best in French music, hit the nail on the head when he wrote that it seems to protest too much that it is the finale of a symphony; one might add that its most satisfying moment comes when a tune from the (outstanding) second movement provides a thumping climax.

The string quartet has claims to be considered Franck's *chef d'oeuvre* for here, while harmonic individualism yields no whit, there is a refreshingly original approach to the formal problems of chamber music; moreover anyone who has patiently schooled himself to accept the Franck idiom will acknowledge that a touch of genius is evident almost throughout and that mastery of the medium puts to flight the notion that he was mentally as well as physically cooped up in an organ-loft all his life. The four movements are well contrasted and some of the harmonic progressions in the third might come near to convincing an unbeliever that Franck's specialized form of chromaticism had something to be said for it after all; it is only in the finale, a rather self-conscious attempt to do a late-Beethoven, that the composer slightly lets everyone down – Beethoven included.

The string quartet, when first played in public early in 1890, brought Franck a greater measure of applause from the Parisian musicians of his day than had any of his previous works and it looked as though he might be turning the corner of their esteem. Soon afterwards however, in a regrettable fit of the absentmindedness to which he was always prone, he crossed a busy street without looking where he was going and collided painfully with the shaft of a horse-omnibus. Minimizing his injuries he carried on his way – and indeed for a few weeks carried on his work – but lack of proper medical treatment resulted in the onset of pleurisy and he died the following autumn, one month short of his sixty-ninth birthday.

During the last fifteen years or so of his life Cesar Franck exerted a considerable influence on a younger generation of French composers: among his pupils and disciples were Vincent d'Indy (a good friend but an undiscriminating admirer), Ernest Chausson, Alfred Bruneau and Gabriel Pierne. If since then his reputation has had its ups and downs on the stock exchange of responsible musical opinion it can be seen in retrospect that he was as significant a figure in the musical life of Paris during the first two decades of the Third Republic as Berlioz had been during the more hectic days of the Second Empire.

CHAPTER TWENTY-FOUR

BRUCKNER

Seven pages of W. H. Hadow's admirable little book *Music* (Home University Library, 1924) were devoted to Brahms, for whom his adulation stopped not far short of idolatry. There then followed, as in sonata-form, a bridge passage leading to the second subject (Dvorak, two pages).

In Vienna itself there is not much more to tell: there were the two Johann Strausses, much beloved of Viennese ball-rooms; there was an amiable and industrious com poser named Anton Bruckner whom his contemporaries endeavoured to place in rivalry with Brahms; there was the true song-writer Hugo Wolf, whose eager and hectic genius wore him out before his time; there was Carl Gold-mark, suave, polished and efficient, a typical example of the second order of composition. Of more moment than these was the growth of the Nationalist School in Boh emia, inaugurated by Bedřich Smetana, whose *Bartered Bride* is still upheld as a standard, and continued by his greater disciple, Antonín Dvorak.[1]

Bruckner, earning this brief mention as amiable and in dustrious, was at least luckier than Mahler who earned none at all, although the author admitted such relatively undistinguished contemporaries as Charles Martin Loeffler and Edward Macdowell and was sufficiently up-to-date to deal with Arnold Bax and Serge Prokofiev. Hadow typified the outlook of his generation, for Bruckner's name (let alone Mahler's) appeared very seldom on British concert pro grammes until 1930 or thereabouts and it is only of recent years – in this country – that his stock has risen to present

[1] For Brahms see chapter 25; for Dvorak chapter 29; for Smetana page 176; for Wolf page 220; for Johann Strauss the younger recall *Die Fledermaus*; for Johann Strauss the elder and Goldmark let Hadow's comments suffice.

heights: it is significant that in the third edition of Grove's *Dictionary of Music and Musicians* (1927) two pages were deemed sufficient for a discussion of his work whereas by the fifth edition (1953) the allowance had been doubled. Though a late entrant to the arena of public esteem he can no longer be denied recognition alongside the old war-horses.

Like his compatriot Franz Schubert (whose page-allocation in *Grove*, by the way, has dropped from fifty-five to thirty-five) ANTON BRUCKNER (1824-96) was the son of a schoolmaster and became one himself at seventeen. There the biographical similarity ends, for Schubert abandoned the drudgery at eighteen and Bruckner supported it till he was thirty-two (an age which Schubert never attained). Born at the pretty hillside village of Ansfelden, seven miles south of Linz and now lying alongside the Vienna-Salzburg *Autobahn*, he stayed in that region of Upper Austria (except for occasional visits to Vienna) until he was forty-four: he was schoolmaster-cum-organist at the villages of Windhaag (two years), Kronstorf (two years) and St Florian (eleven years) in turn, and from 1856 to 1868 organist (without school-teaching) at Linz Cathedral. During his twenties and early thirties he wrote some mediocre choral music and a handful of organ and piano pieces but his creative powers were slow to develop. (Compare his fellow organist and close contemporary Cesar Franck, chapter 23.) St Florian, to this day a picturesque centre of monasticism, might be regarded as the spiritual home of Bruckner the organist, but it was not until he settled in Linz that Bruckner the composer began a meticulous study of harmony, counterpoint, fugue, form and orchestration; by 1862 he was armed with a portfolio of academic certificates which gave him greater confidence. The first few works of his maturity – three masses and three symphonies (the third of which is that now known as no. 1) – were completed before he left Linz in 1868 on being appointed professor of counterpoint and fugue at the Vienna Conservatoire. The remainder – notably eight more symphonies (nos. 2 to 9) – all belong to Vienna, where he lived for the rest of his life.

Meanwhile he made several trips abroad: he visited Nancy and Paris in 1869 and London in 1871 as a practising organist; Bayreuth in 1873, 1876, 1882, 1886 and 1892 as a devoted Wagnerite; Berlin in 1891 and 1894 as a distin guished composer. During his late sixties he suffered from ill-health and was obliged to resign his professorship, but he went on composing until his death at the age of seventy-two.

From the writings of friends and foes – and he had plenty of both – Bruckner emerges as a simple-minded countryman, clean-living and devout; he cuts an incon gruous figure beside Schubert the engaging bohemian, Mendelssohn the spoilt darling of society, Liszt the cos mopolitan man-of-the-world, Wagner the turbulent rebel and Verdi the earnest freethinker. From his forties onward he was continually offering marriage to young girls and being refused; the nearest he came to matrimony was when a chambermaid at a Berlin hotel proposed to *him* and was accepted – but her Lutheran father put his foot down when he realized that she would have to become a Catholic.

Anecdotes abound of Bruckner's rustic gaucherie and some of them are well-authenticated: it is a fact that after the successful first performance of his so-called 'Romantic' symphony (no. 4) he pressed a small coin into the hand of the conductor – Hans Richter – with the words 'that was splendid, my man; go and buy yourself a glass of beer'. One of his most ardent admirers, Franz Brunner, in a mono graph published during Bruckner's lifetime and paying high tribute to his artistic idealism, recognized – and excused – his social imperfections.

Regarded by his colleagues as a shy simpleton and by the leaders of society as a boor, he is in truth a typical Austrian: warm-blooded, excitable, kindhearted, gen erous to a fault – and altogether a most worthy fellow.

Ill-wishers chose to make out that this most worthy fellow was little better than a village idiot, but village idiots do not write symphonies which posterity acclaims as masterpieces and so the unworldly Bruckner has the last laugh over spiteful sniggerers.

A turning-point in his career came in 1863 when he heard *Tannhäuser* for the first time; he promptly conceived an intense admiration for its composer and thereafter sought him out on every possible occasion. (Wagner treated him no better and no worse than one might treat an embarrass ingly affectionate spaniel.) But he did himself more harm than good by naively glorifying his idol in Vienna at a time when Viennese musicians and music-critics were predominantly anti-Wagner: for instance Wagner's arch enemy Eduard Hanslick of the *Neue freie Presse*, having been lampooned as Beckmesser in *The Mastersingers*, revenged himself on poor unsophisticated Bruckner.

> He seems to have accepted certain Wagnerian pieces as models for symphonic construction. . . . Tossed about between intoxication and desolation, we arrive at no definite impression and enjoy no artistic pleasure. It is not out of the question that the future belongs to this muddled hang-over style – which is no reason to regard the future with envy. Wagnerian orchestral effects are met on every hand; one would prefer that symphonic music remain undefiled by a style only relatively justified as an illustrative device for certain dramatic situations. . . . The finale, with its baroque themes, its confused structures and inhuman din, strikes us only as a model of tastelessness.

Bruckner was very sensitive to criticism and this sort of thing sapped his self-assurance, driving him to spend much time on revision: several of his symphonies were played during his lifetime in two or three distinct versions, added to which he never ceased making minor corrections and even allowed well-meaning friends to tamper with nos. 5 and 6. During the nineteen-thirties and -forties a measure of order was brought to the chaotic pile of issues and re-issues by the Austrian musicologist Robert Haas, whose knowledge and understanding of his subject enabled him to disentangle spontaneous alterations from those which were made, as it were, under duress – or by colleagues. It would be going too far to say that Haas's editions are definitive, but they are as near to true Bruckner as we are likely to get.

His symphonies – each one of which holds its moments of loveliness – are cast in the classic mould of late Beethoven and late Schubert, carrying the style of their famous no. 9's to a logical conclusion, but they are laid out on an even larger scale: no vocalists are required but playing-time is anything from an hour to an hour-and-a-half. Moreover the quick movements (leaving aside the scherzos which usually rely on wild energy) seem to adhere to the *festina lente* principle; this is partly because of Bruckner's habit of introducing solemn chorales or other ecclesiastical strains (including orchestral transcriptions of passages from his own masses); partly because of their constructional disjointedness – which is typified by frequent pauses for breath (or, if you prefer, pregnant silences); partly because of the prevailing squareness of the rhythm. (Only in the scherzos – and in the middle sections of the slow movements of nos. 1 and 3 – does he escape from 2/2 or 4/4 time, and the tyranny of the four-bar phrase is almost everywhere apparent.) Perhaps the slow movements make the strongest appeal, particularly those of nos. 7, 8 and 9 which display a resource of rhapsodic eloquence hitherto shrouded by a veil of formality. (No. 9 has no finale; Bruckner sketched one but did not live to finish it.) Although his three masses (all originally completed before he left Linz but later revised) contain fine individual sections – especially the first, in D minor – and the *Te Deum* (1881) is almost suggestive of Berlioz in its emancipation from convention, Anton Bruckner's church music has justly been put in the shade by the hefty and beautiful symphonies (religious symphonies as Alfred Einstein called them) to which he devoted himself during the last thirty years of his life as whole-heartedly and exclusively as his adored Richard Wagner did to his hefty and beautiful (but not always religious) music dramas.

CHAPTER TWENTY-FIVE

BRAHMS

It was unfortunate for Bruckner that during the twenty-eight years which he spent in Vienna the city also housed another master-musician. There is no need to recount here the activities of the rival Brucknerite and 'Brahmin' factions; the principals (like Gluck and Piccinni in Paris a century earlier – see page 49) tried to stand aloof from the warring of their partisans but were inevitably involved from time to time. Their profound differences of approach have been analysed by many historians; Bruckner and Brahms themselves, when dragged willy-nilly into the fray, put the matter in two small nutshells with their pithy and unconsciously self-revealing comments.

Bruckner:

> He is Brahms – my profound respect. But I am Bruckner and I prefer my own stuff.

Brahms:

> Bruckner writes only for effect; his symphonies are a colossal swindle.

It should be stressed that both were extremely good-natured individuals and that neither cherished personal animosity but Bruckner, with his limited intellectual capacity, understood no musical idiom but his own, while his high-minded adversary might have been an even greater composer than he was had he not regarded it as dishonest to write for effect.

JOHANNES BRAHMS (1833-96) was born at Hamburg, to be precise at 24 Schlüterhof just off the Speckgang, a narrow slum midway between the Alster and the Lower Port. (The tenement was destroyed by bombing in 1944, and the site is now occupied by a new building – 60 Speckstrasse.) His father was a double-bass player and though far from affluent somehow managed to ensure that Johannes received a sound musical education. At first he had to be content with entertaining the sailors who frequented the neighbouring brothels, but between the ages of fourteen and nineteen he made several public appearances as a pianist in more respectable surroundings and composed a handful of songs and piano pieces – including three sonatas; in 1853 he travelled Germany with the young Hungarian violinist Eduard Remenyi, giving joint recitals at Hanover, Gottingen, Weimar and elsewhere. When the tour ended they parted company and Brahms made his way to Düsseldorf, armed with a letter of introduction to Robert Schumann. Schumann promptly formed a high opinion of his talent and suggested that he should write a symphony, whereupon Brahms started work on one but only completed two movements. Over the next year or so he repaid kindness and hospitality by befriending Clara Schumann during her husband's distressing last illness (see page 105) and subsequently she helped him to find part-time employment as piano-teacher at the court of Lippe-Detmold (a small principality lying in what is today the north-eastern corner of the province of North-Rhine Westphalia) which remained his headquarters until 1860. Further concert tours followed, one of which took him to Vienna; like Beethoven before him he found the atmosphere so congenial that he settled there permanently.

Brahms the man was as level-headed as Brahms the composer (which is saying a lot) – and never married. Not that he was unattracted by women: since his mother was seventeen years older than his father it may have been a hereditary kink that drove him as a youngster to nourish a hopeless passion for Clara Schumann, a mere fourteen years his senior, but it is known, too, that in later life he had three less calf-like (though probably equally innocent) love affairs. It may be significant that in each case the object of his affection was a mezzo-soprano, for moderation in all things was his motto. It is impossible to imagine such a steady middle-of-the-road character becoming involved (like Liszt) with a princess or (like Bruckner) with a chambermaid, and by the same token much of his music achieves its desired effect at somewhere between *mezzo piano* and *mezzo forte*. (How different from his rival's! When listening to a Bruckner symphony on the radio one has to tune up the quiet passages in order to hear them at all and tune down the Wagnerian climaxes in order to avoid complaints from the neighbours.)

During the six years that elapsed between his departure from Dusseldorf and his arrival in Vienna Brahms steadily added to his reputation as a composer – not only with more songs and piano pieces but also with chamber and orchestral works. Among them were a piano trio, two piano quartets, a string sextet, two (lengthy) orchestral serenades and – most important of all – a fine piano concerto in D minor, largely based on the uncompleted symphony of Dusseldorf days and dedicated in effect though not in superscripture to Schumann's memory. Like Berlioz in the *Symphony fantastique* (written at the same age, twenty-six), Brahms in this concerto established once and for all his true quality, since it displayed many of the features which one associates with nearly all the music of his full maturity: sincerity of expression; earnest striving after absolute beauty with con sequent deliberate avoidance of anything approaching facile charm; a mastery of symphonic form; forthright theme-presentation *a la* Beethoven (*pianissimo* openings, much favoured by Bruckner, are rare in Brahms); a strongly developed sense of harmonic contrast (coupled with an irritating predilection for consecutive sixths, a German characteristic); complete freedom from the four-square rigidity which afflicted Wagner until middle-age and Bruckner throughout his life; an astonishing flair for effec tive off-beat rhythmic accentuations, often of complex pattern; workmanlike but somewhat thick orchestration – more skilful than Schumann's but not to be compared with Mendelssohn's or Wagner's.

During his first five years in Vienna Brahms was still active as a concert pianist in which capacity he paid several visits to his native Germany, to Switzerland and to Hungary. From about 1868 however, he devoted himself almost entirely to composition and presently produced four big choral works – the Requiem (with soprano and baritone solo), *Harz Journey in Winter* (with contralto solo, and commonly known as the alto rhapsody), *Song of Destiny* and *Song of Triumph* (i.e. the triumph of Prussia in the Franco-Prussian war of 1870/71). With all respect to admirers of these works and especially of the Requiem – which was a setting not of the liturgy but of a biblical text – this was a field in which he was never quite at home, despite the fact that his vocal writing was extremely competent. 'Bach brought up to date' it was said, but 'Handel brought up to date' would be a more accurate parallel, since Brahms relied more on harmony than on counterpoint and the contrapuntal passages, when they came, were more note worthy for solidity than for virtuosity. (One is glad to point out that he was a *rara avis* among the German musicians of his day in showing a proper appreciation of Handel.)

To the next period, 1873-86, belong Brahm's eight orch estral masterpieces – the 'St Anthony' variations on a theme of Haydn, the four symphonies, the violin concerto, the piano concerto in B flat major and the double concerto for violin and cello. In these works the strengths and weak nesses noted in the earlier D minor piano concerto (see page 152) are still apparent; bearing them in mind, only a few further remarks are necessary.

(1) It is an apt if cruel comment on his orchestration that the Haydn variations are even more effective in their original form – a piano duet.

(2) The first movement of symphony no. 1 displays genius, for although there is hardly a vestige of a tune it is nevertheless a highly-organized entity and far from boring.

(3) The cyclic key-sequence of the four movements of this same symphony – each up-grading by a major third (C minor, E major, A flat major, C major) – is unconven tional but logical.

(4) The tremendous opening of no. 3, while unmistakably

Brahmsian when it throws into relief the significance of a chromatic A flat in the key of F major, clearly derives from the opening of Schumann's no. 3 in its melody – and even more so in its almost identical rhythm.

(5) The finale of no. 4 is unique: it is an extended passacaglia (i.e. variations on a continually-repeated 'ground bass') – and possibly the most satisfying last movement in eighteenth- and nineteenth-century symphony.

(6) In his second piano concerto Brahms broke new ground by writing four movements instead of the customary three; the extra one, an *allegro appassionato* placed second and not third, is in parts excitingly tempestuous.

(7) Even when in light-hearted mood he was rarely light-handed and as a rule only qualified praise can be given to his attempts at sprightliness – e.g. in the third movements of symphonies 1, 2 and 4, and in the finales of all three concertos. (For the same reason one prefers the characteristic *Tragic* overture to its companion the *Academic Festival,* which is based on German student-songs of ponderous jollity.)

(8) Possible exceptions to the generalization implied in (7) are the lovely second movement of the violin concerto (a gift to the oboist) and the suave third movement of symphony no. 3; they are not exactly light-handed, but here Brahms did achieve a high measure of lyrical charm. (This *poco allegretto* from no. 3, incidentally, provides a straightforward example of the composer's *penchant* for ambiguous rhythmic accentuation.)

Brahms was last in the line of illustrious Viennese musicians who composed string quartets in the classical manner. He produced only three – as against eighty-two by Haydn, twenty-three by Mozart, sixteen by Beethoven and fifteen by Schubert; they were all written in his late thirties or early forties and were noteworthy for the prominence given to the viola – often regarded as the ugly duckling of the ensemble. Brahms added a second viola for two string quintets and a second cello (as well) for two sextets; in all these works he demonstrated a sure instinct for the medium. Two piano trios (ops. 87 and 101) were better still, showing him to greater advantage than the early piano quartets (see page 152); but the piano quintet cannot quite hold its own beside those of Schumann (page 106), Franck (page 140) and Dvorak (page 181). On the other hand in his violin sonatas (ops. 78, 100, 108) Brahms was on top form; I am surprised to find myself in a minority when rating op. 100 (in A major) the best of the three: this sonata and the admirable clarinet quintet op. 115 are to my mind the composer's finest achievements in chamber music, for they exhibit most of the typical strengths and few of the typical weaknesses which have already been enumerated. Outstand ing among his piano pieces are the rhapsodies, capriccios and *intermezzi* comprised in ops. 79, 116 and 119 and the deservedly popular waltzes op. 39 – which were originally written for piano duet. So too were the *Hungarian Dances*, skilful arrangements of traditional or contemporarily popular Magyar tunes; these are often played nowadays in orchestral transcriptions.

There are those to whom Brahms's music, taken by and large, makes little appeal; they are often the very people who tend to overrate the worth of his songs and vocal duets, maintaining that here alone did he prove himself consistently capable of expressing human emotion or achieve any delicacy of touch. Others aver that his genius was more fully conveyed in the symphonies, concertos and chamber music, and are not prepared to concede that as a song-writer he came into the same category as Schubert. If Brahms's idea of human emotion was the *Wiegenlied* ('Guten Abend. gut' Nacht'), they feel, so much the worse for him; as for delicacy of touch, it is understandable that fastidious listeners should find themselves embarrassed by the archness of *Vergebliches Standchen*, the *Liebeslieder* waltzes, and some of the folk-song arrangements. For tunately this is not the whole story: out of Brahms's two hundred or so songs there are many which defy such criti cism and a round dozen at least which deserve to rank with the finest *Lieder* ever written: the love songs *Wie bist du, meine Konigen; Von ewiger Liebe; Meine Liebe ist grun; Wir wandelten*: in more sombre mood *Die Mainacht,*

Feldeinsamkeit, Im Waldeinsamkeit and *Der Tod, das ist die kuhle Nacht*; above all the *Four Serious Songs*, with scriptural words, composed during the last year of his life when he knew that he was dying of cancer. Although he belonged to no religious denomination, refusing to accept *in toto* the doctrines of either Catholicism or Protes tantism, he was a sincere Christian and in the *Four Serious Songs* his deep convictions found personal expression; the fourth and last of them – *Wenn ich mit Menschen- und mit Engelzungen redete* ('Though I speak with the tongues of men and of angels') – was an abbreviated setting of the famous thirteenth chapter of St. Paul's first epistle to the Corinthians. Johannes Brahms may have had it in mind that its closing strain would serve as his epitaph: 'Nun aber bleibet Glaube, Hoffnung, Liebe, diese drei; die Liebe ist die grosste unter ihnen' – in the words of the Authorised Version: 'But now abideth faith, hope and charity, these three, and the greatest of these is charity'.

CHAPTER TWENTY-SIX

BORODIN

That national or regional characteristics in music must in and of themselves be worthy of admiration is a popular fallacy. Of the folk-songs, for instance, that have sprung from Somerset, the Hebrides, Ireland, Spain, Yugoslavia and – at second-hand, as it were – from the deep south of the United States of America, some are truly beautiful by any standard, but many others if judged objectively are not: their sole interest lies in the national or regional character istic itself. Sometimes the vicarious nostalgia of xenophile enthusiasts is tinged with misapprehension, misapprehen sion which is particularly noticeable in the attitude of a certain school of music lovers in western Europe towards Russian composers. There are those who incline to shrug Tchaikovsky aside as a cosmopolitan (which he was) and an artistic renegade (which he wasn't), who acclaim Mikhail Ivanovitch Glinka (1803-57) as the father of modern Russian music for the wrong reason: he was just that, but he only became so because during the course of his career he travelled and studied in the west; while never forsaking his native idiom he was as much influenced by the popular music of Spain (where he lived for two years) as by Russian folk-song – and certainly owed more to his familiarity with Mozart, Weber and Schubert than to the inheritance of obscure eighteenth-century compatriots like Mikhail Matinsky, Stepanovitch Bortniansky and Vassily Alexeievitch Paskevitch. Glinka's lineal successor ALEXANDER PORPHYRIEVITCH BORODIN (1833-87) was also endowed both with a wanderlust and with an artistic probity which took little heed of national or regional frontiers – and he steadfastly if unconsciously pursued Glinka's healthy policy of integration.

Borodin was born at St. Petersburg (now Leningrad); he was the illegitimate son of the aging Prince Luka Semeno-

vitch Gedeanov through the youthful Avdotya Konstantin-
ova Kleinecke, daughter of a soldier. As was usual in such
cases the baby was registered as the child of one of his
father's serfs (Porphyri Borodin), but since his mother was
well-provided-for there was nothing serf-like about his
upbringing: he was treated with every consideration and
instead of being sent to school was educated by a succession
of private tutors. It was at the age of about ten that he first
began to develop side by side the two great interests of his
life – chemistry and music. At seventeen he entered the St.
Petersburg Academy of Medicine and Surgery and six
years later (having passed all examinations with distinction
and thereafter attended a conference of scientists at Brussels)
was practising at an army hospital. Next came a period
abroad, 1859-62, much of which was spent at the university
of Heidelberg but which also included an extended tour of
France, Switzerland, Italy and Austria. On returning home
he married a Moscow girl of gentle birth named Ekaterina
Sergeyevna Protopopova whom he had met while on his
travels; she was a very good pianist and during a some
what protracted courtship had introduced her future hus
band to the music of Chopin, Schumann and Liszt. In 1864
Borodin was appointed professor of organic chemistry at
the Academy and as a respected and valued member of
the teaching staff (he spoke German and Italian fluently
and had a good working knowledge of French and English)
was accommodated rent-free in a flat on the premises –
which was to be his home for the rest of his life.

Thus far he had devoted more time to listening to music
than to making it, although he played both cello and organ
with great enthusiasm and had written some chamber
works – of which only a piano quintet is preserved com
plete (in manuscript). About the time that he became a
professor of chemistry however, he also became the junior
member – junior by date of admission that is, not by age –
of the *kutchka*, a select company of musicians who met
under the leadership of Mily Alexeievitch Balakirev – the
uncompromisingly nationalistic composer of the symphonic
poem *Tamara* and the piano-fantasy *Islamey*. The other

three members of the group (sometimes referred to as 'the five') were all, like Borodin himself, amateurs: Cesar Antonovitch Cui (see page 164) was by profession a military engineer, Mussorgsky (chapter 27) a clerk in the civil ser vice, Rimsky-Korsakov (chapter 30) a naval officer. Thence forth Borodin, encouraged by Balakirev, became a week end composer; in view of his other commitments it is not altogether surprising that his first symphony took five years to complete, his second seven years and the two string quartets four years each; *Prince Igor*, on which he began work in 1869, was still unfinished when he died – eighteen years later. The wonder is that he was ever able to compose at all, for the easy-going and ill-managed Borodin house hold – where the tables were always littered with retorts and test-tubes, the floors strewn with half-unpacked suit cases and piles of music-manuscript, the corners cluttered with the rubbish of months – was regarded as a home from home by innumerable friends and relations (all impover ished), by absent-minded scholars, by penniless students and by all manner of stray cats (animal and human); it was rarely that Borodin himself, hoping for a good night's rest, found his own bed unoccupied when at last he reached it. This was *la vie de boheme* on a scale never envisaged by Henri Murger (although sometimes portrayed by Tchekhov) and Mrs. Borodin, driven nearly out of her mind by the constant succession of unwelcome guests, came to spend more and more of her time with her parents in Moscow. Presently her husband fell ill with cholera and although he recovered sufficiently to make two more trips abroad (to Belgium) he was thereafter obliged to restrict his activities – both scientific and musical. A few years later, at the age of fifty-three, he fell dead of a sudden heart-attack while attending a fancy-dress ball.

For reasons which have already been made abundantly clear Borodin's musical output was not large, and little more than a line will suffice to catalogue the mature works upon which his immortality depends: one unfinished opera, two symphonies, one 'tone-poem' for orchestra, two string quartets and eleven songs. Of the songs *The Sleeping*

Princess (where like Glinka before him in the opera *Russlan and Ludmilla* he anticipated Debussy's use of a whole-tone scale – see page 214), *Dissonance* and *The Sea* (all with words by Borodin himself) were perhaps the best; the three completed orchestral works, the two quartets and the opera call for rather more detailed comment.

Borodin's symphony no. 1 in E flat major has been described as immature, but the adjective can be applied only in a relative sense. The first movement, indeed, is in one respect ahead of its time, for it develops vigorously out of strands of theme in the manner which Sibelius later made his own and ends, most originally and effectively, with a very tranquil summing-up. The second movement is a scherzo of Mendelssohnian lightness, contrast being provided by a middle section which is the most characteristically Russian part of the whole work. The rhapsodic third movement firmly stresses throughout the extremely unconventional key (in the E flat context) of D major and the finale is full of uninhibited vitality.

During one of his visits to the west Borodin met Liszt and showed him the manuscript of his recently completed symphony no. 2 in B minor. The old man was fulsome in his praise; one wonders whether he noticed that the first ten bars recalled the opening of his own piano concerto in E flat major (see page 110). Borodin's arresting motto-theme, whether presented in 2/2 or 3/2 time, in diminution or augmentation, whether marked *allegro, poco meno mosso, animato assai* or (as at the finish) *poco a poco allargando e pesante*, formed the basis of a wonderfully exciting movement. As in the first symphony the scherzo came next, a *prestissimo* one-beat-to-the-bar (four crotchets) affair in the remote key of F major; the slow third movement, extraordinarily impressive in its sombre solemnity, was one of the composer's finest achievements and a truly great work was rounded off with a finale which – with its frequent changes of time-signature (2/4, 3/4, 4/4) – was a lively and stirring evocation of Slavonic dance rhythms.

Borodin's tone-poem *In the Steppes of Central Asia* gave him a chance to prove that when he wished he could be as

national at Balakirev or anyone else. Here is his own pro
gramme-note in which I have inserted, parenthetically,
the instrumental means by which he evoked the appropri
ate atmosphere.

In the silence of the monotonous steppes of central Asia
[two solo violins in the highest register] is heard the un
familiar sound of a peaceful Russian song [clarinet, then
horn, virtually unaccompanied]. From the distance we
hear the approach of horses and camels [*pizzicato* cellos
and double basses] and the bizarre and melancholy notes
of an oriental melody [cor anglais]. A caravan approaches,
escorted by Russian soldiers [opening theme repeated
with full orchestra], and continues on its long way through
the immense desert. The notes of the Russian and Asiatic
melodies join in a common harmony [alternating instru
mental combinations], which dies away as the caravan
disappears in the distance [flute and four solo, muted,
violins].

Besides being straightforward in construction this poetic
little work is admirably concise; it lasts only about six
minutes.

By comparison Borodin's first string quartet (in A major)
– although not completed until 1879 by which time he was
already planning *The Steppes* – is almost *un*-Russian, being
in some places reminiscent of Beethoven and in others of
Mendelssohn once again. Perhaps its most interesting
feature is the up-to-date exploitation of improved string
practice to obtain modern effects, e.g. the sweeping-back-
and-forth arpeggios of the first movement (between letters
F and G) and the extensive use of artificial harmonics in the
trio of the scherzo. In the second quartet (D major), on the
other hand, Borodin as in his second symphony successfully
combined native inspiration with western technique: except
perhaps in the charming waltz-like scherzo (cf. Tchaikov
sky, page 174) the mood was as Russian as anyone could
wish for, but the delicately-adjusted instrumental balance
displayed an understanding of the medium more often

associated with the Viennese masters. The wonderfully expressive melody of the nocturne has brought this move ment a large measure of popular recognition outside its context and it cannot be denied that it represents Borodin, in romantic frame of mind, to perfection.

At times Borodin showed less assurance in his handling of an orchestra and his friendly colleague Rimsky-Korsakov (see chapter 30) along with the younger Alexander Kon-stantinovitch Glazunov (a talented composer of the next generation who never quite fulfilled early promise) 'revised' the two symphonies. Both were expert orchestrators and if they had confined themselves to surface matters there might be little cause for complaint (although I maintain private doubts about certain passages); unfortunately they also took it upon themselves to 'improve the harmony' where they judged that Borodin's progressions were too harsh to suit contemporary taste. However well-meant at the time such editing can be seen in retrospect to have been mis guided; some would say inexcusable. Nevertheless praise should not be grudged the same pair for having evolved *Prince Igor* from the tangled collection of shreds and patches which Borodin left behind at his death, a task which occupied them for three years. As presented to the public in 1890 the constructional basis of the opera was the responsibility of the composer and his associate-librettist (Vladimir Stassov) only to a very small degree. So far as the music is concerned the melodic content was probably about 90 per cent Borodin (it was often reminiscent of his second symphony), 10 per cent Rimsky or Glazunov; the harmoni zation 60 per cent Borodin, 40 per cent Rimsky or Glazunov; the orchestration 10 per cent Borodin, 20 per cent Glazunov (which included the overture) and 70 per cent Rimsky. Borodin's spontaneous melodies (spirited, tender, voluptu ous) were often embellished by appropriate oriental touches – in Konstchakovna's cavatina at the opening of Act II for instance; Rimsky-Korsakov's flair for orchestration was never better demonstrated than in the superb sequence known to concertgoers as the 'Polovtsian Dances'. Indeed *Prince Igor*, rather than turning out to be the amorphous pasticcio which might have been expected, soon became recognized as one of the finest operas of the late nineteenth century. To admit that this was partly due to the able abetting of the junior collaborators need imply no diminution of respect or admiration for the achievements of Alexander Borodin himself – both here and elsewhere. Although he may not have been the greatest and was certainly not the most prolific composer ever to emerge from Russia, he was eminently successful in forging a strong musical link between his own country and the rest of Europe.

CHAPTER TWENTY-SEVEN

MUSSORGSKY

MODEST PETROVITCH MUSSORGSKY (1839-81) was born at Kareva, a village lying roughly two-hundred-and-fifty miles south of St. Petersburg, two-hundred-and-fifty miles west of Moscow, two-hundred-and-fifty miles east of Riga and a hundred miles north of Smolensk. Apart from the fact that his paternal grandmother had been a common serf the family escutcheon was untarnished, many of his ancestors having been army officers loyally serving a succession of imperial czars and his father being a socially acceptable landowner. At the age of ten he accompanied his parents when they moved to St. Petersburg – and it was there that he spent the rest of his life. Unlike Borodin (who knew his way round Brussels, Paris, Rome and Vienna), let alone Tchaikovsky and Rimsky-Korsakov (who, as we shall see presently, penetrated as far afield as London and New York), Mussorgsky never left Russia and indeed only once left the surroundings of St. Petersburg – when in 1879 he undertook a joint concert tour of the Ukraine and the Crimea with the contralto singer Daria Mikhailovna Leonova. It is therefore not surprising that he ultimately proved to be more aggressively nationalistic than the other mem bers of Balakirev's *kutchka* – Borodin, Rimsky-Korsakov and Cui. (Cui, of French descent, never quite kept up with the rest; but he was by no means a negligible figure in the history of Russian music, for although his operas were failures he remained an ardent propagandist of Borodin and up to a point of Mussorgsky. Furthermore he wrote some pleasant chamber music and even those who normally appreciate the punster's art may be inclined to regret that Ernest Newman, whose critical erudition was matched only by his fondness for a joke, yielded to the temptation of prefacing his notice of a recital of Cui's compositions with the headline '*Cui bono?*'.)

As a boy Mussorgsky learnt to play the piano remark ably well but at seventeen – in accordance with family tradition – he enlisted as cadet in a famous regiment known as the Preobrazhensky Guards where he acquired the habit of hard drinking that was later to cause his downfall. He maintained an interest in music however, sought acquaint ance with Balakirev, prevailed upon that enthusiast to give him lessons and was so satisfied with the results that he soon left the army and set out confidently to earn fame as a composer. But some of the ground was cut from under his feet when in 1861, by decree of the reigning Czar Alex ander II, the hitherto knout-bound serfs of Russia were emancipated while the idle and wealthy land-owning class, to which Mussorgsky belonged, was largely dispossessed of its vested interest in property. Thereafter he was obliged to earn his living in the ill-paid though not over-worked clerical grade of the civil service, first in the Ministry of Transport and later in the Ministry of Agriculture. Mean while he composed about eighty songs, a collection of piano pieces entitled *Pictures at an Exhibition* and the tone-poem *Night on the Bare Mountain*. He also planned half-a-dozen or so operas; he made fair progress with *Salambo*, *The Marriage*, *Khovanshtchina* and *Sorochintsky Fair*, but the only one he ever finished was *Boris Godunov*. The pity was that he drowned himself in drink: although he pulled round during the early eighteen-seventies when he was engrossed in *Boris*, he soon relapsed once more into chronic alcoholism. The last six years of his life have been described as a protracted debauch; this is an exaggeration, since he behaved well enough on the Ukrainian tour which has already been referred to, but in the long run nothing could check the miserable sequence: *delirium tremens* – epilepsy – premature death at the age of forty-two.

So much for the *personal* tragedy of Mussorgsky. It was an *artistic* tragedy that he was born when he was, rather than fifty years later, for he was an intrusive realist in a predominantly romantic age. No previous composer had adopted such a stark approach to the problems of aesthetic interpretation; there was very rarely any appeal to sentiment – even in his songs. Admittedly a lyric strain was noticeable in *The Garden by the Don, The Hebrew Song* and the song-cycle *Sunless,* but Mussorgsky's real *forte* lay in his ability to paint a scene or an incident with a few deft strokes of impressionism – often pointing a satirical con trast. Some of his songs ran into trouble with ecclesiastical or military censors: *The Seminarist* for instance (in which the priestly devotions of a divinity student are interrupted by erotic visions), and *Forgotten* (a soldier's rotting corpse is pecked by vultures while far away his wife croons their baby to sleep with a lullaby of which the burden is 'daddy will soon be home'). Less extravagant in conception – and therefore more genuinely moving – are *Darling Savishna* (in which the village idiot stammers out his love to the vill age beauty) and *Kalistratuschk* (a poverty-stricken peasant compares the happy sort of life envisaged for him by his mother with the wretched existence he now has to endure). When humour emerges it is nearly always bitter: in *Hopak* a lively young woman dances away from her elderly hus band and abandons herself to a 'handsome lad'; in *The He-Goat* a girl eludes a lecherous old goat and then marries a lecherous old man with a goatee-beard. Mussorgsky's last and most familiar song, *The Flea,* can perhaps be taken to typify his approach to this branch of composition. He tried to exploit the tone-quality and dynamic potentialities of a solo piano to the same end in *Pictures at an Exhibition* (inspired by the paintings of his artist friend Victor Alex-androvitch Hartmann) and although he was not completely successful there can be no denying the forceful realism of picture no. 1 (a mis-shapen gnome) and the sardonic intent of picture no. 6 (a rich Jew and a poor Jew).[1]

The tone-poem *Night on the Bare Mountain* (1867) depicted the witches' sabbath popularly supposed to take place each midsummer's eve on Mount Triglav near Kiev in the Ukraine. Unfortunately not even Balakirev, though he praised its power and originality, was sufficiently advanced to stomach its harsh dissonances and what he

[1] *Pictures at an Exhibition* was orchestrated by Maurice Ravel, a great admirer of Mussorgsky.

found its 'barbaric disorder'; when several years later Mussorgsky revised the score with a ballet production in view nothing came of it, and the work was never performed complete during his lifetime. After his death, however, Rimsky-Korsakov fashioned a new tone-poem built on the same thematic material and it is this crafty version of *Night on the Bare Mountain* which is known to present-day listeners. (Rimsky's night was not so dark as Mussorgsky's, his mountain not so bare, his witches not so obscene in their orgies.)

It was not long before Mussorgsky abandoned his first serious operatic venture *Salambo* (after Gustave Flaubert), for which he had written only a few short scenes. In 1868 he completed a piano score of the first act of *The Marriage* (after Nikolai Vassilievitch Gogol) but he laid this aside too when his imagination was inflamed with the idea of transmuting Alexander Pushkin's forty-five-year-old historical drama *Boris Godunov* into an opera. The huge task occupied him little more than a year (despite civil service distractions) and in 1870 he submitted the score to the directors of the St. Petersburg Imperial Theatre, who to do them justice seem to have given it careful consideration but in the event turned it down – (a) because the subject was too sombre and there was no love interest and (b) because the music was too 'modernistic'. The composer accepted their decision in good part; his heart and soul were in *Boris* and in order to secure a production he now substituted lighter scenes for some of the more sombre and augmented the feminine interest by introducing a totally new character – the Polish princess Marina Minschek. This second version of *Boris* – modernism and all – was accepted by the theatre's directorate and the first performance took place in 1874. Not surprisingly it had a mixed reception: *kutchka* members (bar one) were enthusiastic, none more so than Rimsky-Korsakov, but the opera-going public was puzzled and suspicious. *Boris* was not an utter failure however and was played now and again during the next few years, but by the time its composer was dead and buried it too had sunk into a half-forgotten limbo. The excitement lay ahead.

In 1896, fifteen years after Mussorgsky's death, the inde
fatigable Rimsky-Korsakov rescued *Boris Godunov* from
oblivion; whatever criticism one may feel disposed to level
at him an an editor, let that sentence be repeated in italics:
Rimsky-Korsakov rescued Boris Godunov from oblivion.
Without such an experienced public relations officer this
fine opera might never have attained recognition, its com
poser's name today means nothing to most music lovers –
and little to most students. But the other side of the medal
is inescapable: Rimsky-Korsakov, like the rest, ascribed
Mussorgsky's unorthodox approach to the problems of
harmony, orchestration and technique in general to lack of
musical education rather than to exceptional genius sub
consciously striving to burst conventional bonds. As a
musician of impeccable taste he found it inconceivable that
Mussorgsky really meant everything that he put down on
paper; he was doing a favour, he thought, when for the
sake of his old friend's posthumous reputation he replaced
so-and-so with such-and-such. His authority to tamper with
the 1874 edition was almost immediately challenged by the
French musicologist Pierre d'Alheim and other critics
followed suit about fifteen years later; since then the con
troversy has raged furiously, fuel being added to the fire
when in 1928 it was discovered that some of Rimsky's
tamperings with the 1874 edition had in fact been reversions
to the original of 1869. Most of us prefer to take no active
part in this dispute; we freely concede that the 1896 *Boris
Godunov* differs in many details (constructional, stylistic,
orchestral) from both the 1869 and 1874 versions, yet we
feel we can acclaim Mussorgsky for a supreme achievement
and at the same time spare a word of thanks for the well-
meaning adaptor who gave us the opportunity to acquaint
ourselves with such a masterwork.

It was Rimsky-Korsakov again who completed and other
wise ministered to Mussorgsky's second historical opera
Khovanshtchina, based on a libretto of his own contriving
and but a pale reflection of *Boris* – although the scene
where the drunken Khovanschky meets his doom (while
being carried off the stage after clumsily cavorting with a

bevy of dancing-girls) is extraordinarily effective in its restraint. In the unfinished comic opera *Sorochintsky Fair* (after Gogol) Mussorgsky struck an unwonted lyrical vein, but Rimsky-Korsakov never bothered with it and of the half-dozen or so completions by less accomplished crafts men none have done much credit either to the composer or to the craftsmen.

In a prefatory note to this book it was hinted that pos terity cannot normally form a reasoned judgment on the ultimate worth of a composer's contribution to music until perhaps fifty years or so after his death. But Modest Mus sorgsky was so far ahead of his time that in his case the margin should be doubled at least; perhaps only when the world is old enough to assess the achievements of Aram Ilyitch Khatchaturian and Dmitri Shostakovich will it be prudent to assert (or deny) with confidence that the genius of their predecessor was both rare and prophetic.

CHAPTER TWENTY-EIGHT

TCHAIKOVSKY

Whereas Borodin was born in St. Petersburg itself and Mussorgsky within its orbit, PETER ILYITCH TCHAIKOVSKY first saw the light a thousand miles away to the east at Votinsk, an iron-and-steel centre in the basin of the river Kama which winds its way through the Ural foothills to join the Volga some fifty miles south of Kazan. His father Ilya Petrovitch Tchaikovsky, a mining engineer, was thrice married – in 1827, 1833 and 1865; the composer, born in 1840, was the second of six children by his middle wife Alexandra Andreevna *nee* d'Assier (French by ancestry). In 1849 tne family moved to Alaparev near Nizhny-Novgorod and the following year Peter, a gifted child already showing signs of musical ability, was sent to St. Petersburg where he stayed with friends and continued his education with a view to becoming a lawyer. Morbidly sensitive, his regard for his mother as an ideal woman surpassed the bounds of normal filial affection and suggested an Oedipus complex; her death in 1854 (he later confessed) might have driven him literally mad but that he was able to immerse himself in music – not, be it noted, in legal studies. A few immature compositions do indeed date from this adolescent period; nevertheless he stuck to his allotted task, passed his law examinations and shortly after his nineteenth birthday secured a clerical post in the Ministry of Justice. But like other minor bureaucrats he seems to have spent most of his office hours playing darts and drinking tea, and in 1861 he took a long holiday abroad during the course of which he visited Berlin, Brussels and Paris. On his return he entered the St. Petersburg Conservatoire recently founded by Anton Rubinstein, applied himself seriously to music – and form ally resigned from the civil service. By 1866 he was suffi ciently established as an oncoming musician to be appointed to the teaching staff of the Moscow Conservatoire under the direction of Anton Rubinstein's brother Nicolas. (The Rubinsteins were of German-Polish descent and their outlook on music differed radically from that of Balakirev or Mussorgsky; both were distinguished pianists and in addition Anton was a prolific composer whose piano con certos were long favoured by *virtuosi*.) Moscow remained Tchaikovsky's headquarters for the rest of his life, but from 1873 onwards he travelled much abroad – to Germany, Switzerland, Italy, France and Britain on several occasions and to the United States once; meanwhile (except for a period of comparative stagnation in the early eighteen-eighties) compositions flowed fast from his pen. Thanks to this extensive travel he was even more influenced than Borodin by western music; for all their individuality his symphonies, taken as a whole, owed much to the classic Viennese models, his operas to the Italian, his ballets to the French; he was never a member of the *kutchka* and maintained little contact with his St Petersburg colleagues.

Perhaps it was Tchaikovsky's idolization of his mother – and to a lesser extent of his sister, also christened Alexandra – which rendered him immune from feminine blandishment outside the family circle and led him to homosexuality. Unfortunately he was indiscreet in his *amours* and pre sently realized that he would have to take drastic action if he wished to avoid being involved in a first-class scandal. In 1877, therefore, he put up a smoke-screen by marrying Antonina Inanovna Milyukova, a vain and importunate young lady who had persistently been setting her cap at him. Three days after the wedding he wrote a distressing and distasteful letter to his young brother Anatole.

I have taken no advantage of her, for I warned her from the outset to expect no more than brotherly affec tion. Physically, she revolts me.

Brotherly affection was not what Antonina had been looking for, and the whole deplorable episode ended in utter and near-tragic fiasco: the remorseful husband had a mental breakdown and tried to commit suicide by immersing himself in an ice-cold river – but only succeeded in catching pneumonia (from which he duly recovered). Meanwhile he had already embarked upon intimate pen-friend intercourse with Nadezhda Philaretovna von Meck – whom he never met face to face although she was often present in the audience when his works were played in public. She was the rich widow of a railway tycoon and the mother of twelve children, but her outlook on life was one more usually associated with a frustrated old maid: she was very much in love – at a safe distance.

> I want you to speak to me, and to no one else, of nature and destiny, of heart-break, trampled faith, wounded pride, of happiness irretrievably lost, of self-abandonment to despair. No art can express all this like music can, and no one understands *me* better than you do.

How right she was! Tchaikovsky understood her perfectly and for fourteen years fed her starved emotions with pseudo-passionate songs and piano pieces – in return for substantial financial patronage. Eventually, as might have been foreseen, Nadezhda's descendants, resentful that their inheritance was being frittered away on a composer with a dubious moral character, opened her eyes to the more un-romantic aspects of her protege's private life; the love letters and the generous pension ceased forthwith – and the toucher was deeply touched.

> My faith in my fellow-humans and my confidence in the world itself are undermined. I have lost my tran quillity, and the happiness that fate might yet have held in store for me is gone for ever.

Tchaikovsky was always subject to moods of extreme depression and it could have been with deliberate intent that while on a visit to St. Petersburg in 1893 (three years after his break with Nadezhda von Meck) he drank a glass of unboiled tap-water; a few days later he was dead of cholera.

Beside Beethoven's 'Emperor' concerto, seventh sym- phony, 'Waldstein' sonata and *Adelaide*, Tchaikovsky's first piano concerto, fifth symphony, *Chant sans paroles* and *None but the weary heart* cannot be accounted master pieces, but judged by any other standard they are admir able compositions and need not be disparaged because they are popular; moreover Tchaikovsky lovers are at liberty to point out that *Eugen Onegin* is a better opera, *qua opera*, than *Fidelio*. (And furthermore let me draw attention to the charming and accomplished vocal quartet in Act I scene 1 and to Lensky's fine dramatic aria in Act II scene 2.) But there was never a composer whose temperament was more closely reflected in his music, much of which was redolent of self-pity – self-pity finding expression as early as the *Romance in F minor* for piano (1868) and the song *E'en though my heart should break* (1869). Later it reared its head in the third movement of the otherwise light- hearted symphony no. 3, in two movements of the string quartet in E flat minor op. 30, in the technically accomp lished concert-overture *Francesca da Rimini* and in the tear-away treatment of the motto-themes of symphonies 4 and 5. It reached a climax in the last two operas (*The Queen of Spades* and *Iolanta*), in the elegiac gloom of the first movement of symphony no. 6 (the 'Pathetic') and in the almost unrelieved pessimism of its finale. (Tchaikovsky deserves credit, however, for having thus ventured to con clude the 'Pathetic' with a slow movement, a precedent of which Gustav Mahler and our own Ralph Vaughan Williams showed themselves fully conscious.) On the other hand it would be a very squeamish critic who failed to appreciate the altogether healthier sentiment of the *Serenade for Strings*, the orchestral suite in G major op. 55, the concert-overture *Romeo and Juliet*, parts at least of the symphonic poem *Manfred*, a handful of the hun dred or so songs – *The Corals*, for instance, and *Does the day reign*. And although, as we have seen, Tchaikovsky was not a strongly nationalist composer he often made effective use of Russian folk-idiom: notably almost throughout symphonies nos. 1 and 2, the string sextet curiously entitled

Souvenir de Florence and the opera *Vakula the Smith*; as well as in the favourite *andante cantabile* from the string quartet in D major op. 11, the finale of the violin concerto and several scenes from two other little-known operas, *The Oprichnik* and *Mazeppa*.

But when all is said Tchaikovsky's main hold on one's affections depends upon his ballet-music, where delicacy of touch and superb orchestral technique combined to make him a master. I am thinking not only of *Swan Lake*, *The Sleeping Beauty* and *Casse-Noisette* (which are *hors concours* in that field), but also of the unconventional ballet-like intrusions on other media – e.g. the waltzes of the *Serenade for Strings* and symphonies nos. 2 and 5, the so-called scherzos of the piano sonata op. 37 and of sym phony no. 4. For simultaneous exposure of nearly all his qualities good and bad one must turn however to the first movement of this same symphony (no. 4), where echoes of the bleak Russian countryside and the gilded Russian ball room are heard against a background of barely repressed hysteria; yet all these elements are incorporated in a frame work of classical sonata-form skilfully adapted to the needs of the moment. Peter Tchaikovsky's approach to his art was in almost every respect the exact antithesis to that of his German contemporary Johannes Brahms, but his music has given pleasure to countless thousands and only high brows will complain if it continues to do so.

CHAPTER TWENTY-NINE

DVOŘÁK

From 1620 until the dissolution of the Habsburg Empire in 1918 the Czechs, racially allied with the Russians and in habiting Bohemia and Moravia, were subject to foreign domination. For all those three hundred years nationalism in politics was harshly stamped out; until 1860 or there abouts nationalism in art survived only as a picturesque feature of the Empire's provincial backwoods and so far as culture was concerned Prague, the Bohemian capital, was a mere outpost of Vienna. (Compare Dublin and London prior to 1922.) The late nineteenth century, however, brought improved communications and greater oppor tunity for spreading propaganda abroad, so that at last Czech literature and music began to make more than local impact: it typified the resurgence that ANTONIN DVOŘÁK (1841-1904) was able through sheer ability to rise alongside the most illustrious of *Herrenvolk* composers. In his own field he was as ardent and practical a patriot as his friend Thomas Masaryk, later to be the first president of independent Czechoslovakia.

Observant tourists with a bent for sociology may have noticed that in many continental countries the village pub is often combined with a retail shop of some sort; in Italy one finds perhaps an *osteria/alimentari*, in Central Europe more likely a *Gasthaus/Metzgerei* – or *hostinec/reznicky*. Verdi was the son of the innkeeper-grocer of Roncole; Dvorak of the innkeeper-butcher of Nelahozeves on the banks of the river Vltava – by trunk road no. 8 about eighteen miles north of Prague (not forty-five, as stated by a biographer whose accuracy in every other respect I would not presume to question). He showed early promise as a musician but when the family moved to Zlonice, a nearby mining village, he was obliged to work as assistant butcher-cum-bartender, since his father did not take his artistic aspirations as all seriously. But slicing carcasses and serving beer did not satisfy Dvorak's inner urge and at the age of sixteen he made his way – on a haycart, we are told – to Prague, where after studying for a few years at the Organ School (later absorbed by the Conservatoire) he secured a position as a viola-player in the orchestra of the newly-opened Czech National Theatre not long before Smetana was appointed its conductor. (Bedřich Smetana, Dvorak's senior by seventeen years, was the first outstanding figure in the history of Czech music. His masterpiece was *The Bartered Bride,* one of the most popular operettas ever written, but he deserves to be remembered also for *My Country* – a fine set of six symphonic poems – and the string quartet entitled *From My Life,* which has life-like ups and downs but is as accomplished as any of Mendelssohn's or Schumann's.)

Dvorak remained at the theatre for ten years; meanwhile he established himself as a sought-after music-teacher – and fell in love with Anna Čermakova, a chorus-girl, whom he married in 1873. (They reared six children and were always a devoted couple.) The compositions of this period – his twenties – were strongly influenced by Wagner; many were subsequently thrown on the fire by the composer himself and the few which survive are unrepresentative of the Dvorak who has achieved immortality. In the early eighteen-seventies however, he turned over a new leaf with the cantata *The Heirs of the White Mountain* and the operetta *King and Collier* (a complete re-setting of an earlier and pseudo-Wagnerian essay) where the approach was more spontaneous. Indeed only a Slav idiom (such as Smetana favoured in his most characteristic works) would here have been acceptable, for the White Mountain was the scene of a crucial battle in the Thirty Years' war and symbolized Bohemia's loss of her treasured independence and the libretto of *King and Collier* also had a national istic slant. These were followed by an even better operetta – *The Peasant a Rogue* (sometimes dubbed, not ineptly, the Czech *Figaro*) – and the *Stabat Mater* (1877), which brought its composer recognition far beyond the boundaries of Bohemia; thereafter he never looked back.

In 1884 Dvorak and his growing family established a permanent home at Vysoka near Přibrom, some thirty miles south of Prague, but from then onward he travelled much abroad. Like Mendelssohn he was a great favourite in Britain which he visited on nine separate occasions: the cantata *The Spectre's Bride* was specially written for the Birmingham Festival of 1885, the oratorio *St Ludmilla* for the Leeds Festival of 1891; the Requiem had its world *premiere* at Birmingham in 1890. Dvorak also toured Germany and parts of Russia and went twice to the United States. In 1892-4 he spent much of his time at the Czech settlement of Spillville (Iowa) where he felt at home, but on a return trip the following year, when he was virtually confined to New York, he suffered from nostalgia; humble in origin and pious in (Catholic) religious observance, he was never truly happy when parted from his ain folk. He belonged too to that select community of musicians – and writers on music – who while in other respects staid and responsible members of society cherish an unbridled passion for railways: in January 1904 an orgy of engine-spotting on an exposed snow-bound platform at a main-line station brought on a bad chill which aggravated chronic uraemia and a few months later he died of apoplexy. His widow survived him by twenty-seven years; she and their son-in-law composer Josef Suk carried the family tradition into the nineteen-thirties.

Dvorak's music here and there displayed a 'Brahmsian' depth of feeling, but whereas Brahms appealed to the emotions through the intellect with Dvorak it was the other way round. One can trace technical affinity with his German contemporary in the straightforward expositions of thematic material and the strong sense of harmonic contrast, but on the whole he had more in common with Schubert: notably an unquenchable flow of melody, a natural genius for modulation, an instinct for the right medium of expression – and a tendency to uncontrolled repetition (which to Brahms was anathema). Although nearly all his music, leaving aside the early attempts to emulate Wagner, was typically national, he rarely if ever made use of actual folk- or gipsy-tunes as did Brahms in his German folk-song settings and Hungarian dances. For instance the admirable *Moravian* (vocal) *Duets* – the first of his compositions to attract attention in Vienna – and the even more admirable *Slavonic Dances* – originally written as piano duets and the first to attract attention in London – conformed with Slav tradition in mood and rhythm but were one-hundred-per cent his own work. So were the songs and piano solos, most of which however provide little more than an excuse for pleasant relaxation: unlike both Schubert and Brahms, Dvorak showed his true strength in large-scale choral and operatic works. The British press over-praised *The Spectre's Bride* and *St Ludmilla* but there can be no gain saying the quality of the consistently beautiful *Stabat Mater*; of the unassuming *Mass in D major* to which one is tempted to apply the irreverent epithet charming; of the Requiem with its constantly recurring five-note *idee fixe* which achieves apotheosis in the concluding 'Agnus Dei' section; of the stirring *Te Deum,* Handelian in its sturdy optimism. Of these four works the *Stabat Mater* and the Requiem, at least, have retained their hold on public allegiance; the wholesale neglect of Dvorak's *operas* I find unaccountable. Ten years in a theatre orchestra gave him a sure sense of stage requirements and only when the libretto was hopeless – *Vanda* and *Armida* – did he fail to do it justice. *King and Collier* and *The Peasant a Rogue* have already been briefly noticed; *Dimitrij* (1882) was con cerned with the same episode in Russian history as Mus sorgsky's *Boris Godunov* and in retrospect is subject to unfavourable comparison, but in *The Jacobin* (1888) – an agreeably sentimental evocation of rural Bohemia (perhaps of his birthplace Nelahozeves, as Alec Robertson has per tinently suggested) – Dvorak was on firmer ground and much of the music showed him at his best – e.g. the love duet between Terinka and Jiri in Act II. Round the turn of the century he touched still higher peaks with the rustic comedy *The Devil and Kate* and the fairy-tragedy *Russalka*

– both based on Slav folk-lore – in which initiative was matched by long experience.

By the time he was thirty-eight Dvorak had completed five symphonies. Only one of them – the fifth in F major later published as 'no. 3' – is still in the standard repertory, but the third in E flat major deserves to be played now and again for sake of the unusually concise first movement (the first of three only), which from the point of view of style might be taken to represent the climax of his Wagnerian period. All five however were partly overshadowed by a set of *Slavonic Rhapsodies* and later completely overshadowed by the magnificent *Symphonic Variations*. So far as actual symphonies are concerned his supreme achievements were the sixth (1880, D major, formerly known as 'no. 1') and the seventh (1885, D minor, formerly 'no. 2'). The D major, as Donald Tovey rightly said, shows Dvorak at the height of his power; I would add that in the third and fourth movements at least it gains rather than loses by com parison with Brahm's no. 2 in the same key which is often thought to have provided the stimulus. The seventh symphony is also a masterpiece, but there are occasional signs that the composer's grip on the underlying principles of sonata-form is insecure. (To particularize: the sombre yet passionately masculine opening theme of the first move ment, after firmly establishing D minor, prepares the way for a disarmingly feminine dialogue between horn and oboe in the remote key of E flat major; any first-time listener – bearing in mind the precedent of Schubert's 'Unfinished' – might be excused for assuming that the exposition of the first subject, however terse, was already completed and that the second group of subjects was by now under way in an unconventional key; Dvorak shatters the illusion by scutt ling back to D minor and repeating he opening all over again with heavier scoring. Those captivating horn and oboe phrases are therefore no more than an inconsequent episode – never to be heard again and only momentarily to be referred to.) Structural deficiencies are even more notice able in the eighth symphony (1889, G major, formerly 'no. 4', sometimes called the 'English') and the ninth (1893, E minor, formerly 'no. 5', *always* 'from the New World'). The first and third movements of the G major are close-knit and attractive but the second is long-winded and the finale, which sets forth confidently as though it were to be a theme with variations, ends by chasing its own tail. The 'New World' is justly beloved as a storehouse of memorable tunes (none of them specifically negroid, by the way, although some might be regarded as based on the highest common factor of negro and Slav elements), but once again they tend to run round in circles without getting anywhere; here Dvorak seems to have followed Robert Louis Stevenson's maxim that to travel hopefully is better than to arrive. By this time perhaps, he himself realized that he was a romantic rather than classical composer for in 1896 he entered the field of programme music. The four symphonic poems *The Water Goblin* (its main theme curiously reminiscent of the opening of Act II from Bizet's *Carmen*), *The Noonday Witch, The Golden Spinning-wheel* and *The Wild Dove* were inspired by the folk-ballads of the Czech poet Karel Erben; a fifth, *The Hero's Song,* was neither inspired nor inspiring. Those who are unfamiliar with Erben's fairy-tales may find *The Water Goblin* and company somewhat frustrating. The orchestration is as brilliant as usual (Dvorak was a master in that respect), there are many passages of charm and a few of real beauty; for the uninitiated however, constant repetition is poor compensation for the lack of coherent musical development which one has a right to expect in a symphonic poem: it is rather as though one were listening to Prokofiev's *Peter and the Wolf* without the spoken narrative.

Posterity has properly acclaimed *Carnival* (1891) as the best of Dvorak's concert-overtures and recognized that the cello concerto (1895) surpassed in artistry the piano and violin concertos dated fifteen to twenty years earlier. His chamber music, generally speaking, is more representative of his genius. He wrote fifteen string quartets all told, about half of which belong to his maturity; one would not expect to find there the same depth of expression as in Beethoven's 'Rasumovsky' quartets (see page 72) or the last four of

Schubert (page 86), but ops. 51, 61, 105 and 106 are neverthe less splendid specimens of the genre. The piano trio op. 90 and the piano quintet op. 81 are also admirable works of art; the latter especially is worthy of close study. The smooth-flowing first movement where the long opening melody is characteristically allotted to the cello, the unduly protracted *dumka* (lament) with its alternating moods of resignation and resentment, the bouncing *furiant* (a Czech dance in 3/4 time frequently crossed with 3/2 rhythm), the gay and uninhibited finale; here is a symposium of the methods and style of Antonín Dvorak, one of the most human and most lovable of great composers.

CHAPTER THIRTY

RIMSKY-KORSAKOV

My dictionary defines an amateur as 'one who cultivates a particular study or art for the love of it, and not profession ally'; a professional as 'one who makes his living by an art, game, etc., as opposed to an amateur who practises it merely for pastime'. There is no need to cavil at these admirably concise definitions, although on the cricket field at any rate the two grades are now merged. (And rightly so: erstwhile professionals like Graveney and Statham have yielded to none in cultivating a particular study or art for the love of it; erstwhile amateurs like never-mind-who have not always practised it merely for pastime.) So far as com posers go however, the terms are sometimes used with a slightly different nuance, an amateur being one who has never really learnt the job and relies mainly or inborn flair, a professional being one who knows the job from A to Z even though he may not necessarily earn his living by it. Whether Borodin, in that sense an amateur *par excellence*, was a greater or lesser composer than Mendelssohn, in that sense a professional *par excellence*, I do not propose to argue; but I must record how it came about that at one stage of his career Nikolai Andreievitch Rimsky-Korsakov (1844-1908) changed almost overnight not just from amateur to professional but from clumsy amateur to expert pro fessional.

Born at Tikhvin, not far from Nizhny-Novgorod, he belonged to an aristocratic family with the sea in its blood and at the age of twelve became a naval cadet. For the next five years or so he was stationed at St. Petersburg and spent all his spare time indulging a love of music at concerts and operatic performances; presently he made contact with Balakirev who quickly sensed that here was a likely disciple, gave him a few perfunctory lessons in composition, admitted him to the *kutchka* and encouraged him to embark on a symphony. Almost simultaneously however his admiral summoned him to embark on a warship for a cruise in Atlantic waters which lasted nearly three years and took in London, New York and Rio de Janiero. When eventually allocated to a further spell of shore duty at St. Petersburg, the young hopeful (his outlook now broadened by travel) was able to turn his attention more seriously towards music, and between 1865 and 1870 he produced a fair quantity of vocal and orchestral works which were suffi ciently Russian in character to satisfy his mentor Balakirev. They included a few charming miniatures like the song *The Rose enslaves the Nightingale,* but taken by and large owed more to enthusiasm than to ability, being mostly uneven, diffuse, ill-constructed – in a word, amateurish. Rimsky-Korsakov himself realized that something was lacking and was unhappy about it; fortunately it was not long before he was given an opportunity to alter his course and by so doing become a professional, a professional – as in the event it turned out – in the Mendelssohn category. The *volte-face* took place in 1871, when Anton Rubinstein, who as already hinted (page 171) was out of sympathy with the *kutchka,* surprisingly offered him the post of professor of composition at the St. Petersburg Conservatoire. Rubin stein may have been bluffing, in the expectation that a refusal would help to discredit the activities of Balakirev and his circle; if so Rimsky-Korsakov called the bluff when he accepted – although he knew perfectly well that his qualifications were inadequate. He had never thoroughly studied harmony, counterpoint and such-like, and it was now suddenly borne upon him that his failure to have done so might be the root cause of his prevailing insufficiency. So he promptly resigned his commission in the Navy, shut himself up with a pile of text-books and in an incredibly short space of time (at the age of twenty-seven there was never a quicker or more industrious student) emerged well-equipped as a budding professor of composition – and re-vivified as a composer. (About the same time he married Nadezhda Nikolayevna Purgold, a professional pianist; their son Andrey Nikolaievitch Rimsky-Korsakov, when he reached his thirties, became a music critic.)

After the transformation it was above all in the field of opera that Rimsky distinguished himself. He produced fourteen, ranging from *Ivan the Terrible* (1872) to *The Golden Cockerel* (1907); in between came *A Night in May, The Snow Maiden, Sadko, The Legend of Czar Saltan* and eight others of less significance. Of the six here named *Ivan the Terrible,* roughly contemporaneous with Mussorgsky's *Boris Godunov,* took a more romanticized view of a rather similar episode in Russian history; *A Night in May* (after Gogol) was in essence a peasant opera which might almost remind one of Smetana's *Bartered Bride* or Dvorak's *Jacobin* (see pages 176 and 178) had not the composer also attempted to depict (I quote his own words) 'the ceremonial side of folk-life which gives expression to the survivals of ancient paganism'. The other four all belonged to that half-world which Rimsky-Korsakov made peculiarly his own – a blend of fairy tale with folk-legend, of extravagant fantasy with bucolic humour. They are still played regularly in Russia and occasionally, one is glad to say, in Britain, where however *The Snow Maiden* is mainly remembered for the 'Dance of the Tumblers', *Sadko* for the 'Hindu Song', *Czar Saltan* for the 'Flight of the Bumble Bee' and *The Golden Cockerel* for the 'Hymn to the Sun'. (The libretti of the two last were both after Pushkin – some way after.)

Even after his 1871 regeneration Rimsky-Korsakov found 'absolute' music rather hard going. During the next few years he completed a symphony in C minor, a string quartet in F major, a string sextet in A major and a quintet in B flat major for the unusual combination of flute, clarinet, bassoon, horn and piano, but they aroused little interest and today are almost forgotten. He was far more at home in the programmatic symphony *Antar* (1875), based on an Arabian fairy tale by Brambeus Sankovsky, where he could indulge to the full his love of oriental colour and decoration. (*Antar* was the wholesale revision of an earlier work of amateur days and it is indicative of the composer's praise worthy addiction to self-criticism that even the 1875 version failed to satisfy him: he revised it again in 1897.) Still more successful was the symphonic suite *Scheherazade* (1888) inspired by *The Thousand-and-one Nights*: in this gorgeous evocation of eastern splendour, barbarity, passion and langour Rimsky-Korsakov reached a zenith; it was, one might say, the apotheosis of all he had striven for in *Antar*.

Whereas *Scheherazade* showed him on top form the same could not be said of the *Russian Easter* overture (also 1888). The *Spanish Capriccio* (belonging to the previous year) demands more positive comment and I shall leave it to the composer himself (as detached as ever) to supply it.

> The opinion formed by both critics and the public, that the capriccio is a *magnificently orchestrated piece*, is wrong. It is a brilliant *composition for orchestra*. The change of timbres, the felicitous choice of melodic designs and figuration patterns, exactly suiting each kind of instrument, brief virtuoso cadenzas for instruments solo, the rhythm of the percussion instruments, and so on, constitute here the very *essence* of the composition and not its garb or orchestration. The Spanish themes, of dance character, furnished me with rich material for putting in use multiform orchestral effects. All in all the capriccio is undoubtedly a purely external piece, but vividly brilliant for all that.

Here Rimsky-Korsakov laid a finger on his own most serious shortcoming: it is not in the *Spanish Capriccio* alone that one is disturbingly aware of this tendency to make orchestration the very essence of composition. More often than not, one feels, acquired technique was unmatched by spontaneous inspiration (a common enough failing among professionals); it was only when he partially relaxed control of latter-day inhibitions (thereby giving rein, perhaps, to a resurgence of the spirit of amateurism at its best) that his music reached the heights. What raised *Scheherazade* above *Antar* – and indeed to the level of a masterpiece – was not any added brilliance of treatment but the greater point and attraction of the melodies themselves. For the same reason one is inclined to rank *The Golden Cockerel* (which is full of good tunes) as the best of his operas although, mind you, nearly all have passages of beauty and charm – e.g. the lovely duet between the Princess of the Sea and the King of the Sea which concludes the second scene of *Sadko*.

Nikolai Rimsky-Korsakov died of angina pectoris at the age of sixty-four and is the last Russian we shall meet in this book (since the next who might have won admission on grounds of merit was not born until 1872 and is there fore ineligible on grounds of chronology – see page 7). There are three counts on which he should be remembered: first as a composer who by taking thought or being anxious added cubits to his stature and at times touched greatness (even if he never rose quite high enough to maintain a firm grip on it); secondly as the untiring and effective – if controversial – propagandist of two illustrious contemporaries whose achievements were recorded in chapters 26 and 27; thirdly as a professor of composition who earned the heart-felt gratitude of a long line of distinguished pupils none of whom was more directly influenced by his teaching than Igor Stravinsky – who celebrated his eightieth birthday in 1962 and is happily still with us.

CHAPTER THIRTY-ONE

FAURÉ

The river Ariege has its source on the high plateau of Font Negre (8,000 feet above sea-level) where stands a three-country stone of France, Spain and Andorra; ninety miles away to the north it joins the mightier river Garonne just above Toulouse; meanwhile its initial torrential down-flow and its subsequent meandering lend interest to one of the most unspoilt regions of southern France. It was in this Pyrenean valley that GABRIEL FAURE spent his early boy hood; born 12th May 1845 ne was tne sixtn child of an assistant schoolmaster at Pamiers, the largest town in the *departement* of Ariege although Foix, twelve miles up stream, is its capital. Until he was four years old he was farmed out to foster-parents at the nearby village of Verni-olle, but he rejoined the family in 1849 when his father Toussaint Honore Faure, hitherto very impecunious, was appointed head of a teachers' training-college at Foix. In a district more noteworthy for scenic attraction than for cul tured sophistication a child's talent for music was recogniz able by only the veriest few among the neighbours, but it so happened that in 1854 the Swiss-born Louis Niedermeyer (who had recently taken over directorship of a privately owned and half-moribund academy of church music in Paris) made an exploratory and extensive tour in the course of which he penetrated as far as Foix; he was so much impressed by the potential talent of young Gabriel that he immediately proffered free board, lodging and tuition. So Faure, rescued from the Pyrenean foothills at the age of nine, became a pupil at the École Niedermeyer in Paris (which under the energetic sway of Niedermeyer himself soon became a formidable rival to the Conservatoire); his principal studies were piano, organ and composition. Five years later Camille Saint-Saens joined the teaching staff; he was only twenty-three years old at the time and being of friendly disposition was soon on *tutoyer* terms with his most promising pupil to whom he introduced the works of Beethoven and Schumann – still regarded with grave sus picion by many conventional French musicians.

After leaving the École Niedermeyer in 1865 Faure was organist at the church of St Sauveur at Rennes in Brittany for four years; for the next forty-five he earned his living in Paris – except during the Franco-Prussian war when he served in the field. He was organist at Notre Dame de Clignancourt and at St Honore d'Eylau before becoming C. M. Widor's assistant at St Sulpice, but from 1877 onwards his headquarters were at the Madeleine where he was choir master for seventeen years and was appointed head organist in 1896. Other important posts which he held simultaneously were those of inspector of music to state-aided schools (from 1892), professor of composition at the Conservatoire (1896-1905), director of the Conservatoire (from 1905) and music critic of *Le Figaro* (from 1903).

In character Faure was unassuming to the point of diffi dence and his career was correspondingly uneventful in the sense that there were few dramatic incidents. In his late twenties he (a) went to Weimar with Saint-Saens who there introduced him to Liszt and (b) began a long courtship of Marianne Viardot, daughter of the famous singer Pauline Viardot-Garcia. In his early thirties he (a) paid three more visits to Germany where he heard at least one complete cycle of Wagner's *Ring of the Nibelung* and (b) at last became betrothed to Marianne, who however broke the engagement a few months later. In 1883, at the age of thirty-eight, he married instead Marie Fremiet, daughter of the sculptor Emmanuel Fremiet. This was a marriage of convenience in the best sense of the term: no one suggested that the bridal pair were passionately devoted to one another but they lived amicably together until Faure's death forty-one years later; the tragedy of his life was that from about 1905 onwards he was afflicted by deafness. During the latter part of the 1914-18 war he and his wife stayed with one of his brothers at Pau in Gascony (which was a hundred miles away from his birthplace but where nevertheless he was within sight of the Pyrenees). Soon after the armistice, being by now well on in his seventies and almost completely deaf, he resigned all his official appoint ments and went into semi-retirement at Annecy in Haute-Savoie, but later he returned to Paris and it was there that he died on 4th November 1924.

Fauré, one of the most distinctively French of all French composers in an age when teutonic hegemony in the world of music was still taken for granted, never joined the ranks of the *avant-garde* (although several of his pupils were numbered among them): admittedly he had more sense of style and eventually developed far greater harmonic initia tive than his life-long and more prolific colleagues Saint-Saens and Massenet, but his roots like theirs lay in classical tradition. Although a professional organist he wrote noth ing for organ alone, and indeed his only important contri bution to church music was a Requiem (1887). In extreme contrast to that of his compatriot Berlioz (see page 96) this was a very reticent setting (for soprano, baritone, small chorus, small orchestra and organ), possibly owing some thing to the modal training which was part of the École Niedermeyer curriculum; admirably suited for liturgical purposes it is less satisfying in the concert-hall. The same restraint, almost asceticism, is noticeable in the incidental music for Shakespeare's *Merchant of Venice* (1889, entitled *Shylock*) and Maeterlinck's *Pelleas et Melisande* (1898)[1] as well as in two operas which came soon afterwards, *Prome theus and Penelope* (though here it derived from a different source – a deep admiration for the cultural ideals of ancient Greece). None of Fauré's stage-works made much lasting impression: his genius was lyrical rather than dramatic and inevitably found fuller expression in his piano pieces and songs. Of the former the most ambitious, structurally, was the rather Schumannesque *Theme with variations* op. 73, but his quintessence lay in the better-known nocturnes and barcarolles (thirteen of each); the earlier specimens, as might have been expected, were reminiscent of Chopin but in due course – and notably

[1] For the opera *Pelleas et Mélisande* by Debussy, see page 213.

perhaps in nocturnes nos. 6, 7 and 13 and barcarolles nos. 5 and 9 – he came to combine a Chopin-like melodic fluency with subtle harmonic devices which as a rule were individual and unmistakable. ('As a rule', because now and again there was a tiny echo of Wagner.)

Faure was France's greatest song-writer. Although he left only sixty, as against the six-hundred left by the greatest song-writer the world has ever known, I am tempted to repeat a phrase I used on page 87 and say that although they were not all masterpieces it is astonishing how many of them were. Most – and perhaps all the very best – were quiet and contemplative: Faure usually preferred to set verses fitting that mood and proved himself, in particular, a perfect interpreter of Paul Verlaine in nine songs from *La Bonne chanson*. His first songs were written during his college days, his last shortly before his death, and through out a long career their quality remained amazingly con sistent: among other exquisite gems were *Apres un reve* (which belonged to his twenties), *Le Secret* (his thirties), *En priere* (his forties), *Soir* (his fifties), *Veilles-tu, ma senteur de soleil?* (his sixties) and *Diane, Selene* (his seventies). These six, and many more too numerous to catalogue here, have rarely been surpassed for poetic sensitivity, purity of utterance and polished artistry.

Just after the first world war but before he retired to Annecy, Faure provided music for a hybrid entertainment (ballet-cum-opera) vaguely based on poems of Verlaine and produced at Monte Carlo; he composed an overture and three other new items, filling in the gaps with transcriptions of some of his earlier songs and piano pieces. As originally conceived *Masques et bergamasques* is as dead as a door nail but it survives in the form of an orchestral suite which is light music at its very best, going far to prove that Faure, had he so wished, could in that field have outpaced Leo Delibes (*Coppelia*) and his own pupil Andre Messager (*Veronique*); the significance of *Masques et bergamasques* has sometimes escaped the attention of serious-minded musical historians.

In the main however Faure devoted his last few years

to chamber music. He had previously written two violin sonatas, a cello sonata, two piano quartets and a piano quintet, among which the cello sonata alone had enhanced his reputation to any considerable extent. At Annecy between 1920 and 1923 he composed a second cello sonata, a second piano quintet, a piano trio and a string quartet. All these were imbued with the austerity that had earlier characterized the Requiem and *Penelope* and furthermore aroused speculation as to whether deafness affected him to the same degree as it had affected Beethoven. Analogy was justifiable, for despite the incidence of many obscure passages Beethoven's genius reached a summit-point in the 'cavatina' of his 'deaf' string quartet op. 130 and Faure's in the first movement of his 'deaf' piano quintet op. 115.

During his lifetime Gabriel Faure (like Schumann and Bruckner but in sharp contrast to Berlioz) was rarely acclaimed beyond the frontiers of his own country. Even today, one feels, the outside world is reluctant to grant him the recognition which he deserves. It is true that he did not excel as an all-rounder and by that token can perhaps hardly be rated as the most historically important French composer of his generation; as a miniaturist however he reigned supreme.

CHAPTER THIRTY-TWO

ELGAR

It is twenty-eight chapters since we last welcomed an Eng
lish composer. That the Britain of the interim was unmusical
is a canard which Haydn and Mendelssohn (to name only
two) would have been glad to refute from personal experi
ence, but all this long while creative aspects of the art had
admittedly been meagrely realized. However the sixteen-
year period 1st May 1842 to 30th April 1858 saw the birth
of half-a-dozen very talented native composers, five of
whom later played a part in shaping the musical renais
sance which swept the country in the eighteen-eighties and
eighteen-nineties; the sixth, the odd man out, was still com
paratively unknown at renaissance-time but before the
twentieth century was well under way his achievements had
put those of the other five in the shade and he had clearly
established himself as the first really great British-born
composer since Henry Purcell. (I say British-*born* because it
must always be remembered that Handel, Purcell's junior
by twenty-five years, was for practical purposes at least as
British as his patron King George I, the Hanoverian
Ursprung of our present royal dynasty.)

EDWARD ELGAR, born 2nd June 1857 at Broadheath just
outside Worcester, was the fourth of seven children of
William Henry Elgar (who kept a music shop in the city)
and Anne Elgar *nee* Greening. The father, although he
spent his Sunday mornings playing the organ at a Catholic
church, was himself a member of the Church of England,
but the mother was a Roman Catholic and it was in that
faith that the five children who survived infancy were
educated. (The youngest daughter afterwards became a
nun.) For a time Elgar, like Handel and Schumann and
Tchaikovsky at much the same age, was intended by his
parents to join the legal profession, but Worcester (with its
triennial Three Choirs' Festival – shared with Gloucester

and Hereford) was a centre of musical culture and before he was out of his teens he gave up the law in order to play a fuller part in that activity, both as violinist and accompanist. He soon conceived an ambition to become a composer but had to rely entirely on self-tuition and extensive practice. This is a cardinal factor which should always be borne in mind when any attempt is made to assess his achievements: experience is the best of all teachers, and Elgar might not have acquired such practical knowledge of orchestration at a conservatoire as he did as bandmaster of the county lunatic asylum, as a first violinist in a Birmingham (semi-professional) orchestra and as conductor of the Worcester (amateur) Orchestral Society. On the concert programmes of all three of these organizations his name figured occasionally as composer; presently he succeeded his father as organist at the nearby Catholic church and furthermore built up a good teaching connection. By the time he was thirty he had therefore acquired considerable local reputation as an excellent all-round musician.

In 1889 Elgar married one of his pupils, Caroline Roberts. She was eight years older than he was, the daughter of a major-general and appropriately enough a woman of strong character who had unbounded faith in her husband's capabilities and stoked his ambitions. At first they went to live in London (where she presented him with a daughter, Carice), but the Thames proved less easy to set on fire than the Severn and the only noteworthy happening in the capital, so far as Elgar was concerned, was the sale of the copyright of *Salut d'amour* (which for the last fifty years has been a Corner House 'must' for two guineas. So it was back to Worcestershire and the old routine of teaching, conducting and violin-playing. During the next six or seven years, however, Elgar found time to compose a very charming serenade for string orchestra and (on a larger scale) about half a dozen extended choral works (owing something to the Wagner of *Tannhäuser* days) which were played with fair success at musical festivals in the midlands and north of England; one or two even reached the Crystal Palace in south London. Unfortunately he was misguided in his choice of librettists and it must also be admitted that more often than not the music was as uninspired as the wards were uninspiring. *King Olaf* was the pick of the bunch: it included the 'challenge of Thor' (a magnificent outburst of pagan energy) and the 'ballad of Thyri', which in its happy combination of fluent lyricism and technical accomplishment was an earnest of what was to come.

Yet the fact remains that Elgar, who by the age of thirty had become by diligence a big fish in a little pond, was by forty, despite further diligence, no more than a medium-sized fish in a medium-sized pond. The transformation scene of 19th June 1899 when the *Enigma Variations on an original theme* ('dedicated to my friends pictured within') had a first performance at St James's Hall in London (under the baton of Hans Richter) was so surprising that one is tempted to mix metaphors and declare that the medium-sized fish in the medium-sized pond became overnight the brightest star in the firmament. *Enigma* made its mark not only on Elgar's career but also on the future of British music. Some have found it, on a first hearing, disconcertingly terse (the fourth variation lasts less than half a minute), but surely all must acknowledge that here Elgar provided a masterpiece – and at the same time a yardstick by which his subsequent compositions of comparable magnitude must be judged.

First among these was his only important collection of songs (*Sea Pictures*); next came the incense-laden oratorio *The Dream of Gerontius*, based on the mystical poem of Cardinal Henry Newman. (Elgar himself by the way, although his faith never wavered, was not an *ardent* Catholic; indeed at one time – although he later changed his mind about this – he expressed a wish that his body should be cremated.) The first performance of *Gerontius* (Birmingham, 1900) was under-rehearsed and had a mixed reception; a year later it was acclaimed at Düsseldorf (a success for which the composer had to thank the German conductor Julius Buths) but it did not reach London until 1903. Since then it has never looked back; musicians and public alike are right when they rank it higher than either of the two later oratorios – *The Apostles* (1903) and *The Kingdom* (1906) – for although each of these contains some beautiful music (particularly in the choral sections) the white-heat intensity of *Gerontius* is sadly cooled and there is over-reliance on repetition rather than development of Wagner-like *Leitmotive*. Meanwhile Elgar had also written the *Cockaigne* overture ('capital fun'), the less garish but more original *Introduction and Allegro for Strings* (string quartet plus string orchestra) and the concert-overture *In the South* (*Alassio*) – a glowing and impassioned evocation of

> lands of palms, of orange blossom,
> Of olives, aloe, and maize and vine.[1]

I cannot understand why *In the South* (1904) is nowadays played so infrequently: taken as a whole it is a finer work of art than the first symphony (A flat major) of 1908, which despite an exquisite slow movement (placed third) and a massive display of technical assurance can now be seen as disturbingly redolent of Edwardian opulence.

The violin concerto (1910) fell into a rather different category. It was perhaps the most impersonal of all Elgar's large-scale works: himself a violinist, he was better equipped than most to assess the technical potentialities of the instrument and yet no important solo passage was finally committed to paper until it had been vetted by Fritz Kreisler, to whom the concerto was dedicated and who was the first to play it. Undoubtedly the composer here made a gallant attempt (like Brahms before him) to reconcile artistic integrity with opportunities for executive virtuosity and in the main he succeeded admirably; it may be significant however that in this undeniably great concerto some of the loveliest moments occurred when such problems were cast aside and the composer *per se* came into his own.

Symphony no. 2 (E flat major, 1911) was more consistent than no. 1 yet in performance somehow fails to make the profound impression which a perusal of the score leads one to expect; the first movement is admirable but the others

[1] Tennyson (just in case you didn't know).

seem to develop out of mechanism rather than inspiration. In any case both symphonies – and even the violin con certo – were surpassed by the symphonic poem *Falstaff* (1913), where spontaneity and technique joined hands in full accord, enabling the composer to achieve resounding and unexpected success in a new field. To appreciate all the detailed subtleties of this work one would have to refer to Elgar's own programmatic analysis published in the September 1913 issue of *The Musical Times*, but for any listener remembering that the hero was the classic knightly scoundrel of *King Henry IV* who was inclined to any form of roguery (rather than the inflated caricature of *The Merry Wives of Windsor* who was interested only in cuckoldry) the music itself should suffice; it gives its own account of Falstaff himself, of Prince Hal, of Mistress Quickly and the rest in a manner which a reincarnated William Shakespeare would surely approve. (I cannot forbear to draw special attention to the characteristic 'Falstaff as cajoling and per suasive' theme, first announced by the cellos between figures 7 and 8, and to the wholly captivating dream interlude – figures 76 to 81.)

Nearly all this while the Elgars had been spending their time at either Malvern or Hereford but Sir Edward (he had been knighted in 1904 and awarded the Order of Merit in 1911) was soon increasingly in demand to conduct his works all over Britain and indeed on the continent and in America. So that he could be more conveniently placed for travel they moved once more to London (Hampstead) – and presently acquired a country retreat in Sussex as well. In August 1914, since his patriotism did not stop short with the provision of imperial marches and coronation odes, Elgar enrolled (at the age of fifty-seven) as a special constable; during the war he produced little music of lasting signifi cance. (It is interesting to note however that although he never wrote an opera his musical play for children *The Starlight Express* was played at the Kingsway theatre in 1915 and a ballet, *The Sanguine Fan*, at the Chelsea Palace in 1917.) During the first year or so of peace, however, came some attractively lyrical chamber music (a violin sonata, a string quartet, a piano quintet) and a cello concerto which was more intimately personal than its counterpart for the violin and moreover achieved in the slow movement a level of poetic expression matched only in parts of *Gerontius, In the South* and the slow movement of the first symphony. In effect the cello concerto was Elgar's swan song, for soon after the death of his devoted wife in 1920 he returned to the county of his birth and lived there in semi-retirement, composing meanwhile only a handful of 'occasional' pieces. Further honours were heaped upon him: he was appointed Master of the King's Music in 1924, a K.C.V.O. in 1928, a baronet in 1931, a G.C.V.O. in 1933. In that same year how ever he was attacked by a malignant tumour; an operation to remove it was unsuccessful and the inevitable end came on 23rd February 1934. He died, as he had been born, within sight of the tall tower of Worcester Cathedral and within sound of its bells.

By ancestry and upbringing and temperament Elgar was an open-air-loving countryman: all his life he retained a boyish enthusiasm for fishing, walking, riding, cycling – and later, motoring. He was also a systematic punter, and in his affluent days kept a separate race-going bank account. Nearly all his friends – as distinct from his acquaintances – belonged to this same world; townsfolk and (especially) professional colleagues found him a poor mixer. He was as good-natured a fellow as one could hope to meet in the paddock at Cheltenham or during the course of a day's tramp over the Malvern Hills, but when he strove to uphold the dignity of his art in public company he was apt to appear stand-offish. Matters were not helped when he showed himself extremely sensitive to criticism – which he always ascribed to jealousy or vindictiveness. He mellowed slightly as the years went by and his personal relationship with several contemporary musicians eventually became quite cordial, but the only ones admitted to his circle of intimates were W. H. Reed (a fellow violinist), Henry Walford Davies (who later succeeded him as Master of the King's Music) and Percy Hull (organist of Hereford cathedral) – all three, be it noted, of west-country origin.

At the other extreme the record of his bitter thirty-year long feud with a distinguished but more academically-minded British musician who came near to rivalling his own eminence makes sorry reading.

The idiosyncrasies of Elgar the composer were as easily recognizable as those of Elgar the man – but less irritating; mannerisms they may have been, but the distinctive flavour which they imparted to nearly every page of his music is by no means unattractive. For instance there is a tendency for melodic phrases, rather than going first up and then down, to proceed by alternate rises and falls; then there is that curious insistence on a steady and indeed often stereo typed rhythmic tread, almost every beat of every bar being emphasized by the actual striking of a note or chord. The first six bars of *Enigma* exemplify what I have in mind; this passage represents Elgar in embryo.

So far I have refrained from specific comment on either the Elgar of *Salut d'amour* or the Elgar of 'Land of Hope and Glory', but since he took very seriously everything that he set down on paper a word or so on these aspects of his work is obligatory: it may suffice to say that in *Salut d'amour* – as in the unexceptionable orchestral suites entitled *Wand of Youth* and *Dream Children* – he appeared as the rich man's Edward German; that in the technically impeccable *Pomp and Circumstance* marches he can be seen in retrospect to have been the tycoon's Eric Coates. Lapses in taste need not be forgotten but they should be forgiven; in any case some of his struggles to reconcile poetry with chauvinism ended with poetry coming out on top. To have consistently maintained the high artistic level of *Enigma*, *Gerontius*, *In the South*, the two concertos and *Falstaff* would have been out-of-this-world, and even when his occasional indiscretions are taken into consideration Edward Elgar can be accounted a truly great composer by international standards.

CHAPTER THIRTY-THREE

PUCCINI

A composer of music named Giacomo Puccini, well res
pected in his day, was born in 1712 at Lucca (twelve miles
north-east of Pisa); he died there in 1781. His great-great-
grandson, also named GIACOMO PUCCINI and also a com
poser of music, was born in the same Tuscan town (at 30
via di Poggio, a narrow street leading off the piazza San
Michele) on 22nd December 1858. It was assumed by his
parents that like many of his forbears he would become a
church-organist and so he did – until at the age of twenty-
one he secured admittance to the Milan Conservatoire. His
leaving exercise, a *Capriccio sinfonico* for orchestra (1883),
showed great promise, and presently he completed his first
opera *Le Villi* (originally in one act but later, at the instiga
tion of the publisher Giulio Ricordi, expanded to two
acts); this was played during the next few years at Turin,
Milan, Naples and even abroad – but today is forgotten. So
is *Edgar* (Milan, 1889). The Puccini whom we all know and
whom many of us admire did not emerge until *Manon
Lescaut* (Turin, 1893).

About the time of *Le Villi* Puccini had set up house with
Elvira Gemignani, the wife of a grocer friend, their son
Antonio being born in 1886. Since Elvira was a devout
Catholic divorce was out of the question and the union was
not legalized until the death of her husband in 1904; long
before that (in 1891) Puccini had found a permanent home
for the family. This was a villa at Torre del lago on Lake
Massaciuccoli (about midway between Pisa and Viareggio)
where he could refresh himself by indulging in his favourite
hobby – duck-shooting. (Today visitors to the shrine, after
inspecting the interesting documents which it houses, can
refresh themselves at the adjoining 'Butterfly Bar'.) Al
though during the course of his career Puccini travelled
widely throughout Europe and America it was nearly

always to Torro del lago that he returned when he wanted to apply himself seriously in peace and quiet to composition. Not that he always found *domestic* peace and quiet, for life with Elvira – both before and after marriage – was not free from trouble and noise: being (for an Italian) un musical she gave him little help or encouragement in his work, and moreover was wont to make scenes when as often happened she suspected him of infidelity. In nine cases out of every ten her suspicions were justified, for although Puccini was no great lover by Liszt or Wagner standards (his only *affaire* to ripen into something more permanent was that with Sybil Seligman, wife of a prominent London banker) he held an extraordinary fas cination for pretty women of both high and low estate – who were rarely backward in coming forward to bestow their favours. Though not ill-natured he was extremely self-centred (it may be significant that he was a life-long hypochondriac) and there was a grain of coarseness in his character to which psychologists inevitably attribute his fondness for depicting scenes not only of sensual passion but also of physical suffering. This is what a large section of the public enjoys; since Puccini was a gifted melodist, a very practical if unscholarly craftsman who chose his libretti with extreme care, and since moreover he was blessed with a superb instinct for making the most of a stage situation, it is small wonder that out of the ten operas he composed between 1892 and his death at Brussels on 29th November 1924 – from cancer of the throat – three rank among the 'top pops' of all time and several others still put in a welcome appearance now and again.

At least six operas (plus one ballet) are known to have been based on Antoine François Prevost's novel *Les Aven-tures du Chevalier des Grieux et de Manon Lescaut* (pub lished in 1731) but only two are of historical importance – Massenet's *Manon* (1884) and Puccini's *Manon Lescaut* (1893); both are most enjoyable, and for once comparison can be illuminating rather than odious. *Manon* (composed when Massenet was forty-one) was better constructed and in many ways a maturer work of art than *Manon Lescaut* (composed when Puccini was thirty-four), for Massenet had no peer when it came to the delineation of feminine frailty and his heroine was a more sympathetic figure than Puccini's, who remained strangely anonymous; indeed Puccini seems to have lavished more affection on Des Grieux, whose melodic outburst 'Donna non vidi mai' far outshone Manon's aria 'In quelle trine morbide' – which was tuneful but rather insipid. In their respective Acts I each composer cleverly captured the bustle and excitement of a stage-coach journey-break in the courtyard of an inn at Amiens. Puccini with his Act III at Le Havre and his Act IV outside New Orleans carried the story a stage further than Massenet – who tactfully allowed Manon to expire before being shipped off to America (which in Prevost's day was evidently regarded as a recognized dumping-ground for convicted prostitutes); in these final and tragic scenes of *Manon Lescaut* Puccini displayed a flair for capturing atmosphere which Massenet, for all his talent, was incapable of matching.

La Boheme (Turin, 1896, after Henri Murger) is one of the very few full-length operas belonging to the late nineteenth century which are exempt from criticism on the ground that they go on just a shade too long. (Others that spring to mind are Verdi's *Falstaff* and Humperdinck's *Hansel and Gretel*.) The first two acts show Puccini in his lightest and most lyrical mood, the quartet that concludes Act III rivals in ingenuity and charm the classic 'Bella figlia dell' amore' from Verdi's *Rigoletto* (see page 127), and even if Act IV is accounted a tear-jerker this is surely tear-jerking at its most gracious.

In *Tosca* (Rome, 1900), closely based on a melodrama by Victorien Sardou, Puccini's workmanship shows itself (from the very first two bars) in a rather grim light, being geared not so much to sentiment as to sadism. (C. V. Stanford has reminded us that 'the torture scene in Sardou's *Tosca*, which in itself is horrible enough, becomes ten times more so when Puccini dots the i's and crosses the t's with his vivid score'.) The finale of Act I is a superb technical achievement although personally I wish that it ended three bars before it does, i.e. at the moment where the sinister three-chord theme which opened the opera settles back on B flat major; to my ears the added full close in E flat major sounds artificial and unconvincing. Among the famous arias Cavaradossi's 'Recondita armonia' and 'E lucevan le stelle' are more satisfying than Tosca's 'Vissi d'arte'; one feels that as in *Manon Lescaut* the composer was more in sympathy with his hero than with his heroine.

If so, he made ample amends to the gentler sex in *Madam Butterfly* (Milan, 1904) where the tenor was the merest stooge. (The hero of J. L. Long's magazine novelette on which the opera was based was named Benjamin Franklin Pinkerton; in the opera itself he is referred to by his initials and in this country, to avoid embarrassment, they are usually transposed and he becomes F. B. instead of B. F.) *Madame Butterfly* on its *premiere* was a failure, and it is a tribute to Puccini's determination to maintain his hold on public allegiance that he promptly doctored it, whereupon it became – and has ever since remained – a big box-office draw. There can be no denying its appeal and one's only serious quarrel with the composer over *Butterfly* is that he apparently disregarded the practical diffi culty that whereas the heroine is supposed to be fifteen both 'Un bel di' and 'Che tua madre' demand the lung-power of a thirty-five-year-old. At one time or another over the last forty years I must have seen and heard at least twenty singers of various nationalities attempting to reconcile this discrepancy, but I recall only two – Isabel Rhys-Parker and Sena Jurinac – who came within measurable distance of making Butterfly credible.

Puccini's music, like Elgar's, is full of mannerisms; so much so that one rarely comes across a passage (other than a piece of deliberate pastiche) which is not immediately identifiable as typical Puccini. This does not mean that he stood still. On the contrary: although his methods never changed, no composer was more broad-minded in experi menting with – and sometimes permanently adopting – new idioms. In *Madam Butterfly* he flirted with both genuine and spurious orientalisms and *The Girl of the Golden West*

(New York, 1910) evidenced a further widening of harmonic and rhythmic outlook: the musical treatment of the exciting moments was often reminiscent of *Tosca* but the handling showed greater technical assurance. Unfortunately melodic inspiration was at a comparatively low ebb, which probably explains why *The Girl* (as the composer himself used to call it, rather than *La fanciulla del West*) has failed to rival its immediate predecessors in popularity.

The operetta *La rondine* (Monte Carlo, 1917) was an unfortunate indiscretion, but by-passing this patchwork of cheap sentiment and banality (redeemed only by one superbly uncharacteristic waltz) we come to *Il triticco* (New York, 1918). The 'triptych' consists of three one-act pieces – *Il tabarro*, *Suor Angelica* and *Gianni Schicchi*. (Nowadays they are rarely played straight off the reel; theatrical evenings aren't long enough.) Puccini's constructional flair was admirably suited to the one-act form and it would be hard to fault any of these three works from the dramatic standpoint; musically they were less consistent. It could have been foreseen that he would deal competently with a sordid tale of animal passion and brute violence which might have been sub-titled 'Three on a barge', and technically speaking *Il tabarro* was a fine achievement, a fitting pendant to *Tosca* and *The Girl*. It could also have been foreseen that he would be less at home with a Mother Superior than with a bargee's moll – and indeed *Suor Angelica* was a maudlin affair: Puccini's music could be affecting or even moving – but never ennobling. What could not have been foreseen was that he would excel himself in farce, yet *Gianni Schicchi* – make no mistake – is one of the greatest comic masterpieces in musical history. Here the gradually developing freedom of harmonic expression which had served him well in *The Girl* and *Il tabarro* was exploited to even better purpose; at the same time there was a revival of the lyric strain that had lain relatively dormant since *Tosca*. Despite the light-hearted use of *Leitmotive* a possible quibble is that fetching little tunes sometimes flit across the scene (as in Verdi's *Falstaff*, see page 131) and then vanish for ever. (One such starts at the tenth bar after figure 20.)

And so we reach the Puccini apotheosis – *Turandot*. He did not live to complete the last act of this his last opera, and its first performance (Milan, 1926) ended abruptly when the chorus left the stage after the death of Liu; the conductor, Arturo Toscanini, then turned to the hushed audience and said: 'At this point the Master laid down his pen'. (The final duet between Turandot and Calaf, as we now know it, was pieced together from Puccini's sketches by his pupil Franco Alfano.) *Turandot* was the culmination of its composer's search for new worlds to conquer and not even the dissonances of *Il tabarro* and *Gianni Schicchi* – most appropriate in their context – had quite prepared one for the stark insistence on bi-tonality for its own sake, e.g. the frequently reiterated clashes between the common chords of D minor and C sharp major (or their equivalents). There were in *Turandot* passages of surpassing beauty (notably the miraculous chorus 'Per che tarda la luna' from Act I), but taken as a whole was not the triumph one of brain over heart? All Puccini lovers must decide for themselves whether they prefer the antics of Ping, Pang and Pong to the antics of Marcel, Schaunard and Colline; whether the musical realization of Calaf implanting a kiss on the frozen lips of Turandot as they stand on the steps of an exotic oriental palace gives them more pleasure than the musical realization of Rudolph touching Mimi's frozen hand as they pretend to search for a lost key on the floor of a moonlit Parisian attic; to get down to it, whether they really love *Turandot* better than *La Boheme*.

It would be fair to say in general that every great composer had an element of genius in his make-up but that not every great composer was what the world calls a genius. Giacomo Puccini, always a troublesome customer, confuses the issue: he was undeniably a genius so far as opera was concerned, but whether or not he was also a great composer it may yet be too soon to determine. Until further notice, however, he should be given benefit of the doubt.

MAHLER

GUSTAV MAHLER, born 7th July 1859, was the son of a Moravian Jew who owned a small distillery at Jihlava (Iglau), a medium-sized industrial town seventy miles south east of Prague which was then and for all I know is still one of those isolated outposts of German culture dotted over the predominantly Slavonic, Magyar and Roman lands of central and south-eastern Europe. (Hence the teutonic con ception of *Mitteleuropa*.) The composer's actual birthplace was the Bohemian village of Kaliste a few miles away to the west, but it was in Jihlava itself, just in Moravia, that he spent a rather unhappy childhood (unhappy because his father and mother were an ill-suited and quarrelsome pair), had his first music lessons and went to school. From 1875 until 1880 he was in Vienna, studying first at the Con servatoire and then at the University; thereafter his name became associated with opera, for during the next seven teen years he was either chorus-master or conductor at the municipal or state theatres of Ljubljana (Laibach), Olomouc (Olmütz), Cassel, Prague, Leipzig, Budapest and Hamburg in turn, and in 1897 was appointed artistic director of the Vienna Court Opera. He held this post until 1907 and although he spent the next three winters in the United States as conductor of the New York Philharmonic Orchestra he always returned between-whiles to Vienna; it was there that he succumbed to chronic heart-disease on 18th May 1911. Of his private life it need only be recorded that at the age of about thirty-five (while at Hamburg) he fell in love with a singer named Johanne Richter but noth ing came of the affair; that a year or two later he abandoned the faith of his fathers and became nominally at any rate a Roman Catholic; that in 1902 he married Alma Maria Schindler, a talented amateur musician who thence forth until his death was his prop and stay. They had two daughters: the elder died tragically at the age of five; the younger is now the wife of the Russian-born conductor Anatole Fistoulari. After Mahler's death his widow married the author and poet Franz Werfel; she has long survived her two husbands and today, in her eighties, remains an unfailing champion of them both.

Taking his other commitments into account Mahler's out put as a composer, though not prodigious, was considerable. He only found time for creative work during the summer months – opera's close season – when he was wont to retire to some hide-out in the Austrian alps; yet although he destroyed all his youthful compositions (which he regarded as immature) he left a cantata (*Das klagende Lied*), about forty songs, ten colossal symphonies (including the named but unnumbered *Lied von der Erde*) and copious sketches for an eleventh (no. 10) – which has recently been prepared for performance by the English musicologist Deryck Cooke in a version which will probably have had its *premiere* by the time these words appear in print.

Mahler was completely uninhibited: as a man he was out spoken to the point of ill manners; as a conductor he was ruthless and uncompromising; as a composer he went his own sweet way regardless of opposition. Consequently per sonal acquaintances, opera lovers and concertgoers were either delighted or enraged according to their temperament. Our main concern lies with the composer: why did his music arouse delight in some breasts and anger in others? It was (*a*) because he often flouted convention, e.g. by con cluding songs and symphonies in the 'wrong' key; (*b*) because he came under the influence of both Berlioz and Bruckner who were themselves controversial figures; (*c*) because his thematic material – the basic inspiration – was nearly always simple in the extreme, the simplicity spring ing at times from impeccable classical models but at others from unfashionable folk-song; (*d*) because he adopted an individual approach to the problems of symphonic develop ment, making it episodic rather than continuous; (*e*) because his orchestration, like Rimsky-Korsakov's, was so startlingly brilliant that it sometimes seemed to be the 'essence' of the composition: either *a, b, c, d* or *e*, taken separately, would have been sufficient to cause a narrow cleft in the ranks of responsible musicians and music critics; taken collectively they caused a nuclear fissure. On the wider issue as to whether Mahler's symphonies proved him a genius who in double quick time could raise a huge oak tree from a couple of acorns or a poseur who regularly used an ostentatious sledge-hammer to crack a modest walnut I must leave to his listeners and posterity to decide for themselves, content ing myself meanwhile with a less figurative review of his achievements.

Virtually all Mahler's songs were composed during his twenties and thirties (although some were not published until later) and it is in them that his art can be seen in its purest form. He had a fondness for recreating the moods of childhood and drew largely on *Des Knaben Wunderhorn*, an anthology of juvenile folk-poetry collected by Joachim von Arno and Clemens Brentano. For the four *Lieder eines fahrenden Gesellen*, however, he supplied his own words, while the five *Kindertotenlieder* were settings of verses by the early-nineteenth-century German poet Freidrich Rückert – who had also from time to time inspired Schubert, Schumann and Brahms. In his songs Mahler was con sistently successful in capturing atmosphere by directly musical rather than impressionistic methods: impish humour in *Verlorne Muh'* and *Ablosung im Sommer* for instance; simple piety in *Himmlisches Leben* and *Es sangen drei Engel*; deeper religious feeling in *Um Mitternacht* and *Ich bin der Welt abhanden gekommen*; elegiac pathos in *Das irdische Leben* and *Revelge*. Among them all perhaps *Die zwei blauen Augen von meinem Schatz* and *Ich atmet' einen linden Duft* were unrivalled in their happy blending of poetry with melody.

Mahler also appeared as an apostle of nature in his first four symphonies (all composed between 1886 and 1900 and therefore belonging to the song period), but acorn evolution (or sledge-hammer treatment) was very much in evidence – even in no. 1 (D major) which the composer later described as a youthful try-out. In no. 2 (C minor, known as the

'Resurrection') and no. 3 (D minor) he really let himself go: each required several solo singers and a chorus to help out an orchestra of stupendous proportions; no. 4 (G major) was a comparatively modest affair needing only a single vocalist, triple wood-wind, four horns, trumpet, harp, strings, and a battery of percussion. Of the four, no. 3 was in every sense the greatest: not only does it hold the world's sym phonic endurance record (two hours); it is also the apotheosis of nineteenth-century Mahler. (We shall come to twentieth-century Mahler presently.) The first movement – itself more than twice as long as the entire symphony in the same key by Cesar Franck – is admittedly an aesthetic puzzle, but once one is acclimatized to the scale of the whole concep tion the remaining five movements, which are played with out a break, are consistently satisfying and in places very moving: here the composer is almost (though not com pletely) successful in conveying to the audience his musical interpretation of the ever-changing miracles of nature – the flowers, the forest, the twilight, human joy, human grief. In these four symphonies there are other (separate) movements that are truly beautiful, notably the second movement of no. 2 and the third of no. 4; but in much of no. 1, in the third and fourth movements of no. 2 and in the finale of no. 4 Mahler fell between two stools: the simple measures of *Des Knaben Wunderhorn* were not at home in the trappings of affluence – nor, for that matter, was the even simpler measure of *frere Jacques*.

About the time of his first meeting with Alma Schindler (I am not suggesting that this had anything to do with it) Mahler turned from nature to metaphysics, from personal introspection to cosmic speculation, and in his next three symphonies (all restricted to orchestra alone and where the stylistic influence of Bruckner was paramount) was feeling his way tentatively in a somewhat unfamiliar world. No. 5 (1902, C sharp minor, and incorporating a hauntingly reminiscent 'adagietto' which echoed not only the slow movement of Mahler's own no. 4 but simultaneously the slow movement of Max Bruch's violin concerto in G minor and the 'adagietto' from Bizet's *Arlesienne* and the intermezzo from Mascagni's *Cavelleria rusticana*) alternated between fiery exuberance and tender passion; no. 6 (1904, A minor) rivalled Tchaikovsky's no. 6 in its undiluted pessimism; the three middle movements of no. 7 (1906, E minor) discovered youthful romanticism anew but the first and last were inconsequently demoniac. Mahler himself was never really satisfied with these transitional works; he revised them continually and his final intentions with regard to no. 5 are uncertain to this day. With no. 8 (1907, E flat major) he came back into his own. This was the symphony of the thousand: for its first performance the sponsors engaged eight soloists and eight-hundred-and-fifty choristers and an orchestra of one-hundred-and-forty-six, so that when the composer/conductor was included the total number of musicians taking part was precisely one-thousand-and-three. (Compare Leporello's estimate of Don Giovanni's amorous conquests in his homeland.) This no. 8 certainly showed the composer in more assured and more optimistic mood than nos. 6 and 7, but it was soon overtaken by *Das Lied von der Erde* (1908, a capacious setting of six poems by the Chinese poets Li-Tai-Po, Tchang-Tsi, Ming-Kao-Yen and Wang-Wei, translated by Hans Bethge) and was left behind by no. 9 (1910, orchestral only, nominally in D major), which stood in the same relation to no. 3 as did Berlioz' opera *The Trojans* to his *Symphonie fantastique* and Brahms's fourth symphony to his first piano concerto: all three marked a mature culmination of youthful (or comparatively youthful) ardour. In Mahler's case the doubts of the interim were resolved and retrospective realization of physical phenomena became imperceptibly merged (so far as a detached listener could judge) with a more recently acquired recognition of spiritual values. Gustav Mahler's third and ninth symphonies were indeed masterworks of their kind, yet although prophecy is a dangerous game I shall for once take it upon myself to play the part of a long-term Old Moore by venturing to foretell, in defiance of many distinguished colleagues, that in years to come this enigmatic composer is less likely to be revered as a symphonist than as a song-writer.

CHAPTER THIRTY-FIVE

DEBUSSY

No doubt many of my readers will have admired the famous view from the *jardin anglais* at St Germain-en-Laye, which covers a wide reach of the Seine valley with the Eiffel Tower and Montmartre visible on the distant horizon; few may have realized that they were within a few minutes' walk of the *maison natale* of CLAUDE DEBUSSY, who was born on 22nd August 1862 over a china shop kept by his parents at 38 rue au Pain. Somewhere about 1865 the family moved to Paris. Manuel Debussy and his wife Victorine (*nee* Manoury) were evidently a rather disreputable couple, and although they treated their five children kindly it was a well-disposed aunt who taught Claude to read and write and arranged for him to have his first piano lessons. He showed such promise that at ten he was admitted to the Con servatoire, where he made slow but reasonably steady pro gress and presently began to compose. A stroke of good fortune came in 1880 when he attracted the attention of none other than Tchaikovsky's wealthy patron Nadezhda von Meck – whom we met in chapter 28; she engaged Debussy to give piano lessons to her younger children and took a personal interest in him that may not have been entirely motherly. That autumn his duties were carried out in such pleasant spots as Interlaken, Arcachon (a seaside resort near Bordeaux), Venice and Florence; in each of the two succeeding summers he joined the von Meck entourage in Moscow itself. Here he became acquainted with the music not only of Tchaikovsky but also of Borodin and possibly of Mussorgsky; moreover on his way home in 1882 he called at Vienna in order to hear *Tristan and Isolde*. Seeds were being sown. Back in Paris he was befriended by Maurice Vasnier, civil servant by profession but in private life a *litterateur* and lover of the arts who was sufficiently well-off to maintain both a flat in town and a villa near

Versailles. He also had a very pretty wife, Marguerite, and some of Debussy's most enjoyable visits to the Vasnier household took place during Maurice's office hours. This happy association came to an end when having won the Prix de Rome (see page 93 footnote) he set out for Italy in January 1885.

The work which had gained him the prize was a cantata, *L'Enfant prodigue*, lyrical throughout and almost every bar reminiscent of Massenet, but in Rome itself Debussy never settled down and produced nothing of importance. Soon after his return to Paris in 1887, however, he got into his stride with another cantata (*The Blessed Damozel*), a dozen or so piano pieces and twenty songs – all composed during the next four or five years. *The Blessed Damozel* was a rather restrained setting of the poem by Dante Gabriel Rossetti, none the worse because there was no attempt to capture the preciousness of the original. Of the early piano pieces the popular *Clair de lune* is the best-known, but the *Petite suite* for piano duet (sometimes heard in an orchestral version) deserves to be. Here Debussy expressed in practical terms his indebtedness to Lalo, Bizet, Chabrier and early Faure. More significant were some settings of verses by Charles Baudelaire and Paul Verlaine, two writers with whom he had more temperamental affinity than with Rosetti (although he admired pre-Raphaelite painting); in these songs one can trace the influence of both Wagner and Borodin, but what really matters is that Debussy was by now showing himself to be an impressionist of the first order, whether evoking Baudelaire's voluptuously alternat ing moods of ecstasy and despair – as in *Le Balcon* – or the unashamed sensuality of Verlaine's *Green*.

His first characteristic masterwork, however, did not come until 1892: this was *Prelude a l'apres-midi d'un faune* (inspired by a poem of Stephane Mallarme) which might be described in the same words that Rimsky-Korsakov applied to his own *Spanish Capriccio* (see page 185): a brilliant composition for orchestra. Yet the two works were utterly dissimilar: Rimsky-Korsakov deliberately gave each instru mentalist an opportunity to display his executive prowess in contribution to overall *brilliance*, while Debussy exploited the virtuosity of the whole orchestra, individually and collectively, to purvey *subtle* sound-effects; furthermore the *Spanish Capriccio* was based – most emphatically based – on definable thematic material whereas *L'apres-midi* was based on practically *no* definable thematic material. The excellent string quartet in G minor of 1893 was also largely dependent (like all good string quartets) on the composer's perfect understanding of his medium, but for all its origin ality in detail the conception taken as a whole appears formal when set beside *L'apres-midi* and the three so-called *Nocturnes* which followed it. These were originally planned for solo violin and orchestra but in the event were recast for orchestra alone – plus a women's chorus in the last of the three. Debussy may here be allowed, like Rimsky-Korsakov in chapter 30, to describe his own achievement.

The title is not meant to designate the usual form of nocturne, but rather all the various impressions and the special effects of light that the word suggests. *Nuages* renders the immutable aspect of the sky and the slow, solemn motion of the clouds, fading away in grey tones lightly tinged with white. *Fetes* gives us the vibrating atmosphere with sudden flashes of light. There is also the episode of the procession (a dazzling fantastic vision) which passes through the festive scene and becomes merged in it. But the background remains persistently the same: the festival, with its blending of music and luminous dust, participating in the cosmic rhythm. *Sirenes* depicts the sea and its countless rhythms and presently, amongst the waves silvered by the moonlight, is heard the mysterious song of the Sirens as they laugh and pass on.

(It is interesting to compare this with Berlioz' analysis of his own *Symphonie fantastique* – see page 95; both composers took themselves seriously, but it will be noticed that Debussy's approach to the problems of programme music was very different from that of Berlioz.)

Although *L'apres-midi d'un faune*, the quartet and *Nocturnes* – together with a further handful of songs and piano pieces – were the only compositions which Debussy completed during the eighteen-nineties, for most of the decade he was simultaneously engaged on a more ambitious work – the opera *Pelléas et Melisande*. The drama of the great Belgian poet and essayist Maurice Maeterlinck was first published in 1892; Debussy picked up a copy at a book stall and promptly conceived the idea of setting it to music. After seeing it performed on a Paris stage in May 1893 he made a few preliminary sketches; the following autumn he journeyed to Ghent to discuss his proposition with the author (who incidentally was exactly the same age – thirty-one). No one could have been more co-operative than Maeterlinck; he knew nothing of music, but instinct told him that *Pelléas* cried out for musical treatment (which it did) and that Debussy was the right man to provide it (which he was). Having been given virtual *carte blanche* to make any cuts he wished to fit the work for operatic produc tion the composer returned home in high good humour. It was eight years before the opera was finished but it was then almost immediately accepted by the Opera Comique, thanks largely to the interest and good offices of the theatre's principal conductor, Andre Messager. At this juncture, however, a storm-cloud passed across the sky. Maeterlinck, who now lived in the Paris outskirts and was married to a French soprano named Gabrielle Leblanc, had apparently assumed that his wife would play Melisande. When he learnt that the role had been allotted to the young Scottish singer Mary Garden (who had recently made a big hit in Gustave Charpentier's opera *Louise*) his fury knew no bounds and drove him to disassociate himself from the whole venture. As it might have been embarrassing for him to disclose the true cause of vexation he adopted a different line of attack: at this late stage in the proceedings he shrugged aside his earlier assurances to Debussy by publicly declaring that the opera was a travesty of his play and that he could only pray 'for its immediate and decided failure'. So far as the *premiere* (30th April 1902) was concerned his prayer was answered, but with each succeeding performance there was a growth in public interest and it was not long before *Pelleas et Melisande* became – by Opera Comique standards – a money-spinner.

Let it be stressed right away that this opera is not everyone's cup of tea, and that many excellent musicians find themselves unable to appreciate its shadowy and elusive quality: there are no 'good tunes' and although the whole is held together by a discreet use of *Leitmotive* the influence of Wagner is stylistically almost indiscernible (except perhaps in the sharply abrupt endings of Acts III and IV). Debussy's purpose – admirably suited to the libretto and splendidly translated into practice – was to intensify in song (not necessarily in melody) the underlying rhythm and meaning and emotion of the words and to provide an orchestral accompaniment which while remaining judiciously subservient would be more than mere background and would help to point the unfolding of the drama. The term 'operatic realism' is often applied to high-pressure works like Mascagni's *Cavalleria rusticana*, but *Pelleas et Melisande* is in truth far more 'realistic' – by reason of its reticence.

(It was during the eighteen-nineties that Debussy first began to exploit the potentialities of the whole-tone scales: *viz.* C, D, E, F sharp, G sharp, A sharp, C; and D flat, E flat, F, G, A, B, D flat; these were a logical if somewhat artificial evolution of 'equal temperament' – for which see page 43. It would be virtually impossible to construct any but the most monotonous piece of music *entirely* on a whole-tone scale because of the limited opportunities for modulation, but it can be used with great effect to add characteristic touches of melodic or harmonic colour-contrast. The opening of *Pelleas et Melisande* exemplifies Debussy's methods: bars 1 to 4 are strictly diatonic, bars 5 to 7 strictly whole-tone, bars 8 to 11 diatonic again; from bar 12 onwards the whole-tone melodic pattern of bars 5 to 7 is retained, but it is both softened and enriched by harmonic treatment that might be called compromise-chromatic.)

Meanwhile Debussy's domestic affairs were becoming

more tangled than those of any operatic character. From 1888 until 1898 he had lived – on and off – with a sophisti cated green-eyed blonde named Gabrielle Dupont but in 1899 he married Rosalie Texier, an unaffected and rather simple country girl who came from Montereau-fault-Yonne and was working in Paris as a dressmaker's assistant. Soon afterwards he entered into a simultaneous *liaison* with Emma Bardac, the wife of a wealthy banker, a woman-of-the-world, an enthusiastic musician and an excellent cook. When the desirable attributes of his latest *inamorata* led him to leave poor ineffective little Rosalie for ever the latter tried to commit suicide and wounded herself so seriously that she had to be taken to hospital. The next complication was that Emma Bardac became pregnant – and it was com mon knowledge who was responsible. By this time Debussy's personal friends and acquaintances, even the most broad-minded among them, were beginning to raise eyebrows and display cold shoulders; to get away from it all he crossed the Channel and spent the summer of 1905 at Eastbourne, where no doubt he was regarded as an eccentric but amiable foreigner. He returned to Paris just in time to attend (*a*) the birth of an illegitimate daughter and (*b*) the first perform ance of a recently completed orchestral work which shared the frigid reception accorded by press and public alike to the composer himself. Indeed it was only after Debussy's death that *La Mer* came to be recognized as the master piece that it is. In construction (three separate movements subtitled 'De l'aube a midi sur la mer', 'Jeux de vagues' and 'Dialogue du vent et de la mer') it reverts to something like the form of a classical symphony: the instrumental effects, as skilfully planned as ever, are even more varied than in *Nocturnes* but the whole is based on identifiable themes – many of them of striking vitality – which are subjected to the process of exposition, development and recapitulation almost in accordance with the tenets of sonata-form. To paraphrase Rimsky-Korsakov once again, *La Mer* is some thing more than a brilliant composition for orchestra; it is a magnificently-orchestrated composition. (About the same time Debussy wrote two of his most characteristically impressionistic piano pieces – *Jardins sous la pluie* and *Reflets dans l'eau*.)

Soon after the arrival of his little daughter two divorce decrees were made absolute and Claude was able to marry his Emma. During the next seven or eight years he paid several more visits to Britain and one each at least to Italy, Austria, Hungary and Russia, and seems to have lost the taste for tackling large-scale compositions with the old integrity and determination. Admittedly the pseudo-Spanish *Iberia* (one of three 'Images' for orchestra) was a clever piece of work of its kind; so was the almost surrealistic ballet *Jeux* (the 'jeux' concerned being 'l'amour' and 'le tennis'); so too was the incidental music for Gabriele d'Annunzio's play *Le Martyre de saint Sebastien* in which the composer was surprisingly successful in reconciling his own panthe istic outlook with a background of Christian suffering and sacrifice. But the most representative works of this period were the late piano pieces ranging from *Golliwog's Cake walk* to *La Cathedrale engloutie*, from *La Fille aux cheveux de lin* to a set of *etudes* dedicated to the memory of Chopin. The best of the last few songs (*Trois ballades de François Villon*) were touched with irony; the last of all (*Noel des enfants qui n'ont plus de maison*) was written and com posed during the autumn of 1915 in a mood of bitterness engendered by French sufferings under enemy invasion: here the innocent victims of war implore Father Christmas in carol-like phrases not to take presents to *German* child ren. But now Debussy was attacked by cancer; he worked intermittently on a projected opera based on Edgar Allan Poe's *Fall of the House of Usher* – but it was never com pleted. From the end of 1917 onwards he was confined to his house (near the Porte Dauphine), presently to his room, eventually to his bed. He died on 25th March 1918 (while Paris was undergoing long-range artillery bombardment by the Germans). Pathetically enough, his daughter Emma-Claude (nicknamed Chou-chou) followed him a year later – at the age of fourteen. They had always been devoted to one another and at the risk of being accounted a senti mentalist I make so bold as to suggest that Debussy the man, always a hedonist, was more to be admired as an affectionate father than as a semi-reluctant husband.

What of Debussy the composer? One will start by saying that his style, in the first instance, was influenced by Bizet and Faure and several other compatriots (notably Massenet and Chabrier), all of whom played an honourable part in striving to make France a first-class power in the world of music; one will go on to say that Debussy – when he struck out a line of his own – clinched the issue, thereby earning the gratitude of all Frenchmen imbued with a sense of national pride (and what Frenchman isn't?). On an international level his achievements were no less significant. The four composers who share with him the five concluding chapters of this book, for all that they provide plenty of contrast, each inherited a measure of the classical tradition; it was transmitted to Elgar through early Wagner, to Puccini through Verdi, to Mahler through Schubert and Bruckner, to Strauss through almost everyone. Claude Debussy in his maturity belonged to a different world: set *L'apres-midi d'un faune* (1892) alongside *Don Juan* (1889), *Nocturnes* (1899) alongside the 'Resurrection' symphony (1894), *Pelleas et Melisande* (1902) alongside *Tosca* (1900), *La Mer* (1905) alongside *In the South* (1904); you will then agree, I think, that among our last five great composers he stood in isolation. Whether or not it was *glorious* isolation I shall not presume to judge. (The only close contemporary of even comparable calibre to adopt a similarly individualistic approach was the Yorkshire-born Frederic Delius, who wrote his finest works during the last thirty-seven years of his life when he was resident in France; had he been endowed with sufficient genius to crown an undoubted flair for impressionism he could have become Debussy's most formidable rival.)

CHAPTER THIRTY-SIX

STRAUSS

Munich has always been noted for the baroque splendour of its public buildings (among them the opera-house, now rebuilt after suffering bomb damage in 1944), for the excel lence of its beer and for the ability of its citizens to reap a financially satisfactory harvest from their manifold activi ties. These three traditions were fused when the opera-house's leading horn-player Franz Strauss married Jose phine, daughter of Georg Schorr, the city's wealthiest brewer. Their son RICHARD STRAUSS (1864-1949) may have given up serious beer-drinking at an early age, but he spent most of the rest of his life composing and conducting music and making money thereby (it has been estimated that he was a millionaire by the time he was fifty), so that take him for all in all he can be accounted a Muchener through and through.

He composed his first piano piece (a polka) at six, his first symphony at sixteen; then after two years' study at Munich University he went to Berlin where he was befriended by the conductor Hans von Bülow – long since rid of his erst while helpmeet Cosima who by now was widow Wagner (see chapter 20). Presently young Strauss took over his patron's directorship of a small but expert orchestra at Meiningen (in the south-western corner of Thuringia), where he had the satisfaction of conducting several of his own works including a second symphony – which showed the influence of both Brahms and Wagner. In the following year, 1886, Strauss the conductor and Strauss the composer each reached a turning-point in his career, for the former was appointed deputy at Munich opera-house (how appropriate!) and the latter completed the compatatively mature *Sym phonie aus Italien* – which contained some original ideas and owed less to Brahms or even Wagner than had his two previous essays in that form. In 1889 the composer/conductor moved to Weimar where in 1894 he produced his first opera *Guntram* and married its leading soprano – Pauline de Ahna. (Fifty years later they celebrated their golden wedding; Pauline survived her husband by a few months.) Not long after his marriage Strauss again succeeded von Bülow but this time it was in a more remunerative job – no less than the conductorship of the Berlin Philharmonic Orchestra. Meanwhile he had completed four out of the eight symphonic tone-poems which it would be fair to say held the quintessence of his youth. (Strauss, like many others among us elders, did not enter middle-age until he reached his forties.) The eight were

> *Don Juan* (first played at Weimar in 1889)
> *Tod und Verklarlung* (Eisenach, 1890)
> *Macbeth* (Weimar, 1890)[1]
> *Till Eulenspiegel* (Cologne, 1895)
> *Also sprach Zarathustra* (Frankfort, 1896)
> *Don Quixote* (Cologne, 1898)
> *Ein Heldenleben* (Frankfort, 1899)
> *Symphonia domestica* (New York, 1904).

In these remarkable works (some in one movement only, others in more than one) Strauss was brilliant enough to combine a descriptive power that was all his own with the inspiration of a Berlioz, the initiative of a Liszt and the technique of a Wagner; also apparent was the influence of Berlioz the mixed-up kid, Liszt the flashy showman and Wagner the second-hand philosopher. I shall confine myself to very brief comment on those which to my way of thinking were pre-eminent among them.

If one remembers that *Don Juan* (based neither on the old legend directly nor on Mozart's librettist Lorenzo da Ponte, nor on Byron, but on the more idealistic conception of the German poet Nikolaus Lenau) was composed at the age of twenty-four, one must acclaim it as a masterpiece. The superbly virile opening, the lovely oboe *cantabile* which in performance is sometimes almost overwhelmed by

[1] *Macbeth* was the first in order of composition.

the weight of the throbbing orchestral accompaniment – a rare instance, for Strauss, of instrumental miscalculation), the rousing horn tune which heralds the peroration; these were all the stuff of which youthful genius is made. *Till Eulenspiegel*, a venture into the field of humour, was a *tour de force*; fastidious musicians should excuse the brass-band intrusions (cf. Elgar's *Cockaigne*) which after all were a programmatic necessity. There was also plenty of humour in *Don Quixote* ('fantastic variations on a theme of knightly character' in which a solo cello represented the Don and a solo viola Sancho Panza), notably in variation no. 7 'the adventure of the magic horse' and no. 9 'the adventure of the two monks'. *Ein Heldenleben* was admittedly a bit of a hotch-potch but anyone who disparages it thereby dispar ages Strauss himself, since its inconsequence was utterly characteristic: the nostalgic recollections of voluptuous love-making *a la* Don Juan and the bitterly clever allusions to nattering critics did at least as much to illuminate the composer's outlook on his own life and work as did the allegedly autobiographical *Symphonia Domestica*.[1]

It was during this period that Strauss earned distinction as a song-writer, distinction comparable with that of his predecessor Johannes Brahms and of his contemporaries Gustav Mahler and Hugo Wolf (who incidentally deserves to be remembered also for his only opera, *Der Corregidor*). Like Brahms's and Wolf's and by contrast with Mahler's, Strauss's songs (about a-hundred-and-fifty all told) were uneven in quality, but singers and the world at large would be poorer without *Standchen* ('Mach' auf!'), *Heimliche Aufforderung, Fruhlingsgedrange, Morgen* (is there not an echo here of Brahms's *Feldeinsamkeit?*), *Traum durch die Dammerung* and a good few others. Nearly all the best belonged however to the eighteen-nineties: after the turn of the century Strauss was fully occupied in other pastures. From 1898 until 1910 he was director of the Berlin Opera and although his second essay in the genre, *Feuersnot*

[1] Perhaps the composer himself would have included his later *Alpine Symphony* in the same category as the tone-poems, but this work (dated 1915) has found few admirers.

(Dresden, 1901), made little more impression than had *Guntram* it was on opera that he thereafter concentrated his attention. The one-act *Salome* (Dresden, 1905, based on Oscar Wilde), displayed far greater dramatic sensitivity than had either *Guntram* or *Feuersnot*; subject and treatment alike helped to earn it a *succes de scandale*. And about the same time Strauss became acquainted with the Austrian dramatist Hugo von Hofmannsthal with whom he soon found himself completely *en rapport*: between them they fashioned

Elektra (first played at Dresden in 1909)
Der Rosenkavalier (Dresden, 1911)
Ariadne auf Naxos (final version, Vienna, 1916)
Die Frau ohne Schatten (Vienna, 1919)
Die ägyptische Helena (Dresden, 1928)
Arabella (Dresden, 1933).

Of these six operas the first three, in their different ways, were masterpieces. *Elektra* was an electrifying assault on the nerves: some adjudged it depraved and gruesome, others vivid and realistic, for librettist and composer forced their own interpretation of Sophocles on listeners who were at first too startled either to accept or reject it. By complete contrast *Der Rosenkavalier* was an operatic comedy standing in the category of Wagner's *Mastersingers* and Verdi's *Falstaff*; that in this work Strauss tried here and there, very successfully, to emulate his namesake Johann the younger – no relation – should in theory be beside the point but in practice cannot be disregarded, since its Viennese waltzes have certainly helped to further the opera's popularity.

In *Der Rosenkavalier* Strauss had paid tribute not only to the waltz king but also to Mozart, Schubert and Mendelssohn. He did so again, with even greater panache, in *Ariadne auf Naxos*; this is one of the most engaging of all his large-scale compositions. Unfortunately that cannot be said of any of the three subsequent Hofmannsthal operas nor of *Intermezzo* (1924), where the composer provided his own libretto and once again inclined towards autobiography. The melancholy truth must be faced that the plush world to which Strauss's art belonged collapsed in 1918 along with the German Empire; nothing was ever again the same. So before chronicling his sad decline let us take a quick look at one or two of the finger prints embossed on the representative works of his heyday.

It would perhaps be unfair to describe Strauss as an eclectic and yet although he was a great composer he was not, in essence, a very original one: his mentality was imbued with late-nineteenth-century and early-twentieth-century sophistication but his aesthetic consciousness was partly that of a late-eighteenth-century classic and partly that of an early-nineteenth-century romantic. A flair for conceiving (or contriving) sensuously expressive tunes was his strongest card and he was more successful than Wagner in superimposing pleasing vocal lines on a significant and often turbulent orchestral background. No less than Elgar and Puccini he had easily recognizable mannerisms – not ably that unmistakably characteristic upward melodic sweep of a major sixth or an octave at an anacrusis – but his approach to harmonic problems was more advanced than that of Elgar and less crude than that of Puccini: his polytonal effects derived less from setting two or more keys against one another (so typical of Puccini) than from setting them side by side (e.g. the common chords of D sharp minor, B minor and F minor at Elektra's first en trance). One hopes therefore, without confidence, that in years to come he may be remembered as something more than Liszt plus one (as Vaughan Williams called him).

From 1909 onwards Strauss lived at Garmisch-Parten-kirchen in the Bavarian alps, where he owned a luxurious villa and could compose to his heart's content, but during the years of the Weimar Republic after the first world war he made several tours abroad and apart from a few uncon-sidered trifles wrote only *Intermezzo, Die agyptische Helena* and *Arabella* (see page 221), a ballet entitled *Schlagobers* (*Whipped Cream*) which was produced at Vienna in 1924 and a symphony for sixteen wind instruments. (This last, sub-titled 'a light-hearted piece of work' was composed in

1933 as a tribute to his beloved Mozart, but on his own instructions was not published until after his death.) After Hitler came to power Strauss faced a situation fraught with difficulty, even danger: his latest opera (*Die schweigsame Frau*) had a *premiere* at Dresden in 1935 but was almost immediately withdrawn because the librettist, Stefan Zweig, was a Jew; the composer himself was under suspicion too, because his son Franz had married a Jewess. Furious at first, Strauss was presently obliged to compromise with authority: in return for undertaking that in future he would collaborate with an aryan hack named Josef Gregor he was allowed to remain in untroubled peace and quiet at Garmisch. The arrangement suited both sides: the Nazis could (and did) claim that the greatest living German composer supported the regime; Strauss could (and did) claim that so long as he stayed in Germany German culture was protected. In Britain and the United States, either of which would no doubt have been proud to grant him asylum as a refugee, his equivocal behaviour was widely criticized, an understandable attitude but one which failed to take into consideration a point of cardinal importance. Virtually all the thousands of men and women – including many distinguished writers, artists, musicians and scientists – who voluntarily left or escaped from Germany during those dark years had the shadow of the concentration camp looming over them because they were either Jewish or left-wing. Strauss was neither, and once the government had agreed to overlook the indiscretion of his short-lived association with Zweig no shadow loomed over *him* and he had no strong incentive (as had the Jews and left-wingers) to up root himself. Had he done so it would have been welcomed abroad as the magnificent gesture of a world-famous composer more than seventy years old, but anyone who feels inclined to blame Strauss for lack of moral courage should search deep in his own conscience before glibly asserting that at that age and in similar circumstances he would have acted differently.

Strauss spent the war years at Garmisch, but when in 1945 the United States army of occupation in the American zone of Germany established divisional headquarters at that attractive tourist centre its most distinguished inhabitant was unable to convince the ruling guests that he was no Nazi sympathizer; finding the atmosphere uncongenial he betook himself to Switzerland. (Although a very old man he was by no means either decrepit or penurious and came and went as he pleased between Zurich, the Engadine and Lake Geneva.) In 1948, however, his political record was examined by an international court which ultimately exonerated him from the charge of active participation in the Nazi movement and so at last he felt free to return to Garmisch; he died there the following year at the ripe age of eighty-five.

The three operas in which Strauss had collaborated with Gregor (*Friedenstag, Daphne, Die Liebe der Danae*) were not surprisingly uninspired, and none of them is likely to enjoy frequent revival; nevertheless (like *Die schweigsame Frau*) all three contain some pleasant music recalling the sentimental rather than the more brilliant scenes of *Der Rosenkavalier* and *Ariadne auf Naxos*. More satisfying on the whole were (*a*) his last opera of all *Capriccio* (the libretto of the conductor Clemens Kraus dealt with the tribulations of those who set out to produce an opera), (*b*) a work for twenty-three solo stringed-instruments entitled *Metamorphosen* and (*c*) an oboe concerto. These were all composed during or just after the second world war and as might have been expected from a musician of vast experience who was still in full possession of his faculties they were well-constructed, fluent, and highly polished; but spontaneity was lacking and furthermore they belonged in spirit to a bygone era. Although it was a chronological chance which determined that the final chapter of this book should be devoted to Richard Strauss the fortuitous choice was not entirely inappropriate, for this one-time *enfant terrible*, as things turned out, was the last great composer to fly the flag of nineteenth-century romanticism in an age of realism, atonality and pseudo-jazz – and he flew it to the end.

(continued from front flap)

born before 1864 because, he explains, ". . . the true stature of a creative artist rarely becomes apparent until after the lapse of a generation or two," and he is well aware of the pomposities critics let fall when they confuse argu ment with personal taste. Not that Mr. Hughes avoids expression of taste. He is far too enthusiastic for that, but he never tries to disguise it as dogma.

This is a reference book. It is also a witty, informative, ear-opening com panion to European music, a book to turn to before a concert and to return to after it.

GERVASE HUGHES was born in 1905 and received his M.A. and his B.Mus. from Oxford University. A well-known conductor, composer, and author, he conducted for several sea sons with the British National Opera Company, and arranged and conduc ted Handel's *Julius Caesar* for the Lon don Opera Festival. His compositions include operatic and orchestral works, compositions for the piano, and songs. He has contributed articles on musical topics to various periodicals and refer ence books, and is the author of *The Music of Arthur Sullivan* and *Com posers of Operetta.*

Printed in Great Britain
by Amazon.co.uk, Ltd.,
Marston Gate.